William Russell, James Rush, James E. Murdoch, George James Webb

**Orthophony**

The Cultivation of the Voice in Elocution

William Russell, James Rush, James E. Murdoch, George James Webb

**Orthophony**

*The Cultivation of the Voice in Elocution*

ISBN/EAN: 9783337367060

Printed in Europe, USA, Canada, Australia, Japan

Cover: Foto ©Thomas Meinert / pixelio.de

More available books at **www.hansebooks.com**

# ORTHOPHONY;

OR, THE

# CULTIVATION OF THE VOICE

## IN ELOCUTION.

### A Manual of Elementary Exercises,

ADAPTED TO DR. RUSH'S "PHILOSOPHY OF THE HUMAN VOICE," AND
THE SYSTEM OF VOCAL CULTURE INTRODUCED BY

MR. JAMES E. MURDOCH.

DESIGNED AS AN INTRODUCTION TO

### RUSSELL'S "AMERICAN ELOCUTIONIST."

COMPILED BY

### WILLIAM RUSSELL,
AUTHOR OF "LESSONS IN ENUNCIATION," ETC.

---

WITH A SUPPLEMENT ON PURITY OF TONE,

BY G. J. WEBB,
PROF. BOSTON ACADEMY OF MUSIC.

FORTY-NINTH EDITION.

BOSTON:
JAMES R. OSGOOD AND COMPANY,
LATE TICKNOR & FIELDS, AND FIELDS, OSGOOD, & CO.
1878.

TO

# DR. JAMES RUSH,

WHOSE WORK ON

## THE PHILOSOPHY OF THE HUMAN VOICE

HAS RENDERED DEFINITE AND EXACT INSTRUCTION PRACTICABLE IN

ELOCUTION,

THE FOLLOWING MANUAL

IS

RESPECTFULLY DEDICATED.

# PREFACE.

The design of the exercises presented in this manual, is to furnish the groundwork of *practical elocution*, and whatever *explanations* are needed for *the training of the organs and the cultivation of the voice.* — The system of instruction, adopted in the present volume, is founded on Dr. Rush's treatise, "The Philosophy of the Human Voice," and is designed as a practical synopsis of that work, with the addition of copious examples and exercises, selected for the purpose of facilitating the application of theory to practice. We hope, however, that the use of this manual will induce students and teachers to consult, for themselves, that invaluable source of instruction, for an ample and complete statement of the theory of vocal culture, in connection with an exact analysis of the vocal functions.

The manual now offered as an aid to the business of instruction, contains, — besides a compendious view of the system of Dr. Rush, — the practical methods of instruction introduced by Mr. James E. Murdoch, and taught by Mr. Francis T. Russell, in that part of elocution which comprises *phonation*, or the formation of vocal tone, and *orthophony*, or the training of the vocal organs, on the rudiments of articulation, force, "stress," pitch, and the other elements of "expression," — including the whole organic discipline of "vocal gymnastics."

The exercises imbodied in the following pages, are designed equally for the assistance of two classes of students, — at very different stages of progress in general education, but requiring, alike, the benefit of a thorough-going course of practice in elocution; — young learners, whose habits of utterance are, as yet, forming; and adults, whose professional duties involve the exercise of public speaking. To the former, this manual will furnish the materials for a progressive cultivation and development of the vocal organs, for the useful purposes of education, and as a graceful accomplishment. To the latter, it affords the means of correcting erroneous habit in the use of the organs of speech, and of acquiring the command of an easy, healthful, and effective mode of managing the voice, in the act of reading or speaking in public.

The plan adopted, in arranging the subsequent exercises, presents the various departments of elocution in the following order

[1] 1. The function of BREATHING, as a preliminary to the use of the voice; — 2. The practice of ENUNCIATION, in the act of articulating elementary sounds and syllables, and of pronouncing words. — 3. The study of the various "QUALITIES" of the voice, as an instrument of sound, and the training of the organs, with reference to the formation of "*purity*," *fulness*, *vigor*, and *pliancy* of voice. — 4. The study and practice of FORCE, 'STRESS," "MELODY," *pitch*, "*slide*," "*wave*," "*monotone*," and "*semitone*," "TIME," "*quantity*," "*movement*," "*rhythm*," *metre*, and *pause*, — with a view to organic discipline and the command of the voice, in EMPHASIS and "EXPRESSION," — the appropriate utterance of thought and emotion.

To adapt the work to the purposes of *practical instruction*, and to render it convenient, as a *class-book*, those parts which are most important to learners, are distinguished by "*leaded*" lines, and larger type; and these are intended either to be impressed, in substance, on the *memory*, or to be practised as exercises. The portions of the work which are in smaller type, contain the theory and the explanations requisite for the guidance of the adult student and the teacher.

The sentential or grammatical department of elocution, — that which concerns the modifications of voice, for the purposes of strictly *intellectual* communication, the adapting of the voice to the structure of sentences in prose, and stanzas in poetry, — involves a more extensive study of "*slides*," (inflections,) *emphasis*, and *pausing*, together with *prosodial* elocution, or the regulation of the voice in the reading of verse. The full discussion and practice of these branches, are reserved for a separate course of study, as prescribed in the "American Elocutionist," to which the present manual is intended as an introduction. In that volume will also be found an extended course of practice in *articulation* and in *pronunciation*, with remarks on the character of *cadence;* and, in addition to the vocal part of elocution, an outline of the principles of *gesture*, and a collection of *pieces* for practice in *reading* and *declamation*.

The stereotype process, adopted in this new edition of the present work, enables the publishers to offer it in a more compact shape, without diminishing the actual extent of the matter; while the new arrangement of the chapters, and the addition of the Tables of Orthophony, will, it is thought, render the volume more useful as a manual for schools and academies.

---

[1] The arrangement adopted in this improved edition of the Orthophony, is intended to facilitate the business of instruction by presenting more prominently those parts of elocution which are most important in practice. The chapter on the structure and action of the vocal organs, has been transferred, therefore, to the appendix. But adult students may derive advantage from perusing it, before commencing the practice of the various exercises.

# INTRODUCTORY OBSERVATIONS.

## ORTHOPHONY,[1] OR THE SYSTEMATIC CULTIVATION OF THE VOICE.

THE term orthophony is used to designate the art of cultivating the voice, for the purposes of speech, reading, declamation, recitation, or singing. This art, like all others, is founded on certain principles, the knowledge of which constitutes science. The principles of orthophony, are derived from the sciences of anatomy and physiology, as regards the structure and action of the vocal organs, from the science of acoustics, as regards the formation of sound, in general, and from the science and art of music, as regards the regulation of vocal sound, in particular.

Orthophony is, to elocution, what *solfeggi*, and other rudimental exercises, are to music, — a course of elementary discipline, for the systematic cultivation of the voice. We may, it is true, read well, just as we may sing well, "by ear," or the teaching of nature, merely. But cultivation gives us, in both these uses of the voice, the immense advantages of knowledge, science, and skill. Furnished with these aids, and directed by discerning judgment and good taste, the cultivated reader or speaker has all the advantages of the cultivated singer, as regards the true and effective use of his organs.

The preparatory training and discipline of the voice, for the purposes of reading, recitation, and declamation, are of incalculable value, whether as regards the organic results connected with the

---

[1] The terms *phonation*, (the act of producing vocal sound,) and *phonology*, (the science of voice,) are in current use among physiologists. But the systematic cultivation of the vocal organs, on the elements of expressive utterance, is a branch of education for which our own language furnishes no appropriate designation. The compiler of this manual has ventured to adopt, as a term convenient for this purpose, the word *orthophony*, — a modification of the corresponding French word, "*orthophonie*," used to designate the art of training the vocal organs. The etymology of this term, when traced to the original Greek words, — signifying *correct* and *voice*, — sanctions its use in elocution, on the same ground with that of "orthoëpy," in grammar.

easy, vigorous, and salutary exertion of the voice, or the healthy expansion of the chest, and the inspiring glow of vivid emotion, which is indispensable to effective expression. Dr. Rush's exact and scientific analysis of elocution, in its connection with the action of the organs of voice, enables the teacher to carry elementary cultivation to an extent previously unattainable, and, even yet, too little known by those who have not paid special attention to the subject. The actual benefits, however, arising from the practical applications of Dr. Rush's system, are equally felt in the exactness of intelligence, which it imparts, regarding all the expressive uses of the voice, and the force, freedom, and brilliancy of effect, which it gives to the action of the vocal organs, whether in the utterance of expressive emotion, or of distinctive meaning addressed to the understanding, by the process of unimpassioned articulation.

The methods of practical training, founded on the theory and the suggestions of Dr. Rush, are attended by a permanent salutary influence of the highest value. They produce a free and powerful exertion of the organs of respiration, a buoyancy of animal life, an exhilaration of spirits, and an energetic activity of the whole corporeal frame, — all highly conducive to the well-being of the *juvenile* pupil, not less than to his attainment of a spirited, effective, and graceful elocution. The correspondent benefits conferred on *adults*, by a vigorous course of vocal gymnastics, are of perhaps still higher moment, for the immediate purposes of life and usefulness. The sedentary habits of students and professional men, render them liable not only to organic disability of utterance, and to injury of the lungs, but to numerous faults of habit, in their modes of exerting the organs of speech, — faults which impair or counteract the intended effect of all their efforts in the form of public reading or speaking. The daily practice of vocal exercises, is the only effectual means of invigorating the organic system, or correcting faults of habit in utterance, and the surest means, at the same time, of fortifying the inward frame against the exhausting effects of professional exertion, when either pursued too long in succession, or practised at too distant intervals, — both serious evils, and nearly equal in the amount of injury which they occasion.

The compiler of the present work, could enumerate many cases in which, voice and health, equally impaired, have been restored in a few months, or even weeks, of vocal training, — and still more in which new and brilliant powers of expression, have been elicited in individuals who have commenced practice with little hope of success, and with little previous ground for such hope, — confirmed wrong habits of utterance, debilitated organs, and sinking health having all united their depressing and nearly ruinous influence on the whole man.[1]

It will be perceived, by referring to the subjoined expressions of opinion, that, in pressing this subject on general attention, there is ample professional authority for the expectation of invaluable benefits, as the result of the systematic vocal training recommended in this volume.

*Opinions of Gentlemen of the Medical Profession regarding Mr. Murdoch's System for the Cultivation of the Voice.*

"BOSTON, July 29, 1842.

"I have carefully examined Mr. Murdoch's system of Vocal Gymnastics. It is based upon an accurate knowledge of the anatomy and physiology of the larynx, or organ of the voice. All the details of the system seem to me to be practical, ingenious, interesting, and in accurate conformity to scientific principles. Its obvious utility in developing the functions of the human larynx, and giving flexibility, beauty, facility, and permanent power to the voice; and its eminent effect both in the prevention and cure of the diseases to which public speakers are liable, give it a strong claim upon the attention of the Teachers in our Schools and Colleges, our Youth, and all whose duties demand a frequent & great use of the voice. EDWARD REYNOLDS, Jr."

"We fully concur with Dr. Reynolds in the opinions above expressed.
GEO. HAYWARD,
D. HUMPHREYS STORER."

"July 30, 1842.

"The exercise of Vocal Gymnastics, as recommended by James E Murdoch, being founded on a correct knowledge of the anatomy and physiology of the vocal apparatus, cannot fail, if properly practised under his direction, to develop and strengthen the voice. Persons of

---

[1] Mr. Murdoch, — whose system of orthophony is imbodied in this volume — seemed, at one time, while pursuing a profession in which the most intense exertion of the vocal organs is perpetually required, destined to sink under the effects of over-exertion; but, having seasonably turned his attention to the systematic practice of vocal gymnastics, he recovered his tone of health, and gained, to such an extent, in power and depth of voice, as to add to his previous range in the latter, a full octave, within the space of some months. On devoting himself to the daily occupation of conducting classes in the practice of regulated vocal exercise, the result continued to be a constant accession of vocal power and compass; and on returning to the practice of his early profession, in which he is now so distinguished, his utterance was at once remarked for its round, deep, rich, and full tone.

delicate constitutions and feeble voices, will receive great benefit from the practice of his system; as it is well calculated to give a healthy action to the vocal and pulmonary organs; and, in this particular, it is well worthy the attention of parents  WINSLOW LEWIS, Jr."

"I have had the pleasure of a long interview with Mr. J. E. Murdoch, in which he illustrated his principles of managing and giving strength to the voice; and I am very happy to say, that I can fully concur with Dr. Lewis in his statement of Mr. M.'s system of Voco-Gymnastics.  W. CHANNING."

---

We smile at the enumeration of the formal apparatus of Athenian rhetorical education, which, in addition to its long and classified array of grammarians and rhetoricians, furnished, it is said, *five* gradations of schools for different species of muscular exercise, and *three* distinct classes of instructors for the voice: one, to superintend practice in *pitch;* another, to conduct the exercises in *force;* and a third, to regulate vocal *melody* and *inflections.* Modern taste forbids this fastidious multiplicity and minuteness of appliances; but it makes, as yet, no adequate provision for the acquiring of that moral and intellectual power, and that expressive force, which result from the blending of a high-toned physical and mental training. The customary routine of academic declamation, consists in permitting or compelling a student to "speak," and pointing out his faults, after they have been committed. But it offers no genial inducement to the exercise, and provides no preventive training by which faults might be avoided. Eloquence, in his habits of voice and action, a student may bring with him to our literary institutions; but he will find little opportunity, there, of acquiring or of perfecting such accomplishments, till a correct and graceful elocution is duly recognized as a part of liberal education.

# CONTENTS

|  | Page |
|---|---|
| PREFACE, | 5 |
| INTRODUCTION, | 7 |
| CHAPTER I. RESPIRATION, | 13 |
| Exercises in Breathing, | 14 |
| FIRST TABLE OF ORTHOPHONY, | 16 |
| SECOND, | 17 |
| CHAPTER II. ORTHOEPY, | 18 |
| Tonic Elements, | 19 |
| Subtonic " | 22 |
| Atonic " | 23 |
| Vowels and Diphthongs, | 24 |
| Consonants, | 26 |
| Labial Sounds, | 26 |
| Dental " | 27 |
| Palatic " | 28 |
| Aspirated Element, | 28 |
| Nasal Sounds, | 28 |
| Lingual, " | 29 |
| Exercises in Enunciation, | 30 |
| Words containing "tonic" elements, | 30 |
| Words containing "subtonic" elements, | 34 |
| Words containing "atonic" elements, | 37 |
| Words containing syllabic combinations, | 37 |
| Words containing classified elements, | 40 |
| CHAPTER III. "QUALITY" OF VOICE, | 44 |
| Whispering, | 45 |
| "Pure" Tone, | 48 |
| Faults in "Quality," | 49 |
| Examples of "Pure tone," | 53 |
| "Subdued" Force, | 53 |
| "Moderate" " | 54 |
| "Sustained" Force, | 61 |

|  | Page |
|---|---|
| "Orotund Quality," | 62 |
| "Effusive Orotund,' | 64 |
| "Expulsive" " | 68 |
| "Explosive" " | 70 |
| "Aspirated Quality,' | 73 |
| CHAPTER IV. FORCE, | 75 |
| Degrees of Force, | 77 |
| CHAPTER V. "STRESS," | 78 |
| "Radical Stress," | 79 |
| "Median" " | 84 |
| "Vanishing" " | 91 |
| "Compound" " | 96 |
| "Thorough" " | 98 |
| "Tremor," | 100 |
| Analytic Exercises on "Stress," | 103 |
| CHAPTER VI. "MELODY," | 105 |
| Pitch, | 106 |
| "Middle" Pitch, | 107 |
| "Low" " | 113 |
| "Very Low" " | 115 |
| "High" " | 117 |
| "Very High" " | 120 |
| "Transition" in Pitch, | 122 |
| "Phrases" of "Sentential Melody," | 126 |
| The "Slide," | 130 |
| The "Slide" of Emotion | 133 |
| The "Distinctive Slide," | 136 |
| The "Mechanical" " | 139 |
| CHAPTER VII. TIME, | 141 |
| "Quantity," | 141 |
| Exercises in "Quantity," | 144 |
| Pauses, | 152 |
| Poetic and Oratorical Pauses, | 154 |

| | Page | | Page |
|---|---|---|---|
| Rhetorical Pauses, | 157 | DESCRIPTION OF THE ORGANS | |
| Movement," | 162 | OF VOICE, | 211 |
| Examples of "Slowest Movement," | 164 | ADDITIONAL BREATHING EXERCISES | 218 |
| Examples of "Slow Movement,' | 165 | | |
| Examples of "Moderate Movement," | 167 | ANALYSIS OF "SLIDES," | 219 |
| | | Scale of "Slides," | 220 |
| Examples of "Animated Movement," | 169 | The "Wave," | 221 |
| | | The "Monotone," | 223 |
| Examples of "Brisk Movement," | 171 | The "Semitone," | 231 |
| Examples of "Rapid Movement," | 173 | CULTIVATION OF "PURE TONE, | 239 |
| Accent, | 174 | EXTRACTS FOR PRACTICE, | 24? |
| "Syllabic" Accent, | 174 | Exercises in "Pure Tone," | 242 |
| "Rhythmical" " | 176 | Exercises in "Orotund" Utterance, | 253 |
| Examples of "Rhythmical" Accent, | 179 | Exercises in "Aspirated Quality," | 262 |
| Prosodial Accent, | 183 | | |
| "Iambic" Metre, | 184 | Exercises in Force, | 267 |
| "Trochaic" " | 186 | | |
| "Anapæstic" " | 186 | MISCELLANEOUS EXERCISES, | 277 |
| "Rhythmical" and Prosodial Accent combined, | 187 | I. A Sea-voyage. *Irving.* | 277 |
| | | II. Death of Morris. *Scott.* | 280 |
| | | III. The Planetary Systems. *Hervey.* | 282 |
| CHAPTER VIII. EMPHASIS AND "EXPRESSION," | 190 | IV. Chatham's Rebuke of Lord Suffolk. | 283 |
| Impassioned Emphasis, | 190 | V. Speech of Patrick Henry. | 284 |
| Unimpassioned " | 191 | VI. The Ocean. *Byron.* | 285 |
| Examples, | 193 | VII. Battle of Waterloo. *Byron.* | 286 |
| "Arbitrary" Emphasis, | 196 | | |
| "Expression," | 200 | VIII. Satan Rallying the Fallen Angels. *Milton.* | 287 |
| Third Table of Orthophony, Elements of "Expression," | 202 | IX. Hymn to Mont Blanc. *Coleridge.* | 289 |
| Fourth Table of Orthophony, Combinations of "Expression," | 204 | X. Ode on the Passions. *Collins.* | 291 |
| Fifth Table of Orthophony, Metre, | 205 | XI. The Uses of Knowledge. *Alison.* | 293 |
| | | XII. Scene of Scottish Life. *Wilson.* | 294 |
| APPENDIX, | 206 | XIII. Eloquence of John Adams. *Webster.* | 296 |
| ENGRAVED ILLUSTRATIONS OF THE VOCAL ORGANS, | 206 | XIV. Heroism of the Pilgrims. *E. Everett.* | 29? |

# CHAPTER I.

## RESPIRATION, OR EXERCISES IN BREATHING.[1]

The organs of voice, in common with all other parts of the bodily frame, require the vigor and pliancy of muscle, and the elasticity and animation of nerve, which result from good health, in order to perform their appropriate functions with energy and effect. But these indispensable conditions to the exercise of the vocal organs, are, in the case of most learners, very imperfectly supplied. A sedentary mode of life, the want of invigorating exercise, close and long continued application of mind, and, perhaps, an impaired state of health, or a feeble constitution, prevent, in many instances, the free and forcible use of those muscles on which voice is dependent. Hence arises, to students of elocution, the necessity of practising physical exercises, adapted to promote general muscular vigor, as a means of attaining energy in vocal functions; the power of any class of muscles, being dependent on the tone of the whole system.

The art of cultivating the voice, however, has, in addition to the various forms of corporeal exercise, practised for the general purpose of promoting health, its own specific prescriptions for securing the vigor of the vocal organs, and modes of exercise adapted to the training of each class of organs separately.

The results of such practice are of indefinite extent: they are limited only by the energy and perseverance of the student, excepting, perhaps, in some instances of imperfect organization. A few weeks of diligent cultivation, are usually sufficient to produce such an effect on the vocal organs, that persons who commence practice, with a feeble and ineffective utterance, attain, in that short period, the full command of clear, forcible, and varied tone.

*Gymnastic and calisthenic exercises are invaluable aids to the culture and development of the voice*, and should be sedulously practised, when opportunity renders them accessible. But even a slight degree of physical exercise, in any form adapted to the expansion of the chest, and to the freedom and force of the circulation, will serve to impart energy and glow to the muscular apparatus of voice, and clearness to its sound.

*There is, therefore, a great advantage in always practising some preliminary muscular actions, as an immediate preparation for vocal exercise.* These actions may be selected from the system of preparatory movements, taught at gymnastic establishments; or they may be made to consist in regulated walking, with a view to the acquisi-

---

[1] For a description of the vocal organs, see Appendix

tion of a firm, easy, and graceful carriage of the body, with appropriate motion of the arms and limbs,— in the systematic practice of gesture, in its various forms, for the purpose of obtaining a free, forcible, and effective use of the arm, as a natural accompaniment to speech,— or in the practice of attitude and action combined, in the most vivid style of lyric and dramatic recitation, so as to attain a perfect control over the whole corporeal frame, for the purposes of visible expression.

Some preliminary exercises, such as the preceding, having been performed, and a sufficient period for rest and tranquil breathing having elapsed, the next stage of preparatory action may be as in the following directions:

1. *Attitude of the Body, and Position of the Organs.*

Place yourself in a perfectly erect, but easy posture; the weight of the body resting on one foot; the feet at a moderate distance, the one in advance of the other;[1] the arms akimbo: the fingers pressing on the abdominal muscles, in front, and the thumbs on the dorsal muscles, on each side of the spine; the chest freely expanded and fully projected; the shoulders held backward and downward, the head perfectly vertical

2. *Exercises in Deep Breathing.*

Having thus complied with the preliminary conditions of a free and unembarrassed action of the organs, draw in and give out the breath very fully, and very slowly, about a dozen times in succession. Let the breathing be deep and tranquil, but such as to cause the chest to rise fully, and fall freely, at every effort.

3. *Exercise in " Effusive," or tranquil Breathing.*

Draw in a very full breath, and send it forth in a prolonged sound of the letter $h$. In the act of inspiration, take in as much breath as you can contain. In that of expiration, retain all you can, and give out as little as possible,— merely sufficient to keep the sound of $h$ audible. But keep it going on as long as you can sustain it. In this style of respiration, the breath merely *effuses* itself into the surrounding air.

---

[1] The object in view, in this apparently minute direction, is, to secure perfect freedom and repose of body. A constrained or a lounging posture, is utterly at variance with a free, unembarrassed use of the voice, or the production of a clear and full sound.

4. *Exercise in "Expulsive," or forcible Breathing.*

Draw in a very full breath, as before, and emit it, with a lively expulsive force, in the sound of *h*, but little prolonged —in the style of a moderate whispered cough. The breath in this style of expiration, is *projected* into the air. Repeat this exercise, as directed, in the statement preceding.

5. *Exercise in "Explosive," or abrupt Breathing.*

Draw in the breath, as already directed, and emit it with a sudden and violent explosion, in a very brief sound of the letter *h*,— in the style of an abrupt and forcible, but whispered cough. The breath is, in this mode of expiration, thrown out with abrupt *violence*. Repeat this exercise, as before directed.

*Note to Adult Students and Teachers.*

The habit of keeping the chest open and erect, is indispensable to the production of a full, round tone of voice. But it is of still higher value, as one of the main sources of health, animation, and activity.

The effect, on the student, of the preceding exercises in breathing, is usually soon perceptible in an obvious enlargement of the chest, an habitually erect attitude, an enlivened style of movement, a great accession of general bodily vigor, an exhilarated state of feeling, and an augmented activity of mind. To persons whose habits are studious and sedentary, and especially to females, the vigorous exercise of the organs of respiration and of voice, is, in very point of view, an invaluable discipline.

## FIRST TABLE OF ORTHOPHONY.

## ORTHOËPY.

ELEMENTS OF THE ENGLISH LANGUAGE,

*Classified by the Ear, as Sounds.*

I. TONIC,[1] OR VOCAL AND DIPHTHONGAL ELEMENTS.

SIMPLE,— *having one unchanging sound.*

The element of sound, in every instance, is indicated by *italic* type, and should be repeated, by itself, after the pronunciation of the whole word, in a *full, clear, exact,* and *distinct* style.

1, *A*-ll; 2, *A*-rm; 3, *A*-n; 4, *E*-ve; 5, *Oo*-ze, (long;) L-*oo*-k, (short;)[2] 6, *E*-rr;[3] 7, *E*-nd; 8, *I*-n; 9, *Ai*-r;[4] 10, *U*-p; 11, *O*-r;[5] 12, *O*-n.[6]
COMPOUND,— *beginning with one sound and ending in another*
13, *A*-le; 14, *I*-ce; 15, *O*-ld; 16, *Ou*-r; 17, *Oi*-l; 18, *U*-se, '(verb, *long*;) *U*-se, (noun, *short*.)

II. SUBTONIC,[7] SUBVOCAL, OR SEMIVOWEL[8] ELEMENTS.

SIMPLE.— 1, *L*-u-*ll*; 2, *M*-ai-*m*; 3, *N*-u-*n*; 4, *R*-ap, (*hard* but not *rolled*;) 5, Fa-*r*, (soft, not *silent*;) 6, Si-*ng*; 7, *B*-a-*be* 8, *D*-i-*d*; 9, *G*-a-*g*; 10, *V*-al-*ve*; 11, *Z*-one; 12, A-*z*-ure 13, *Y*-e; 14, *W*-oe; 15, *TH*-en. COMPOUND.— 16, *J*-oy.

III. ATONIC,[9] ASPIRATE,[10] OR MUTE[11] ELEMENTS.

SIMPLE.— 1, *P*-i-*pe*; 2, *T*-en-*t*; 3, *C*-a-*ke*; 4, *F*-i-*fe*; 5 *C*-ea-*se*; 6, *H*-e; 7, *Th*-in; 8, Pu-*sh*. COMPOUND.— 9 *Ch*-ur-*ch*.

[1] So called from their comparatively musical sound, and susceptibility of *tone. See pages* 19, 20.
[2] The same in *quality*, but not in *quantity*, with the preceding.
[3] Middle sound, between *ur* and *air*.
[4] Middle sound, between *a*-le and *e*-nd.
[5] A sound closer than that of *a* in *a*-ll.
[6] Closer than *o* in *o*-r.
[7] So called from their *inferiority* in *tone*, when contrasted with tonics
[8] So called from their *partial vocality*, when contrasted with *atonics* or *mutes*.
[9] So called from their *want* of *tone*.
[10] Formed by a process of *breathing*.
[11] *Deficient* in *sound*.

## SECOND TABLE OF ORTHOPHONY

## ORTHOËPY.

ELEMENTS OF THE ENGLISH LANGUAGE,

*Classified according to the action of the Organs of Speech in Articulation.*

I. ORAL AND LARYNGIAL SOUNDS.

[*Formed by the mouth and larynx.*]

In practising the sounds, the mouth should be freely opened, and firmly held in the position proper for the formation of each sound, and every position carefully observed.

1, *A*-ll; 2, *A*-rm; 3, *A*-n; 4, *E*-ve; 5, *Oo*-ze, L-*oo*-k; 6, *E*-rr; 7, *E*-nd; 8, *I*-n; 9, *Ai*-r; 10, *U*-p; 11, *O*-r; 12, *O*-n 13, *A*-le; 14, *I*-ce; 15, *O*-ld; 16, *Ou*-r; 17, *Oi*-l; 18, *U*-se (verb, *long* ;) *U*-se, (noun, *short.*)

II. LABIAL, OR LIP SOUNDS.

1, *B*-a-*be*; 2, *P*-i-*pe*; 3, *M*-ai-*m*; 4, *W*-oe; 5, *V*-al-*ve* 6, *F*-i-*fe*.

III. PALATIC, OR PALATE SOUNDS.

1, *C*-a-*ke*; 2, *G*-a-*g*; 3, *Y*-e.

IV. ASPIRATE, OR BREATHING SOUND

*H*-e.

V. NASAL, OR NOSTRIL SOUNDS.

1, *N*-u-*n*; 2, Si-*ng*.

VI. LINGUAL, OR TONGUE SOUNDS

1, *L*-u-*ll*; 2, *R*-ap; 3, Fa-*r*.

SYLLABIC COMBINATIONS,

To be practised with great *force, precision,* and *distinctness*

I. INITIAL SYLLABLES.

Bl, cl, fl, gl, pl, spl; Br, cr, dr, fr, gr, pr, spr, tr, str, shr Sm, sn, sp, sk, st.

II. FINAL SYLLABLES.

Ld, lf, lk, lm, lp, lse, ls, (lz,) lt, lve; m'd, nd, nce, ns, (nz, nk, (ngk,) nt; rb, rd, rk, rm, rn, rse, rs, (rz,) rt, rve, rb'd rk'd, rm'd, rn'd, rs'd, rv'd; sm, (zm,) s'n, (zn,) sp, st; ks, ct k'd, (kt,) f'd, (ft,) p'd, (pt ;) d'n, k'n, p'n, v'n ; ble, (bl,) fle (fl,) gle, (gl,) ple, (pl,) dle, (dl,) tle, (tl,) rl; lst, nst, rst, dst rdst rmdst, rndst; bl'd, pl'd, rl'd; ngs, ngst, ng'd; bles (blz,) cles, (clz,) fles, (flz,) gles, (glz ;) sms (zmz,) s'ns, (znz, sps, sts; stles, (slz,) stens, (snz.)

2*

# CHAPTER II.

## ORTHOËPY.

THE term orthoëpy[1] comprehends all that part of elocution which pertains to the organic functions of *articulation*, and its audible result, which we term *enunciation*. It will be a matter of convenience, at the same time, to take into view the subject of *pronunciation*, or, in other words, enunciation as modified by *the rules of sound and accent* which are drawn from the usage of a particular language. To *pronounce* a *word* properly, implies that we *enunciate* correctly all its *syllables*, and *articulate* distinctly the sounds of its *letters*.

We commence with the study of *articulation*, as a function of the smaller organs of voice, including the larynx and the circumjacent parts, the *mouth* and its various portions and appurtenances. Our preceding observations applied to the use of the *larger* organs, — the cavity and muscles of the *chest*, &c., and referred to the act of respiration, preparatory to the production of vocal *sound*, whether in speech or in music. We are now occupied with the functions of *speech*.

Propriety of pronunciation is justly regarded as an inseparable result of cultivation and taste. We recognize an educated person by his mode of pronouncing words; and we detect slovenliness in mental habit, or the absence of culture, with no less certainty, in the same way. Whatever thus holds true of pronunciation, — a thing subject to the law of prevailing good custom, merely, and liable, therefore, to various interpretations in detail, — is still more emphatically applicable to distinct enunciation, the unfailing characteristic of correct intellectual habits, and the only means of exact and intelligible communication by speech.

But a distinct enunciation is wholly dependent on the action of the organs, — on their positions and their movements, — on the force and precision of their execution. The breath having been converted into sound by the use of the component portions of the larynx, passes on to be modified or articulated into definite forms by the various portions of the mouth, and by the action of the tongue.

A person of perfect organization and in perfect health, — in an undisturbed condition of feeling, and, consequently, with a clear state of thought, — utters his ideas distinctly and impressively, without special study. But defective organization, neglected habit, false tendencies of feeling, and confused conceptions, are so prevalent, that very few individuals in a community, can be selected as naturally perfect in the function of articulation. With most persons, and especially in youth, the negligence of unguarded habit impairs the distinctness and clearness of oral expression. The comparatively inactive life of the student, subjects him, usually, to imperfection in this, as in most other active uses of the organic frame; and every individual, — whatever be his advantages, as such, — needs a tho-

---

[1] A term derived from the Greek language, and compounded of two words signifying *correct speech*.

ւ ..gh organic training, before he can pass successfully to the comparatively forcible and exact mode of using the organs, which distinguishes public reading and speaking from private communication. The latter occupies but little space, and needs but a slight effort of attention or of will, to effect it: the former implies large space, and correspondent voluntary exertion of the organs, with the due precision which stamps, at once, every sound distinctly on the ear, and renders unnecessary any repetition of an imperfectly understood word or phrase,— a thing allowable in conversation, but impracticable in public speaking.

The functions of the organs in articulation, must obviously be determined by the character of the sound which, in any case, is to be executed. We shall find advantage, therefore, in first considering the character of the component elementary sounds of our language, as a guide to the mode of exerting the organs in producing them.

Dr. Rush, in his Philosophy of the Voice, has adopted an arrangement of the elementary sounds of our language, which differs from that of grammarians, and is founded on a more strict regard to the vocal properties of each element,— a classification which is more convenient for the purposes of elocution, as well as more exact in relation to the facts of speech. Dr. Rush's arrangement we shall follow in this branch of our subject; as it is best adapted to the purposes of instruction.

On a very few points of detail, however, we shall take the liberty to vary from Dr. Rush's system, where precision and accuracy of instruction seem to require such variation.

Dr. Rush's mode of classifying the elementary sounds of our language, presents, first, those which he has denominated "*Tonic*" elements, as possessing the largest capacity for prolongation of sound, and other modifications of *tone*. The following are the

"TONIC" ELEMENTS.

I. *Simple Sounds.*

1. *A*,   as in *A*-ll.
2. *A*    as in *A*-rm.
3. *A*    as in *A*-n.
4. *E*,   as in *E*-ve.
5. *OO*,  as in *Oo*-ze.
   *OO*,[1] as in L-*oo*-k.
6. *E*,   as in *E*-rr.
7. *E*,   as in *E*-nd.
8. *I*,   as in *I*-n.

9. *Ai*,  as in *Ai*-r.
10. *U*,  as in *U*-p.
11. *O*,  as in *O*-r.
12. *O*,  as in *O*-n.

II. *Compound Sounds.*

13. *A*,  as in *A*-le.
14. *I*,  as in *I*-ce.
15. *O*,  as in *O*-ld.
16. *Ou*  as in *Ou*-r

The following elements of the same class, are omitted by Dr. Rush. But they seem to be indispensable in teaching, which

[1] A shorter *quantity*, but the same in *quality*, with *oo* in *ooze*

requires exact and close discriminations, in order to obtain accuracy in practice.

17 *Oi*, as in *Oi*-l.   18. *U*, as in *U*-se, sounding *long* in the *verb*, *short* in the *noun*.

[The student's attention should be directed to the following observations, previous to practising the preceding sounds.]

The *a*, in such words as *ale*, Dr. Rush has very justly represented as consisting of *two* elements: — 1. The " radical," or initial sound with which the name of the letter *a* commences; and 2. The delicate " vanish," or final sound, with which, in full pronunciation, and in singing, it closes, — bordering on *e*, as in *eve*, — but barely perceptible to the ear. This element obviously differs, in this respect, from the acute *é* of the French language, which begins and ends with precisely the same form of sound, and position of the organs of speech; while the English *a*, as in *ale*, requires a slight upward movement of the tongue, to close it with propriety; and hence its " vanish," approaches to the sound of *e*.

The *i* of *ice*, in like manner, will, on attentive analysis, be found to consist of two simple elements: — 1st, *a*, as in *at*; 2d, *i*, as in *in*. Walker, in his system of orthoëpy, defines this element as commencing with the *a* in *father*. But such breadth of sound, is, in our own day, justly regarded as the mark of a drawling and rustic pronunciation, while good taste always shrinks from the too flat sound, which this element receives in the style of dialectic error in Scotland or Ireland, or in the style of fastidious and affected refinement, as if " *āyee*."

The *o* of *old*, although not so commonly recognized as a compound element, will be found, on analysis, to belong properly to that class. Thus, if we observe closely the pronunciation of a native of continental Europe, in speaking English, we shall find that the letter *o* in such words as *old*, sounds a little too broad, and does not close properly. The foreign pronunciation lacks the delicate " vanish, approaching to *oo*, in *ooze*, although not dwelling on that form of sound, but only, as it were, approximating to it; as the letter *a*, in just and full utterance for public speaking, and for singing, closes with a slight approach to *e*, in *eve*, but does not dwell on that element.

That this compound form of the " tonic " *o*, in *old*, is a genuine tendency of the organs, in the pronunciation of our language, may be observed in the current fault of the utterance which characterizes the popular style of England, and in which the vanish of this element is protruded to such an extent as to justify American caricaturists in representing it by the spelling of " *powst rowd*," for *post road*.

The element *ou*, in *our*, is obviously a compound of *o*, as in *done*, — the same with *u*, in *up*, — and a short, or " vanishing " quantity of *oo* in *ooze*. The negligent style of popular error, makes this element commence with *a*, as in *arm*, or *a* in *at*; and the local style of rustic pronunciation in New England, makes it commence with *e* in *end*.

*Ai*, as in the word *air*, though not recognized by Dr. Rush, nor by many other writers on elocution, as a separate element from *a*, in *ale* is obviously a distinct sound, approaching to that of *e* in *end*, but not forming so close a sound to the ear, nor executed by so much muscular pressure in the organs. The literal flat sound, however, of *a* in *le*, if given in the class of words *air*, *rare*, *care*, &c., constitutes the peculiarity of local usage in Ireland, as contradistinguished from that of England.

Popular usage, in England and America, inclines, no doubt, to the opposite extreme, and makes *a*, in *air* too nearly like a prolonged sound of *a*, as in *an*. In the southern regions of the United States, this sound is even rendered as broad as that of *a* in *arm*. But while good taste avoids such breadth of sound, as coarse and uncouth, it still preserves the peculiar form of this element, as differing both from *a* in *ale*, and *e* in *end*, and lying, as it were, between them.

*U*, in *up*, seems to have been merged by Dr. Rush in the element ., in *err*, which would imply that the latter word is pronounced "*urr*." But this is obviously the error of negligent usage, whether in the United States, or in England. In the latter country, it is the characteristic local error of Wales.

In the usage of New England and of Scotland, there is, no doubt, a too prevalent tendency to pronounce *err*, *earth*, *mercy*, &c., with a sound too rigidly close, like that of *e* in *merit* ; thus, "*Air*," "*airth*," "*maircy*." But cultivated and correct pronunciation, while it avoids this preciseness, draws a clear, though close distinction, between the vowel sounds in *urn* and *earn*.

Mr. Smart, in his Practice of Elocution, describes the element in question, with perfect exactness and just discrimination.

" *Er* and *ir* are pronounced by unpolished speakers just like *ur*, as indeed, in some common words, such as *her*, *sir*, &c., they are pronounced, even by the most cultivated : but in words of less common occurrence, there is a medium between *ur* and *air*, which elegant usage has established, as the just utterance of *e* and *i* joined to the smooth *r*."[1]

*O*, in *or*, and *o*, in *on*, are apparently considered by Dr. Rush and by Walker, as modifications of *a* in *all*. Admitting, however, the identity of quality in these elements, — their obvious difference in quantity, and in the position and pressure of the muscles by which, as sounds, they are formed, together with the precision and correctness of articulation, demand a separate place for them in elementary exercises designed for the purposes of culture, which always implies a definite, exact, and distinctive formation of sounds.

*Oi*, in *oil*, though omitted in the scheme of Dr. Rush, are evidently entitled to a distinct place in the classification of the elements of our language, on the same ground on which a separate designation is assigned to *ou* in *our*.

This compound element, *oi*, is formed by commencing with the *o* in *on*, and terminating with the *i* in *in*. Popular and negligent usage, inclines to two errors in this diphthong : — 1st, that of commencing with *o*, in *own* instead of *o*, in *on ;* 2d, that of terminating

---

[1] Practice of Elocution. By B. H. Smart. London · 1826

with a short sound of *a*, as in *ale*, instead of *i*, in *in*. The appropriate sounds are as mentioned above.

The compound element *u*, as in *use*, although obviously formed of a short quantity of *e*, in *eve*, and of *oo*, in *ooze*, is entitled to a place in the classification of the elements of our language, not merely as being a sound represented by a distinct character, as in the name of the letter *u*, but as constituting a peculiar diphthongal element.

### "SUBTONIC" ELEMENTS.

These elements are so denominated by Dr. Rush " from their inferiority to the ' tonics,' in all the emphatic and elegant purposes of speech, while they admit of being ' intonated,' or carried ' concrete-.y,' (continuously,) through the intervals of pitch."

1. *L*, as in *L*-u*ll*.[1]
2. *M*, as in *M*-ai-*m*.
3. *N*, as in *N*-u-*n*.
4. *R*, as in *R*-ap.
5. *R*, as in Fa-*r*.[2]
6. *Ng*, as in Si-*ng*.
7. *B*, as in *B*-a-*b*e.
8. *D*, as in *D*-i-*d*.

9. *G*, as in *G*-a-*g*.
10. *V*, as in *V*-al-*ve*
11. *Z*, as in *Z*-one.
12. *Z*, as in A-*z*-ure.
13. *Y*, as in *Y*-e.
14. *W*, as in *W*-oe
15. *TH*, as in *TH*-en.

*Compound* of 8. and 12.

16. *J*, as in *J*-oy.

The first six of the "subtonic" elements, *l*, *m*, *n*, *r* (hard,) *r* (soft,) and *ng*, have an unmixed "vocality" throughout: the seventh, eighth and ninth, *b*, *d*, *g*, have a "vocality," terminating in a sudden and explosive force of sound : the remaining " subtonics," *v*, *z*, *zh*, *y*, *w*, *th*, *j*, have an " aspiration," (whispering sound of the breath,) joined with their vocality.

The fourth of these elements, — *r*, as in *rap*, — differs from the fifth, — *r*, as in *far*, in having a harder and clearer sound, executed by a forcible but brief vibration of the tip of the tongue, against the first projecting ridge of the interior gum, immediately over the upper teeth ; while the latter has a soft murmuring sound, caused by a slight vibration of the whole forepart of the tongue, directed towards the middle part of the roof of the mouth.

The common errors of careless usage, substitute the " soft " for the " hard " *r*, and omit the " soft " *r*, entirely ; thus "*fah*," for *far*. Another class of errors, consists in *rolling*, or unduly prolong

---

[1] In arranging the "subtonics," words have, in as many cases as practicable, been selected for examples, which contain a repetition of the element under consideration. The design of this slight deviation from Dr. Rush, is to present each element as impressively as possible to the ear.

[2] Added to Dr. Rush's arrangement, for the reasons mentioned in subsequent observations on this element.—See last paragraph but one of this page.

**"ATONIC" ELEMENTS.**

ing, the sound of the "hard" *r*, and substituting the hard for the "soft" sound.

The greater prolongation of sound, which takes place in the average of *singing* notes, or in impassioned recitation, renders a slight comparative "roll" of the "hard" *r* unavoidable, at the beginning of a word. But it is a gross error of taste, to prolong this sound, in the style of foreign accent, as in French and Italian pronunciation, or to substitute the rough sound of the "hard" *r*, for the delicate murmur of the "soft" *r*.

The "subtonic" elements numbered 13 and 14,—*y*, as in ye and *w* as in *woe*,— are, it may be remarked, not properly separate elements from *e*, in *eve*, and *oo* in *ooze*, but only extremely short "quantities" of the same "qualities" of vowel sound which are exhibited in these words. They require, however, a closer position of the organs for their execution; and, hence, for the purposes of practical instruction, they may be advantageously studied as distinct elementary sounds.

**"ATONIC" ELEMENTS.**

These elements are thus designated by Dr. Rush, from their want of "tonic" property,— "their limited power of variation in pitch." "They are all, properly, 'aspirations,' and have not the sort of sound called 'vocality.' They are produced by a current of the *whispering* breath, through certain positions of parts, in the internal and external mouth."

1. *P*, as in *P*-i-*pe*.
2. *T*, as in *T*-en-*t*.
3. *C*, "hard," and *K*, as in *C*-a-*ke*.
4. *F*, as in *F*-i-*fe*.

5. *C*, "soft," and *S*, as in *C*-ea-*se*.
6. *H*, as in *H*-e.
7. *Th*, as in *Th*-in.
8. *Sh*, as in Pu-*sh*.

*Compound* of 2. and 8.

9. *Ch*, as in *Ch*-ur-*ch*.[1]

To some persons the foregoing analysis may seem unnecessarily minute. But exactness in articulation cannot exist without close discrimination and careful analysis. Many of the worst errors in the enunciation of words, are owing to slight oversights about the true sound of a letter. Without strict attention to details, there can, in this particular, be no security for accurate execution. The very common error, for example, of reading or singing the word *faith* as if it were written "*fai-eeth*," is merely an act of negligence regarding the "vanish," or final portion of sound, in the diphthong, *ai*,

---

[1] *Wh* which Dr. Rush has recognized as a distinct element, are but apparently such. They differ, in no respect, from the separate elements, *w* and *h* — only that, in the *modern orthography* of words, they are inverted, as to their order. The *ancient orthography* of the language, placed them as they stand in *orthoëpy*,— *Hw*; thus *Hweal*, *Hwen*, &c.

which,—although it is unavoidably analyzed by the voice, in the utterance of singing, to a greater extent than in that of reading,— should never be dissected, in the unnatural style which has just been mentioned.

We have omitted,—as will have been observed,—that part of Dr. Rush's analysis which presents the "tonic" elements *a*, as in *awe*, (identical with *a*, in *all*,) *a* in *arm*, and *a* in *an*, as diphthongs'. Correct reading and appropriate singing, alike forbid the "vanish" of these sounds to be rendered apparent to the ear. It is one of the acknowledged improprieties of enunciation, which permits the word *awe* to terminate in any form approaching,—even in the most distant degree,—the negligent style of "*awer*."

Let it be admitted that the "vanish," or final portion of the sound, in such elements, is but an unavoidable, accidental "vocule," inseparably attached to the "radical" or initial sound, when we utter it by itself; and it becomes, from its very nature, a thing which judgment and taste would alike require to be sunk out of notice to the ear, in the enunciation of syllables, or words.

---

The preceding arrangement of the elementary sounds of the language, as presented by Dr. Rush, exhibits them in a manner very clear and distinct, as *results* of organic action,—or as *sounds* formed by the voice. But to ascertain their character, with perfect accuracy of knowledge, for the purposes of vocal practice and culture, it becomes important to examine them closely, in connection with the exact position and movement of the *organs*, during the process of execution.

Classified, in this light, the audible elements of our language may be conveniently designated by the terms in use previous to Dr Rush's arrangement. We will commence with the

#### VOWELS AND DIPHTHONGS.

These elements, generally, are formed by the act of "expiration" modified into vocality by the larynx, and the adjoining organs, aided by the tongue, the palate, the lips, &c., which give definite and distinctive character to the sounds of the voice, as rudiments of speech.

The enunciation of vowels and diphthongs demands attention principally to *the free and expansive opening of the mouth*, together with a strict attention to the action of the particular organ, or organs, by which each element receives its peculiar character as a definite sound Much attention, in the execution of these sounds, is required to the action of the organs at the moment of commencing and at that of closing each sound. The sound of the voice in the utterance of the first audible portion of articulate sounds, Dr. Rush has termed the "radical," (initial,) movement: the sound uttered in the concluding portion of an articulation he has termed the "vanishing," (final,) movement. Each of these points of articulate sound, demands the closest discrimination, as regards both the voice, and the motion or action of the organs. If the latter is not exact, the former will be more or less incorrect or vague, confused, and indefinite. The "radical" movement always demands clearness, force, precision, and spirit, in the execution: the "vanish" requires nice and delicate finish, perfect exactness, but no undue marking or prominence. It should resemble, in its effect on the ear, that of a light but definite touch on the piano.

"In just articulation, the words are not to be hurried over, nor precipitated, syllable over syllable; nor, as it were, melted together into a mass of confusion: they should be neither abridged, nor pro-onged, nor swallowed, nor forced, and,—if I may so express myself,—shot from the mouth: they should not be trailed nor drawled, nor let slip out carelessly, so as to drop unfinished. They are to be delivered out from the lips, as beautiful coins newly issued from the mint, deeply and accurately impressed, perfectly finished, neatly struck by the proper organs, distinct, sharp, in due succession, and of due weight."[1]

The precision and force of the "radical" portion of a sound, are gained by deep inspiration, and a preliminary rallying, or gathering of impulse on the organs,—somewhat as we brace the muscles before the exercise of jumping or diving,—and then causing an instantaneous explosion of the accumulated and compacted breath, in the form of clear, cutting sound. In practising the following elements, this explosive, radical movement should be carried up from the slightest style of a suppressed cough to the most violent exertion, or the loudest style of coughing. The preliminary practice of a repeated actual cough is the best preparatory discipline for the species of organic action which constitutes the "radical" portion of any articulate sound.

VOCAL AND DIPHTHONGAL ELEMENTS,

corresponding to the "tonics" of Dr. Rush, and executed principally by the action of the *larynx*, with *the mouth more or less open.*

I. *Simple Sounds.*
1. *A*-ll;
2. *A*-rm;
3. *A*-n;
4. *E*-ve;
5. *OO*-ze,
" *L*-oo-k,
6 *E*-rr;
7. *E*-nd;
8. *I*-n;
9. *Ai*-r;
10. *U*-p;

11. *O*-r;
12. *O*-n.

II. *Compound Sounds.*
13. *A*-le; (original element and 4.)
14. *I*-ce; (3. and 4.)
15. *O*-ld; (original element and 5.)
16. *Ou*-r; (10. and 5.)
17. *Oi*-l; (12. and 8.)
18. *U*-se; (4. and 5.)

[1] Austin's Chironomia, pp. 38, 39

## CONSONANTAL ELEMENTS,

corresponding to the "subtonic" and "atonic" sounds in the classification of Dr. Rush.

### I. *Labial Sounds.*

These are,—in consonance with their designation —formed b the action of the *lips.* They may be enumerated as follows:

1. B-a-*be*,
2. P-i-*pe*;
3. M-ai-*m*;
4. W-oe;
5. [1]V-al-*ve*;
6. F-i-*fe*.

The "subtonic," *b*, is formed by a firm compression of the lips, which arrests the escape of the breath, and causes, by this occlusion of the mouth, a murmuring resonance of the voice in the cavity of the chest, and in the interior of the head and mouth. The pressure of the lips, in the formation of this sound, is increased to a maximum, or chief point, at which the lips are suddenly opened, and a slight explosive effect produced, which consummates the character of the sound, and causes a "vocule," or slight and obscure vowel sound, resembling *e*, in *err*, to follow the effort of the organs.

The "atonic," *p*, is produced by an intense compression of the lips, which prevents the possibility of any audible sound, till the forcible "aspirated," or whispering, explosion, following the maximum of the pressure, is heard, accompanied by the same "vocule" which attends the sound of *b*, but, in *p*, is only an aspiration, or whisper.

The precision of these two elements of speech, is dependent, wholly, on the full force of the labial compression, and the intensity of the following explosion, by which they are produced. In impassioned utterance, the force of the organic action, in the articulation of these sounds, must be carried to the utmost degree, and executed with instantaneous precision, and the most vivid effect.

The "subtonic," *m*, is articulated by a very gentle compression of the lips, attended by a murmur in the head and chest, resembling somewhat, that which forms the character of the "subtonic" *b*, but differing from it in the sound being accompanied by a free, steady, equable "expiration" through the nostrils. In extremely empassioned utterance, this gentle element is made to assume the character of intensity, by increasing the force of the labial compression to a maximum, and exploding the sound in a manner similar to that of *b*. This element is not *followed*, as *b* or *p*, by a "vocule;" its own distinctive character of sound, throughout, being very nearly of the "tonic," or purely vocal, nature.

The "subtonic" element, *w*, as in *woe*, is formed by rounding the lips, as in articulating *oo*, in *ooze*, but slightly compressing them, and holding them closer to the teeth: a brief vocal murmur is formed by

---

[1] This and the following element, being formed by means both of the lower lip and the upper teeth, are, on this account, sometimes called "**labio dentals**."

the breath, — as modified by the larynx, — escaping through this partial opening of the lips, and at the same time, in a very slight degree, through the nostrils. This sound has not, from its nature, much independent energy; neither does it admit of prolongation. But it becomes forcible and impassioned, to some extent, by increasing the pressure of the lips, and exploding the sound, somewhat in the manner of *m* and *b*, when rendered intense.

The "subtonic," *v*, is articulated by the sound of the voice being modified by bringing the upper fore-teeth close upon the ridge of the under lip, and, at the same time, slightly raising the upper lip, so as to prevent its interfering with the contact of the upper fore-teeth and the lower lip. A murmuring resonance, bordering on aspiration, is thus produced in the head and chest, by the partial escape of breath between the teeth and the lip. This element, — as mentioned before, — has, on this account, been sometimes denominated "labio-dental," — from its dependence on both these organs.

The "atonic," *f*, is executed as *v*, with the difference, only, arising from a closer compression of the teeth and the lip, a more forcible expulsion of the breath, and an aspirated or whispering character, in the sound. This element, also, is sometimes denominated "labio-dental," being formed as the preceding.

## II. *"Dental" Sounds.*

These are all modified, — as their name imports, — by the aid of the *teeth*. But, like many other articulate sounds, they are founded on, and imply, an action of the tongue; although this circumstance is not indicated in the designation of such elements.

1. *D*-i-*d*;
2. *T*-en-*t*;
3. *Th*-in;
4. *TH*-ine;
Compound of 1. and 5.
9. *J*-oy;

5. A-*z*-ure;
6. Pu-*sh*;
7. *C*-ea-*se*;
8. *Z*-one;
Compound of 2. and 6.
10. *Ch*-ur-*ch*.

The "subtonic," *d* is articulated by a partial vocal murmur, modified by pressing the tip of the tongue, with great energy, against the interior ridge of gum, immediately over the upper fore-teeth. This pressure is but an instantaneous effort; yet it evidently comes to a maximum, just before the explosion from which it takes its peculiar character, is executed. This explosion necessarily produces the "vocule," *e*, as in *err*

The "atonic" *t*, is executed in a similar manner, excepting the absence of vocal murmur, an intense percussive pressure of the tongue, and an aspirated explosion, which takes place in the act of withdrawing the tongue from the gum.

The "atonic," *th*, as in *thin*, is executed by a forcible "aspiration," modified by a slight horizontal parting of the lips, and a forcible pressure of the end of the tongue against the upper fore-teeth.

The "subtonic," *TH*, as in *thine*, is executed by a similar position of the organs, but a vocalized emission of the breath, forming a gentle resonance.

The "subtonic," *z*, as in *azure*, is formed by a partially vocal sound, modified by gently raising the whole fore-part of the tongue towards the roof of the mouth, and allowing the breath to escape, between it and the teeth.

The "atonic," *sh*, is formed in a similar manner, as regards the position of the organs, but with more pressure, and by means of 'aspiration," not "vocality," in the emission of the breath.

The "atonic" sound of *s*, or the soft sound of *c*, as in the word *cease*, is articulated by pressing, with intense force, the tip of the tongue against the interior gum, immediately over the fore-teeth. Through the extremely small aperture thus formed, aided by the horizontal parting of the lips, and the cutting effect of the edges of the teeth, the sibilation, or hiss, is formed, which gives the peculiar character of this element.

The "subtonic," *z*, as in *zone*, is formed by nearly the same position of the organs, as the preceding element, but with very slight pressure, and by means of "vocalized," not "aspirated," sound.

### III. "*Palatic*" Sounds.

These are so termed from their depending on the *palate*, for their distinctive character. They are enumerated as follows:

1. *C*, "hard," and *K*, as in *C*-a-*k*e; 2. *G*, as in *G*-a-*g*; 3. *Y*, as in *Y*-e.

The "atonic," *c*, "hard," or *k*, is executed by opening the mouth retracting, and curving the tongue with great force, and exploding an aspiration against the palate.

The "subtonic," *g*, as in *gag*, is formed by similar movements and positions of the organs, but less forcible, and by means of "vocality," instead of "aspiration."

The "subtonic," *y*, is articulated by a similar process, still less forcible, and by means of "expulsion," not "explosion," as regards the character of the function and the sound.

### IV. "*Aspirated*" Element.
### *H*, as in *H*-e.

This sound is formed by a forcible emission of the breath, in the style of a whisper, and a moderate opening of all the organs of speech.

### V. "*Nasal*" Sounds.

1. *N*, as in *N*-u-*n*; 2. *Ng*, as in Si-*ng*; or *N*, as in l-*n*-k.

The "subtonic, *n*, is articulated by a vocalized breathing through the *nose*; the lips parted freely; and the end of the tongue pressing vigorously against the interior ridge of gum, immediately above the upper fore-teeth.

The "subtonic," *ng*, is formed by a vocalized breathing, directed against the nasal passage and the back part of the veil of the palate, and by a retracted and elevated position of the lower part of the tongue, which partly shuts the nasal passage, and causes it, at the same moment, to become resonant.

## VI. *"Lingual" Sounds.*

These elements are so called from their special dependence on the action of the *tongue.* They are the following:

1. *L,* as in *L*-u-*ll ;* 2. *R,* as in *R*-ap ; 3. *R,* as in Fa-*r.*

These are all "subtonic" elements.

The first is formed by a moderate opening of the mouth, and the utterance of a vocalized sound, modified by raising the tongue towards the roof of the mouth, and pressing the end of it, very gently, against the interior ridge of gum, immediately above the upper fore-teeth.

The "subtonic," *r*, as in *rap*, is an element formed by vivid and energetic vibration of the tip of the tongue, against the interior ridge of gum, immediately over the upper fore-teeth, forming a partially vocalized sound, clear and forcible, but very brief. It should never extend to a prolonged trill, or roll. This element is sometimes designated as "initial" *r*, from its occurring at or near the beginning of words and syllables; and sometimes "hard," or "rough," *r*, from its comparative force, as contrasted with *r* at the end of a word, which is always soft in sound. This element follows but never precedes a consonant; thus, *Pray, brass, crape, green, dread, tread, scream, spread,* &c.

The "subtonic," *r*, as in *far*, is a softer sound, of longer duration, modified by a slight and gentle vibration of the whole fore-part of the tongue, retracted, and rising towards the roof of the mouth, but not actually touching it. The just observance of the true character of this and the preceding element, is, as was mentioned before, a point of great moment in enunciation, and decides its style, as regards taste and culture. The designation of "soft," or "smooth," *r*, is sometimes given to the "final" *r;* as it is a more delicate and liquid sound, than the "hard," or "initial," *r*. This element occurs at the end of words, and *before*, but never *after*, a consonant; thus, *War, star, fair, ire, ear, oar, farm, barn, card, harp, part mercy, servant, person,* &c.

*Note.* — It is one of the great inconveniences of our language, that we have so few letters or characters, by which to designate its sounds; and it is not less a defect in it, that we have the same element sometimes represented by a great variety of letters, and combinations of letters. Thus, the element *a*, in *ale*, is heard also in *aid, lay, weigh, survey,* &c.

*A,* in *arm,* is heard, also, in *aunt.*

*A,* in *all,* is heard, in *awe, laud,* &c.

*A,* in *what was, wash,* &c., is used to represent the same sound with *o,* as in *on,* or *not.*

*A,* as in *rare,* is heard, also, in *air, prayer,* &c.

*E*, as in *eve*, occurs, also, in the sound of *ee* in *eel*, *ea*, in *eat*; *ie*, in *field*; *ei*, in *seize*.

*E*, in *end*, occurs in the form of *ea*, in *head*.

*E*, in *err*, is the same sound which occurs in *heard*, and in *firm*.

*Y*, except its peculiar sound in *ye*, is but a repetition of *i*, long or short; thus *rhyme*, *hymn*, &c.

*O*, in *old*, is repeated in *oak*, *course*, *own*, &c.

*Oo*, in *ooze*, and *oo*, in *foot*, recur in the sounds of *o*, in *move*; *u* in *true*; *o*, in *wolf*; *u*, in *pull*; *ui*, in *fruit*, &c.

The diphthongal sound *oi*, as in *oil*, is heard, always, in *oy*. The sound of *u*, in *use*, occurs also in the form of *iew* in *view*; *eau*, in *beauty*.

The diphthong *ou*, in *our*, is repeated in the sound of *ow* in *down* &c.

*F*, as a sound, recurs in the form of *ph* and *gh*; as in *phrase*, *laugh*, &c.

*J*, and *g* "soft," are, on the other hand, but combinations of the sounds of *d*, and of *z*, as in *azure*.

*Ch*, in *church*, are but repetitions of the sound of *t* and *sh*.

The sound of *sh* is found also in the words, *nation*, *gracious*, *ocean*, &c.

*C*, "soft," is identical with *s*.

*S*, is, in multitudes of instances, but a repetition of *z*, as, for example, in *houses*, *diseases*, &c.

The sound of *k* is repeated in the form of *c*, "hard;" *ch*, as in *chorus*; and *q*, as in *queen*.

*N*, in *ink*, is identical with *ng*.

*X*, in either form, is but a repetition, in sound, of *ks* or *gz*; thus, *ex*, *example*, &c.

It is unnecessary, however, to enlarge on these inconsistencies in the forms of our language. It is sufficient, perhaps, for our present purpose, to suggest the fact, that the orthography of words may sometimes afford no guidance to orthoëpy, but, rather, may apparently mislead. The ear should, in all cases, be trained to the utmost exactness and precision, in detecting and seizing the true element of sound, independently of the form or combination of letters, by which it may be represented.

---

WORDS

to be practised in the same style as the exercises on syllables, — each component element kept perfectly clear and distinct.

## I. *Tonic Elements.* — *Simple Sounds.*

One error, often made in the following class of words, is to pronounce them nearly as if written *oall*, &c. Sometimes, we hear the coarse error of dividing the sound of *a*, in such words, into two parts thus *O-ŭll*, *fo-ŭll*, &c. To a cultivated ear, this sound is peculiarly displeasing, as associated with low and slovenly habit.

ENUNCIATION OF WORDS.

1. *A*, as in *A*-ll.

All    War    Law    Awful    Water

2. *A*, as in *A*-rm.

The two current errors in this class of sounds, are, 1st, — as in the local usage of New England, — flattening it down to *a* in *an;* — 2d, as in the custom of the Middle States, making it as broad as *a* in *all.* The former style causes the pronunciation of " fărm," " părt," ' făther ;" the latter, that of " fawrm," " pawrt," " fawther."

Harm    Bar    Mart    Balm    Daunt

3. *A*, as in *A*-n.

Common errors : — 1, *a* flattened down to *e*, in *end*, nearly ; thus, " Dence," " pess,"— the local usage of the Middle States ; — 2d, *a* made as broad as *a*, in *arm;* thus, " Dânce," (as if *darnce,*) " pâss," — the customary fault of New England.

Add    Band    Mass    Last    Slạnt    Dance
had    hand    páss    mást    chant    lance
mad    land    grass    past    gránt    glance

4. *E*, as in *E*-ve.

There is seldom any error made in the enunciation of such words as the following, except the slight one arising from not distinguishing between the longer sound of *ee* before a " subtonic," as in *feel*, and the shorter, before an " atonic," as in *feet*.

The explosive force of the organic action, in executing an " atonic," compresses the preceding vowel : the gentle and gradual sliding of the *ee* into a " subtonic," allows it a longer duration.

Theme    Feel    Heed   |   Week    Feet    Deep

5. *OO*, as in *Oo*-ze ; *OO*, as in *L-oo*-k.

The sound of this element, needs attention to the same distinction as in case of the *ee*. Before a " tonic " element, it is prolonged, — before an " atonic," it is shortened. The difference is exemplified, for the former, in *tool*, — for the latter, in *took*.

Cool    Boom    Moon   |   Hook    Hoop    Boot

*Exceptions.* Good, wood, stood, which have the *oo* short, though before a " subtonic."

6. *E*, as in *E*-rr.

The just, not overdone, distinction between *urn* and *earn*, is the object to be kept in view, in practising on the following words. This class of sounds is so liable to mispronunciation, that it needs close and repeated attention. — See remarks on the " tonic " element, *e* in *err*, — in the discussion of elementary sounds.

| Err | Serve | ¹Earth | ¹Firm | Mercy | Merciful |
|---|---|---|---|---|---|
| erst | verse | earl | gird | person | terminate |
| herk | stern | pearl | girl | servant | perfectly |

### 7. *E*, as in *E*-nd.

The common error in the following class of words, is that of allowing the vowel to approach the sound of *a* in *ale*; thus, "*taill*" for *tell*. Other errors are such as "*stiddy*," for *stĕady*· "*maysure*," for *mĕasure*.

| Elk | Hence | Let | Bell | Den | Bed |
|---|---|---|---|---|---|
| Ready | steady | measure | pleasure | general | genuine |

### 8. *I*, as in *I*-n.

The common error of careless articulation, in this element, makes it approach the *a* of *ale*; thus, "*sainn*," for *sin*. An opposite error in foreign style, or in bad taste, gives "*scenn*," for *sin*; "*ceetee*," for *cĭty*, &c.

| Din | Dim | Bid | Ill | Lip | Bit |

### 9. *A*, as in *Ai*-r.

Sometimes carelessly enunciated as *a* in *an*, prolonged; thus. "*ăer*," for *air*; — sometimes too fastidiously flattened, and reduced to *a* in *ale*; thus, "*ācr*" for *air*. The true sound lies between.

| Bare | Fare | Hair | Stare | Barely | Aware |

### 10. *U*, as in *U*-p.

The error in enunciating this element, is that of forming the sound in a coarse, guttural style, which makes it approach the sound of *o* in *on*. This fault is prevalent in the usage of the Middle States.

| Up | Bud | Gum | Dun | But | Done |

### 11. *O*, as in *O*-r.

Three errors are extensively prevalent in the mode of enunciating this element: — 1st, a local error of New England, which gives a double sound for a single one, — commencing with *o* in *old*, and ending with *u* in *up*, or *a* in *an*, thus "*nŏŭr*," or "*nŏăr*," for *nor*, 2d, a local error of the Middle States, which makes the sound too broad, and resembling the *a* in *arm*; thus, "*năr*," for *nor*; 3d, a long and drawling sound, which has a coarse and slovenly character; thus *cawrd*, for *cord*.

| Orb² | Born | Cork | Sort | Form |

### 12. *O*, as in *O*-n.

A prevalent local error in Massachusetts, in the following class of

---

¹ The same element with *e* in *err*, though differertly spelled.
² The *r* of these words is *soft*, but never *silent*, as in the style of faulty usage.

sounds, exists in the words, *loss, lost, soft,* &c., which are pronounced nearly with *o,* as in *old;* thus "*loass,*" "*loast,*" "*soaft,*" &c., and sometimes with a double, instead of a single sound; thus "*lŏăst,*" &c., for *lŏst.* The local error of usage, in the state of Connecticut, verges to the opposite extreme, in such words, and gives, for *o,* a sound too nearly like that of *a* in *an;* thus "*lăss,*" &c., for *lŏss.*

| On  | Mob | Bog | Rod   | Lop | Loss |
|-----|-----|-----|-------|-----|------|
| odd | rob | dog | god¹  | sop | toss |

### 13. *A,* as in *A*-le.

The common error in the enunciation of this element, is that of making its "vanish" too conspicuous; thus "*aeel*" for *ale.* An opposite error is not uncommon, — that of omitting the delicate "vanishing" sound entirely, which makes the style of enunciation coarse and negligent.

Ace   Day   Hail   Lade   Make   Came

### 14. *I,* as in *I*-ce.

The two errors to be avoided in enunciating this element, are, 1st, that of commencing with too broad a sound; thus, "*âece,*" for *ice* (*ăece;*) 2d, that of commencing it with too flat a sound; thus, "*ăece,*" for *ice.* — See remarks on "tonic" elements.

| Dice | Bide | Life | Lime  | Fight | Dive |
|------|------|------|-------|-------|------|
| rice | ride | rife | time  | light | hive |
| vice | side | wife | prime | might | rive |

### 15. *O,* as in *O*-ld.

A prevalent error in the local usage of New England, makes this *o* too short; thus, "*hom,*" for home. A common error of the Middle States makes the sound too broad; thus "*fûrce*" for *förce.*

| Oh    | Go    | Bold | Home   | Lone  | Hope  |
|-------|-------|------|--------|-------|-------|
| lo    | wo    | cold | loam   | bone  | mope  |
| so    | foe   | hold | foam   | stone | grope |
| both  | ford  | fort | course | gore  | boat  |
| oath  | sword | port | force  | more  | coat  |
| sloth | forge | sport| source | pour  | dote  |

### 16. *Ou,* as in *Ou*-r.

The prevailing errors on this element, are "*âur,*" "*ăur,*" and "*ŭr,*" for *ou*, (*o* sounding as in *done.*) The first two of these

---

¹ Commonly mispronounced "*ga·vd,*" "*goad,*" "*gŏŏd,*" or "*gŭd.*"

errors are current in the pronunciation of the Southern and Middle States; the last, in that of New England.

| Out | How | Loud | Cow | Fowl | Crown |
|-----|-----|------|-----|------|-------|
| ounce | now | cloud | count | howl | drown |
| owl | vow | proud | gown | growl | frown |

17. *Oi*, as in *Oi*-l.

The two errors usually exhibited in enunciating this element, are 1st, beginning the diphthong with the sound of *o*, in *own*, instead of that of *o*, in *on*; 2d, closing with a sound resembling *a*, in *ale*, instead of *i*, in *in*.

| Boil | Toil | Joy | Coin | Broil | Rejoice |
|------|------|-----|------|-------|---------|
| coil | soil | hoy | join | spoil | appoint |
| foil | coy | toy | loin | groin | avoid |

18. *U*, as in *U*-se, [long, as in the *verb*,—short, as in tne *noun*.]

The common errors in articulating this compound element, consist in, 1st, turning the whole sound into *oo*, as in *ooze*; 2d, making the diphthong commence with *a*, in *ale*, instead of *e*, in *eve*, shortened, or the sound of *y*, in *yet*.

| Use | Tune | Feud | Cue | Human | Student | Constitution |
|-----|------|------|-----|-------|---------|--------------|
| cure | dupe | hew | due | useful | stupid | institution |
| lure | fume | few | sue | humor | stewing | revolution |

II. " *Subtonic* " *Elements*.

1. *L* as in *L*-u-*ll*.

| Loll | Lie | Lad | All | Weal | Dull |

2. *M*, as in *M*-ai-*m*.

The common error in the enunciation of this element, is that of sounding it too slightly, and in a slack and lagging style.

| Mime | May | Move | Am | Him | Hum |

3. *N*, as in *N*-u-*n*.

The common fault of enunciation in this, as in the preceding element, is a want of that force which belongs to energetic and animated utterance.

| Nine | Nay | Now | An | Den | Din |

ENUNCIATION OF WORDS.

4. *R*, as in *R*-ap. [*R* initial, *before* a *vowel*, or *after* a *consonant*.]

The error to be avoided in articulating this element, is that of prolonging it into a "roll," or that of substituting for it the soft sound of *r* "final." A correct articulation, in this instance, always presents to the ear a firm, clear, and distinct, but very brief sound.

| Raw | Red | Rid | Ream | Robe | Rude | Rub |
|---|---|---|---|---|---|---|
| rye | rent | rim | reel | rose | rule | ruff |
| ray | rest | rip | reap | roam | rue | rust |
| Brag | Brave | Grave | Crane | Pray | Trade | Stray |
| brass | brain | grim | crag | prate | track | stride |
| brad | braid | groan | cry | prone | tread | strut |

5. *R*, as in Fa-*r* ; [*r* final, or *before* a *consonant*.]

The error most frequent in the articulation of this element, is that of omitting it, through inadvertency. This fault is one of the conspicuous peculiarities of the style of pronunciation prevalent among the uncultivated classes of the city of London. But it is not less so, even among educated people, in the United States. The soft *r*, being one of the few liquid consonants which our language possesses, should never be omitted in enunciation. At the same time, it should never be converted into the opposite *r*, as in *rap*, as it often is, in the style of foreigners; neither should it ever be dwelt upon, or prolonged in sound. It is properly but a "vanish," in its effect on the ear; as its vibrating and murmuring articulation prevents it from becoming forcible or distinct. The tongue should execute it with a delicate motion adapted to its slight and evanescent character.

| Hare | Bar | Ear | Ire | Ore | Lure | Bur |
|---|---|---|---|---|---|---|
| dare | car | fear | hire | core | pure | cur |
| fare | mar | hear | mire | door | sure | pur |
| Orb | Arm | Earn | Dark | Pearl | Art | Burn |
| horn | harm | fern | hark | marl | dart | turn |
| form | farm | learn | lark | whirl | part | churn |
| Murmur | former | charmer | warmer | warbler | burner | forlorn |

*Exercise on words containing both sounds of R.*

. [The difference in the sounds of the *hard* and the *soft* *r* should be exactly observed.]

| Rare | Rear | Roar | Reared | Roared | Rarely | Drier |
|---|---|---|---|---|---|---|
| error | horror | terror | brier | prior | truer | crier |
| regular | barrier | terrier | merrier | forrier | barrier | courser |

# 36   ORTHOPHONY.

6. *Ng*, as in Si-*ng*; [or *n*, before *g* hard or *k*.]

| King | Gong | Hang | Hung | Bank | Ink |
|---|---|---|---|---|---|
| ring | wrong | bang | tongue | rank | sink |
| wing | prong | rang | sprung | drank | wink |
| Hanging | Ringing | Lancing | Mangling | Haranguing | |
| twanging | winging | glancing | dangling | prolonging | |
| swinging | bringing | dancing | wrangling | besprinkling | |

7. *B*, as in *B*-a-*b*e.

The forcible execution of this, and the two following elements, in a very clear and compact form, is often indispensable to the full effect of vivid emotion.

| Babe | Ball | Bead | Blab | Mob | Curb |
|---|---|---|---|---|---|

8. *D*, as in *D*-i-*d*.

| Did | Dawn | Den | Laid | Mad | Bed |
|---|---|---|---|---|---|

9. *G*, as in *G*-a-*g*.

| Gag | Gave | Gall | Gull | Hag | Log |
|---|---|---|---|---|---|

10. *V*, as in *V*-al-*v*e.

| Valve | Vaunt | Cave | Leave | Velvet | Survive |
|---|---|---|---|---|---|

11. *Z*, as in *Z*-one, [or *s* flat.]

| Zone | Maze | Has | Daisies | Disease |
|---|---|---|---|---|

12. *Z*, as in A-*z*-ure, [or *s*, as in *measure*.]

| Seizure | Measure | Vision | Composure | Derision |
|---|---|---|---|---|

13. *Y*, as in *Y*-e.

| | Yes[2] | Young | Yawn | Yearly |
|---|---|---|---|---|
| yea | you | youth | yell | yellow |

14. *W*, as in *W*-oe.

| Way | Was | Ware | Wed | Wine |
|---|---|---|---|---|

15. *TH*, as in *TH*-ine.

| They | Than | Then | Thee | Bathe | Beneath |
|---|---|---|---|---|---|

[1] *Yay*, not "*ye*."  [2] *Yes*, not "*yiss*." In *there* and a few other words, the style recommended by Walker, is now obsolete.

16. *J*, as in *J*-oy, [and *G*, soft.]

Joy . Jar Jilt Page Giant Judge

### III. *"Atonic" Elements.*

[All "atonics," from their utter want of vocality, need great force and precision in their articulation.]

1. *P*, as in *P*-i-*pe*.

Pulp Pall Pile Pale Paper Pulpy

2. *T*, as in *T*-en-*t*.

Tight Tall Top Mat Tatter Total

3. *C*, hard, and *K*, as in *C*-a-*k*e; and *Q*, as in *Q*-ueen.

Key Cane Queen Creak Deck Cork

4. *F*, as in *F*-i-*fe*.

Fade Fell File Off Hoof Fly

5. *S*, (sharp,) and *C*, soft, as in *C*-ea-*se*.

Say See Sauce Mass Source Ceaseless

6. *H*, as in *H*-e.

Hail Had Heel Hit What Whet

7. *Th*, as in *Th*-in.

Thank Through Thong Thrust Hath Breath

8. *Sh*, as in Pu-*sh*.

Sham Shine Share Shroud Ash Hush

9. *Ch*, as in *Ch*-ur-*ch*.

Chair Check March Chine Fetch

### IV. *Syllabic Combinations.*

1. *Initial Syllables.*

The common faults in the enunciation of syllables, consist in a slack, obscure articulation of the single elements of which they are composed, ana, in addition, the fault of negligently allowing a vowel sound to intervene between the consonants; thus, "*bălă*," for *blă*. True taste will never allow a slovenly style of articulation, but wil. always maintain a neat, clear, and exact sound of every element, in whatever combination it may occur.

*Bl, cl, fl, gl, pl, sl, spl.*

Blame, bleed, blow, blest. Claim, clean, clime, close, clot. Flane, flee, fly, flit. Glare, gleam, glide, gloss. Place, plea, p'y, please. Slay, sleep, slide, slew. Spleen, splice, splay.

*Br, cr, dr, fr, gr, pr, spr, tr, str, shr.*

[The following words need attention to a clear, distinct enunciation of the hard *r*,—free, however, from prolongation and roll.]

Brave, bread, brink. Crave, creep, cried, crust. Drain, dream, dry, drop. Frame, free, fro, freeze. Grain, green. grind, ground. Pray, preach, pry, proud. Spray, spring, sprung, sprang. Trace, tree, try, trust, track, tread, trip, true. Stray, street, strife, strength. Shrine, shroud, shrub, shriek

*Sm, sn, sp, st.*

Small, smite, smote. Snare, sneer, snow, snug. Space speed, spike, spear. Stay, steer, stile, stop.

### 2. *Final Syllables.*

*Ld, lf, lk, lm, lp, ls, lt, lve.*

Bold, hailed, tolled. Elf, wolf, gulf, sylph. Milk, silk, bulk, hulk. Elm, helm, whelm, film. Help, gulp, Alp scalp. Falls, tells, toils. Fault, melt, bolt, hilt. Elve, delve revolve.

*M'd, ms, nd, ns, nk, nce, nt.*

Maim'd, claim'd, climb'd, gloom'd. Gleams, streams, climes, stems. And, band, hand, land, lined, moaned. Gains, dens, gleans, suns. Bank, dank, drink, link. Dance, glance hence, ounce. Ant, want, gaunt, point.

*Rb, rd, rk, rm, rn, rse, rs (rz,) rt, rve, rb'd, rk'd, rm'd, rnd, rst, rv'd.*

Barb, orb, herb, curb, barb'd, orb'd, curb'd, disturb'd. Hard

# ENUNCIATION OF WORDS.

herd, hir'd, board, lord, gourd, bar'd, barr'd. Hark, lark, jerk stork, work, mark'd, jerk'd, work'd. Arm, harm, farm, alarm arm'd, harm'd, alarm'd. Earn, learn, scorn, thorn, burn, turn, worn, shorn, earn'd, scorn'd, burn'd, turn'd. Hearse, verse, force, horse, dar'st, burst, first, worst, hears'd, vers'd, forc'd, hors'd. Bars, bears, hears, wears, pairs, tares, snares, repairs. Mart, dart, start, hurt, pert, girt. Carve, curve, serve, starve, carv'd, curv'd, serv'd, starv'd.

*Sm, s'n, sp, st, ss'd, ks, ct, k'd, ft, f'd, pt, p'd, p'n k'n, t'n, v'n, t'n.*

Chasm, schism, prism, criticism, witticism, patriotism. [1]Reas'n, seas'n, ris'n, chos'n. Asp, clasp, grasp, wasp, lisp, crisp. Vast, mast, lest, dost, must, lost, mist; pass'd, bless'd, gloss'd, miss'd. Makes, quakes, likes, looks, streaks, rocks, crooks. Act, fact, respect, reject; wak'd, lik'd, look'd, rock'd. Waft, oft, left, sift, quaff'd, scoff'd, laugh'd. Apt, wept crept; sipp'd, supp'd, slop'd, pip'd, popp'd. [1]Op'n, rip'n, weap'n, happ'n. Tak'n, wak'n, weak'n, tok'n, drunk'n. Sadd'n, gladd'n, lad'n, burd'n, hard'n, gard'n. Grav'n, heav'n, riv'n, ov'n, ev'n, giv'n, wov'n. Bright'n, tight'n whit'n.

*Lst, mst, nst, rst, dst, rdst, rmdst, rndst.*

Call'st, heal'st, till'st, fill'st, roll'st, pull'st. Arm'st charm'st, form'st, harm'st. Can'st, runn'st, gain'st, against. (*agenst.*) Durst, worst, erst, first, bar'st, barr'st, hir'st Midst, call'dst, fill'dst, roll'dst. Heard'st, guard'st, reward'st discard'st. Arm'dst, harm'dst, form'dst, charm'dst. Learn'dst scorn'dst, burn'dst, turn'dst.

*Ble, ple, dle, rl, bl'd, dl'd, pl'd, rld.*

Able, feeble, bible, double; troubl'd, babbl'd, bubbl'd doubl'd. Ample, steeple, triple, topple; tripl'd, toppl'd, dappl'd, crippl'd. Cradle, saddle, idle, bridle; cradl'd saddl'd, idl'd, swaddl'd. Marl, hurl, whirl; world, hurl'd, whirl'd, furl'd.

[1] *O* and *E* should never be heard, in these and similar words, unless in singing and then only when a verse demands the syllable us a requisite to metre

ORTHOPHONY.

*Ngs, ngst, ng'd, ngdst.*

Rings, wrongs, hangs, songs; hang'st, sing'st, wrong'st, bring'st; wrong'd, hang'd, clang'd; wrong'dst, throng'dst.

V. *Exercise in transition from one class of Elements to another.*

The design of this exercise is to impress vividly on the mind the distinctive quality of each species of sound, and the effect of each on the organic action. — The columns are to be read across the page

| "*Tonics.*" | "*Subtonics.*" | "*Atonics.*" |
|---|---|---|
| *A*-ll | *B*-a-*be* | *P*-i-*pe* |
| *A*-m | *D*-i-*d* | *T*-en-*t* |
| *A*-n | *G*-a-*g* | *C*-a-*ke* |
| *E*-ve | *V*-al-*ve* | *F*-i-*fe* |
| *Oo*-ze | *Z*-one | *C*-ea-*se* |
| *E*-rr | *A*-*z*-ure | Pu-*sh* |
| *E*-nd | TH-en | *Th*-in |
| *I*-n | *J*-ud-ge | *Ch*-ur-*ch* |

VI. *Exercise in transition from one class of Organic Actions to another.*

| *Labials.* | *Dentals.* | *Aspirate.* |
|---|---|---|
| *B*-a-*be* | *D*-i-*d* | *H*-e |
| *P*-i-*pe* | *T*-en-*t* | *Nasals.* |
| *M*-ai-*m* | *Th*-in | *N*-u-*n* |
| *W*-oe | *TH*-ine | Si-*ng* |
| *V*-al-*ve* | *J*-oy | *Linguals.* |
| *F*-i-*fe* | *Ch*-ur-*ch* | *L*-u-*ll* |
| *Palatics.* | *A*-*z*-ure | *R*-a-p |
| *C*-a-*ke* | Pu-*sh* | *F*-a-*r* |
| *G*-a-*g* | *C*-ea-*se* | |
| *Y*-e | *Z*-one | |

VII. *Exercise in difficult Combinations of Elements.*

1. U, as in Use.

| L*uc*ubration | Instit*u*tion | Acc*u*mulate | Incalc*u*lably |
|---|---|---|---|
| *u*g*u*brious | constit*u*tion | manip*u*late | s*u*periority |
| incalc*u*lable | revol*u*tion | deglu*u*tition | s*u*premacy |

## 2. Words of many syllables

| | | |
|---|---|---|
| Absolutely | Necessarily | Coextensively |
| abstinently | ordinarily | Annihilation |
| accessory | momentarily | annunciation |
| accurately | temporarily | appreciation |
| agitated | voluntarily | apologetic |
| adequately | Obediently | association |
| angularly | immediately | circumlocution |
| antepenult | innumerable | apocalyptic |
| architecture | intolerable | circumvolution |
| agriculture | dishonorable | coagulation |
| Annihilate | ambiguously | colonization |
| antipathy | articulately | commemoration |
| apocrypha | collaterally | Congratulatory |
| apostatize | colloquially | authoritatively |
| appropriate | Affability | disinterestedly |
| assiduous | agricultural | expostulatory |
| assimilate | allegorical | Dietetically |
| associate | alimentary | disingenuousness |
| auricular | astrological | Immutability |
| Acquiescence | atmospherical | compatibility |
| acquisition | christianity | ecclesiastical |
| alienation | chronological | spirituality |

## 3. Repetition of Elements.

*H*ail! *h*eavenly *h*armony.
Up the *h*igh *h*ill *h*e *h*eaved a *h*uge round stone.
Heaven's fir*st st*ar alike ye see.
Let it wave proudly o'er the good an*d* brave
The supply la*sts st*ill.
An*d* gleamin*g* an*d* streamin*g* an*d* steamin*g* an*d* teamin*g*
An*d* rushin*g* an*d* flushin*g* an*d* brushin*g* an*d* gushin*g*,
An*d* flappin*g* an*d* rappin*g* an*d* clappin*g* an*d* slappin*g*,
An*d* curlin*g* an*d* whirlin*g* an*d* purlin*g* an*d* twirlin*g*,
Retreatin*g* an*d* beatin*g* an*d* meetin*g* an*d* sheetin*g*,
Delayin*g* an*d* strayin*g* an*d* playin*g* an*d* sprayin*g*,
Advancin*g* an*d* glancin*g* an*d* prancin*g* an*d* lancin*g*,

Recoiling, turmoiling and toiling and boiling,
And thumping and flumping and bumping and jumping
And dashing and flashing and splashing and clashing.
And so never ending, but always descending,
Sounds and motions for ever and ever are blending,
All at once and all o'er, with a mighty uproar;
And this way the water comes down at Lodore.

It is the first step that costs.

The deed was done in broad day.

None now was left to tell the mournful tale.

Take care that you be not deceived,—dear friends.

Lie lightly on her, earth! her step was light on thee.

Thou wast struck dumb with amazement.

Can no one be found faithful enough to warn him of his danger? No one dared do it.

A good deal of disturbance ensued.

He gave him good advice which he did not take.

A dark cloud spread over the heavens.

Had he but heeded the counsel of his friend, he might have been saved.

He came at last too late to be of any service.

The magistrates stood on an elevated platform.[1]

---

It is a fact familiar in the experience of most teachers, that, after the utmost care in the systematic cultivation of the utterance of young readers, by regular analytic exercises, such as the preceding, the influence of colloquial negligence in habit, is so powerful, that the same individual who has just articulated, with perfect exactness, the elements on a column,—while he is kept mechanically on his guard against error, by express attention to details,—will, immediately on beginning to read a page of continuous expression of thought, relapse into his wonted errors of enunciation. To correct this tendency, no resort is so effectual as that of studying analytically a few lines, previous to commencing the usual practice of a reading lesson. The attention must first be turned to the words as such,—as forms of articulation,—then to their sounds in connection with their sense.

The following will be found useful modes of practising such exer-

[1] These and similar examples, as they occur in reading lessons, should be repeated till they can be executed with perfect distinctness, and with an easy exertion of the organs. But a hard and labored style should be carefully avoided as a very bad fault.

class as are now suggested. Begin at the end of a line, sentence, or paragraph, so as to prevent the possibility of reading negligently, then, 1st, articulate every *element* in every word, separately and very distinctly, throughout the line or sentence; 2d, enunciate every *syllable* of each word, throughout the line or sentence, clearly and exactly; 3d, pronounce every *word*, in the same style; 4th, read the *line* or *sentence*, from the beginning, forward, with strict attention to the manner of pronouncing every word; 5th, read the whole line or sentence with *an easy fluent enunciation*, paying strict attention to the expression of *the meaning*, but without losing correctness in the style of pronunciation.

This is, apparently, a merely mechanical drill; but its effects are strikingly beneficial, in a very short time. The habits of classes of young readers have thus been, in some instances, effectually changed, within a very few weeks, from slovenliness and indistinctness to perfect precision and propriety, united to fluency and freedom of style.

To adults, also, the practice of such exercises as have been mentioned, proves, in the highest degree, useful, as an effectual means of correcting erroneous habit, and of acquiring that distinctness of utterance which is so important in the exercise of public speaking, or in that of private reading, for social and literary purposes.

An exercise of great practical value, as regards the formation of habit in enunciation, is, to select from every reading lesson, before and after the regular consecutive reading of a piece, all words and phrases which contain difficult combinations, and repeat them often

## PRONUNCIATION.

A full statement of the rules of usage in pronunciation, as regards the accent of polysyllables, does not properly fall within the scope of this work, which is designed rather for the cultivation of the voice, and the discipline of the organs, than as a manual of orthoëpy. The most important classes of errors in pronunciation, have been already indicated. But this branch of the subject is discussed, at greater length, in the " American Elocutionist," to which the present volume is introductory. It occurs in a form adapted to the instruction of young readers, in the " Introduction to the American Common-School Reader and Speaker," and is presented for the use of professional speakers, in the volume entitled " Pulpit Elocution." [1]

For the present purpose it may suffice to suggest the benefit arising from the daily systematic study of a good standard dictionary of orthoëpy; such as Walker's, which, — with due allowance for a very few points in which custom has slightly changed since that work was written, — remains the most accurate report of authorized custom, in the vast majority of places where the English language is spoken. If Dr. Webster's dictionary be preferred, the 8vo edition of it, prepared by Mr. J. E. Worcester, will be found the most useful; as it contains, in the introduction, a full list of all words in

---

[1] The works mentioned in the text, are prepared by the compiler of this manual.

which Dr. Webster's style is peculiar to himself, or merely to the local custom of New England, which, as regards the standard of the genuine pronunciation of the English language, is justly considered, elsewhere, as liable to the same objections with the local peculiarities of Scotland or of Ireland, — current, as sanctioned by respectable authority, in their several regions, but, when referred to the standard of general English usage, to be condemned as faults.

## CHAPTER III.

### "QUALITY" OF VOICE.

The learner, having acquired, by the exercises prescribed in the preceding chapters, a free and forcible use of the breathing apparatus, and of the organs of speech which are employed in articulation, has thus laid the requisite foundation for the course of vocal training in "expression," or the various qualities of utterance, which are the appropriate language of emotion.

The word *utterance*, as a term in elocution, is used to designate the mere act of forming and emitting voice: it does not necessarily imply any of those functions of the organs by which articulate sound is produced; thus we speak of a person uttering a cry, a groan, a sigh, a moan, a sob, or a laugh. In a correspondent use of language, we read that "the seven thunders *uttered* their voices."

The function of utterance is necessarily attended, however, with a given degree of *force* in sound, — from that of whispering, or of any of the intermediate stages, to that of shouting and calling. It implies, also, a certain *note of the scale*, — high, low, or intermediate in pitch. The utterance of successive sounds is, farther, slow, rapid, or moderate, as regards the rate of *movement*. These properties, — force, pitch, and rate, or movement, coexist in one strain of utterance, and are, to the ear, independent of the process of articulation or the function of speech. An example of mere utterance is furnished in the successive notes of a song hummed or sung without words, — or sung at such a distance from us, that we cannot distinguish the words. The case is similar, when we overhear a person reading, or talking, in an adjoining room, but when we do not hear so distinctly as to recognize the enunciation of letters or syllables. We perceive, in such instances, that the voice of the reader or speaker, is soft or loud, high or low, and that it moves fast or slow; but we cannot tell what is said: we hear the utterance, but not the articulation, of vocal sound.

The formation of even a single sound of the human voice, is necessarily attended by yet another property, its predominating quality as

' tone ' - in the popular sense of that word. When we overhear, as already supposed, a person reading or talking, but at such a distance from us, or with such objects intervening, that we cannot make out the articulate character of the sounds which are uttered, we may still be able to say, with confidence, that the voice of the reader or speaker has a cheerful or a mournful tone, a lively or a solemn sound. Farther, we say, perhaps with equal certainty, that the person has a hollow, a guttural, a nasal, a sharp, a thin, a rough, a round, a full, or a smooth voice.

The utterance of even a single exclamation of emotion, may, in this way, enable us to define the feeling of a reader or speaker, and, at the same time, to recognize the " quality," — as it is termed, — of his voice.

## WHISPERING.

The progressive discipline of the organs, for the purposes of utterance, comprises the practice of every stage of audible voice, from whispering to shouting and calling. We proceed, now, to the first stage of utterance, — that of *whispering*, which is the nearest, in style and effect, to breathing, and forms the extreme of " aspirated," or breathing " quality."

The function of whispering lies, as it were, half way between breathing and " vocality," or the actual production of vocal sound, in the form termed by musicians " pure tone." Whispering differs from even the ' explosive," or strongest form of the breathing exercises, in being articulated as a mode of speech, and in taking on, to a certain extent, the qualities of " expression ;" thus we not only use the whisper for secret communication, but for the utterance of excessive fear, or of deep awe, suppressed anger, or any other naturally violent emotion, when it is kept down by some overawing restraint.

Whispering, therefore, as a discipline of the organs of voice, carries on, to a greater extent, and with more special effect, all the beneficial results of the exercises in full, deep, and forcible breathing. The whisper, even in its gentlest or " effusive " form, should, as a vocal exercise, be practised on *the scale of public speaking*, — that is to say, with a force sufficient to create *full and distinct articulation, and intelligible utterance, in a large hall*, or any similar apartment.

The function of whispering, on this scale, it will be easily perceived, demands *the full expansion of the chest, a deep inspiration, a powerful expulsion of the breath, the practice of frequent pausing and renewing the supply of breath*, without which a forcible whisper cannot be sustained.

This species of exercise combines, therefore, the discipline of *full and energetic respiration*, with that of *forcible utterance*. It demands a large and a frequent supply of breath, and trains the student to close attention to his habit of breathing, and to the position of the body and the action of the organs. It thus facilitates the acquisition of a perfect control over the organs of speech, — the prime requisite to easy and effective utterance.

A subsidiary advantage attending this process of powerful whispering, consists in the greatly increased intensity which it produces in the organic function of articulation. The whisper being performed as if addressed to a person at the distance of a hundred feet from the speaker, compels a force of percussion in the tongue and the other minor organs of speech, sufficient to compensate for the absence of the common round tone of the voice. The style of enunciation, accordingly, becomes that of the most intense earnestness. The exercise now prescribed, therefore, is of immense advantage, as a preparatory discipline to the organs of speech, as well as a process of training for full-toned and energetic use of the voice.

Whispering, — like breathing, and like resonant vocal utterance, — has the three forms described under the head of Exercises in Breathing, — " effusive," or tranquil ; " expulsive," or forcible ; and " explosive," or abrupt and violent.

## 1. *"Effusive" Whispering.*

This mode of utterance belongs to tranquil emotion, when expressed in the language of *deep-felt awe* or *profound repose*, which represses, by an approach to fear, at the same time that it excites the voice by its intensity.

The exercise in " effusive " whispering, should be practised with strict attention to full, deliberate breathing, and the exact articulation of every element, — 1st, on all the " tonic "[1] elements of the language ; 2d, on the " subtonics ;" 3d, on the " atonics ;" 4th, on syllables ; 5th, on words, as arranged in the columns of Exercises in Articulation ; 6th, on the following stanza,[2] which should be often repeated.

### *Exercise.*

#### STILLNESS OF NIGHT. — *Byron*

" All heaven and earth are still, — though not in sleep,
  But breathless, as we grow when feeling most ;
  And silent, as we stand in thoughts too deep : —
    All heaven and earth are still : From the high host
    Of stars to the lulled lake, and mountain coast,
  All is concentrated in a life intense,
    Where not a beam, nor air, nor leaf is lost,
  But hath a part of being, and a sense
Of that which is of all Creator and Defence."[3]

---

[1] See Chapter on Orthoëpy, and Tables of Orthophony.
[2] It is not meant that the above stanza is necessarily and uniformly to be whispered, in reading or reciting the passage from which it is taken. The extract is here used as a convenient exercise merely.

## 2. "Expulsive" Whispering.

This species of exercise, being much more forcible than the preceding, and corresponding, in energy, to the style of bold declamatory utterance, when given forth with the full round tone of the voice, has yet a more powerful influence on the action and habits of the vocal organs. It should be repeatedly performed, with the utmost force of the whisper, which the student can command, on the elements, syllables and words, and on the following example, the tone of which implies *the intensest force of earnest utterance*, suppressed by apprehension approaching to *fear*.

### Exercise.

MILITARY COMMAND.—*Anonymous.*

"Soldiers! You are now within a few steps of the enemy's outpost. Our scouts report them as slumbering in parties around their watch-fires, and utterly unprepared for our approach. A swift and noiseless advance around that projecting rock, and we are upon them,—we capture them without the possibility of resistance.—One disorderly noise or motion may leave us at the mercy of their advanced guard. Let every man keep the strictest silence, under pain of instant death!"

## 3. 'Explosive" Whispering.

The "explosive" whisper, like the "explosive" breathing, imparts a still greater power to the vocal organs, by the vivid, abrupt, and instantaneous force, with which it bursts out. The explosive intensity of articulation, which it produces, calls at the same time for the utmost precision in the functions of the tongue, the lips, and all the minor instruments of enunciation. The whisper should, in this form, burst forth as suddenly as if the breath were forced out by the instant effect of a violent blow applied to the back. This style of whispering should be repeatedly practised on the elements, syllables, and words, and on the following exercise, which exemplifies the utterance of *the most abrupt and intense alarm*, at once exciting and suppressing the voice.

### Exercise.

MILITARY COMMAND.—*Anon.*

"Hark! I hear the bugles of the enemy! They are on their march along the bank of the river. We must retreat instantly, or be cut off from our boats. I see the head of their column already ris.ng over the height. Our only safety is in the screen of this hedge. Keep close to it; be silent; and stoop as you run. For the boats! Forward!"

The exercises in whispering may now be repeated, on the preceding examples, in the form of a *half whisper*,—which, as its name imports, lies half way between a whisper and the ordinary " quality " of the voice, or " pure tone."

## PURE TONE.

One of the most important parts of vocal culture, is that which defines the " qualities " of the voice, and prescribes appropriate exercises for the formation of good, and. the eradication of bad, habits of utterance.

A deep, round, clear, full, and sweet voice, is too commonly regarded as one of nature's rare gifts to her few favorites. This popular impression, like many others of a similar nature, proceeds upon the erroneous assumption, that what we observe as fact, is *necessarily* such.

A good voice,—owing to our prevalent deficiency in cultivation, -is a thing so rare, that we are apt to regard it as an original endowment of constitution,—a grace not lying within the scope of acquisition, a charm the absence of which, like that of personal beauty, implies no fault.

Observation, however, will remind us of the fact that all children in good health, and in cheerful or tranquil mood, have, naturally, in their habit of utterance, a round, sweet, and clear tone. The fact continues thus, with every child, in the earliest stage of life. It ceases, when the voice ceases to utter the feelings of the heart,— when the mechanical processes of spelling and syllabication commence, and the voice becomes adapted to the routine of reading, as commonly taught at school.—Judicious culture might evidently preserve, and cherish, and confirm the beautiful tendency of habit, originally implanted in the human voice and ear.

We are familiar with the fact, that true musical cultivation pro ceeds upon the assumption, and insists, with inevitable authority, on the primary rule, that every human voice can and must utter " pure " tone. No failure, no .emissness, in this respect, is ever tolerated in appropriate training in vocal music. The result,—as might be expected,—corresponds to the pains taken to regulate the position and action of the organs, in elementary practice. All who are recognized as even tolerable singers, utter every sound of the voice in the form of. pure tone,—entirely free from pectoral gruffness, guttural suffocation, nasal twang, or oral thinness of quality; and among proficients in the art, whatever personal peculiarity of voice is suffered to exist in such only as keeps within the limits of perfect purity, and serves rather to form a crowning grace from the hand of nature, than in any sense, a defect.[1]—A similar result will always

---

[1] We may refer, here, to familiar examples, in the occasionally rich racy

be found to attend the diligent cultivation of the voice, in the modes of utterance appropriate in reading and conversation.

*Faults in "Quality," which impair "Purity" of Tone.*
The first point to which, in the training of the vocal organs, it becomes important to direct the attention, with a view to render the ear discriminating in relation to the qualities of the voice in utterance, is the exemplification of the common faults in "qua.ity," by which purity of tone is prevented or impaired. These are the following:

1. *A hollow and false pectoral murmur*, arising from an imperfect habit of breathing, in consequence of which, the lungs are not furnished with a sufficient supply of air, to produce full and clear tone.

Another cause of this fault in utterance, usually is the feeble action of the abdominal muscles, and, therefore, an inadequate expulsion of the breath, and a smothered or muffled quality of voice, which makes its sound appear buried within the frame or issuing directly from the chest. This fault of utterance may, from the character of its effect on the ear, be properly denominated *pectoral tone*. It arises, in some instances, from ill health, or a feeble condition of the bodily organs; in others, from the oppressive influence of diffidence and constraint. Students, and other persons of sedentary habit, and female readers, in particular, incline to this faulty mode of utterance. The low note which always accompanies this quality of voice, serves greatly to increase its false and hollow sound, the prevalence of which gives to all reading, indiscriminately, the tones of solemnity and awe. Full inspiration, the expulsive action of the abdominal muscles, and the cultivation of the middle notes of the voice, together with habits of healthful exercise and cheerful emotions, are the best remedies for a tendency to hollow pectoral one

2. A fault which bears a resemblance to the preceding, is that of *aspirated* quality, by which, a half-whispering effect of fear is imparted to every sound of the voice.

This defect of utterance arises, in part, from the want of sufficiently full and deep inspiration, to produce pure and full tone; it arises, sometimes, from organic weakness, or from embarrassment, which causes a slight "rigor" of the organic parts, and consequently allows more breath to escape from the trachea, than is converted into sound by the larynx. The condition of pure tone is, that much

quality, which characterizes the vocalist, Mr. H. Russell; the clear, crystalline points of sound, in that of Madame Caradori Allan; the warm, breathing glow of that of Mrs. Wood, or the exquisite, soft fulness of that of Mr. H. Phi. ips.

breath should be drawn in, but little given out, and that the whole of what is suffered to escape, should be converted into sound; while, in "aspirated quality," little is drawn in, and much is given out In this faulty style of utterance, the due action of the abdominal muscles is neglected, and a forced and exhausting action of the thoracic and intercostal muscles, is substituted, causing an incessant sinking and collapsing of the chest, and a tone of voice such as belongs to sickness and pain. This mode of reading or speaking, is very prevalent, and, especially among the weak and the sedentary: yet no habit is more exhausting to the vocal organs, more injurious to health, or more destructive of life. A due attention to the full expansion of the chest, to deep inspiration, and to the vigorous action of the abdominal muscles, is the chief preventive of the faulty habit of aspirated utterance.

3. Another bad quality of voice consists in what is termed *guttural* tone,—a mode of utterance which seems to make the voice issue from an obstructed throat.

This fault is of a twofold character,—first, the soft, choked sound not unusual in the utterance of persons inclined to fulness of habit and corpulence,—second, the hard, dry, and barking voice, which sometimes characterizes persons of an opposite habit and frame. Both these forms of vocal sound, are disagreeable in their effect; as they indicate a want of ear, coarseness of feeling, or an undue ascendancy of the animal nature. Such properties of tone are not less repulsive and objectionable, in reading and speaking, than in singing, in which they are universally regarded as intolerable to an ear regulated by taste and feeling. The immediate organic cause of this bad quality of tone, is an improper pressure of the muscles around the larynx, and the root of the tongue,—causing the voice in the one case, apparently to issue from the pharynx or swallow instead of the larynx, and, in the other, to originate in the upper part of the throat only, cut off from all communication with either the chest or the mouth. Defective taste or an inadvertent ear, rather than organic necessity, is usually the origin of the guttural tone; and the free expansion of the chest, and the energetic action of the abdominal muscles, with the habit of opening the mouth freely, when reading or speaking, are the surest means of avoiding or removing this great hindrance to purity of tone.

4. Another fault is that commonly termed *nasal* tone,— which makes the voice sound as if it came only through the nose.

Of this fault it is unnecessary to say much. It is a habit of utterance which makes the reader or speaker ridiculous to most hearers and uncomfortable to all; yet it is one which is very prevalent although not always in its worst forms. The chief security against it, consists in the habit of fully expanding the chest, which aids depth of voice and takes off the wiry sound that is otherwise imparted to the tone. Another preventive, of still greater efficacy, is, the free opening of the mouth, not only in front, but in the back part, by raising the veil of the palate, as is mechanically done in the act of coughing, in consequence of which the voice escapes in its proper direction, instead of being allowed to drift with force against the nasal passages, while they remain partially shut. At the same time, care must be taken not to raise the veil of the palate so high as to stop the nasal passage entirely, in the style of obstruction caused by a cold, producing the utterance of "*Cub id,*" for "*Come in.*" A due degree of nasal ring is one of the component elements of a good voice.

5. Both the *guttural* and the *nasal* tones are *combined* in the utterance of some readers and speakers; and the effect is, of course, rendered, in such cases, doubly injurious. Sometimes the *pectoral* tone is blended with the other two, causing the extreme of impure tone, in all its bad properties. The effect of this species of voice, is a grunting utterance, resembling that of the inferior animals, instead of the clear resonant tone of the human being.

6. There is still another fault of utterance, which is yet more prevalent than those which have been described. It consists in what may be termed *oral* tone. It is the slight ineffective voice of indifference, of feebleness, or fatigue, or the mincing tone of false taste. It causes the vocal sound to issue from the mouth, in a style which seems to make it lose all connection with the throat and the chest, and consequently to lose all its natural depth and fulness.

Without these last-mentioned properties, no voice can ever sound earnest or sincere in utterance. Hence we observe "oral" tone always ascribed to the languid beauty or the trifling fop.—The full expansion of the chest, and the vigorous, appulsive action of the abdominal muscles, which ensures the energetic expulsion of the breath,—together with the cultivation of the lower notes of the scale, in the habits of utterance,—are the chief correctives of the tendency to the fault of the slender "oral" tone. The musician, it is true, denominates purity of utterance by the phrase "head-tone." But, in the usages of music, this phrase is not strict or exclusive, in its application: it is used rather in contradistinction to the false and impure tones of the throat and the chest,—the guttural and the pectoral. It is meant to designate that species of tone which rings clearly in the cavity of the head, by the head becoming, as it were, a sounding-board to reflect the voice downward, and secure, at the same time, the resonance of the chest, blended with that of the head.

False utterance, or impure tone, arises, in all instances, from the exclusive or undue, or, it may be, the imperfect use of one portion of the vocal organs, as is intimated in the designation of "pectoral," "guttural," or "nasal" tone.[1] True utterance and "pure tone," on the contrary, employ the whole apparatus of voice, in one consentaneous act, combining in one perfect sphere of sound,—if it may be so expressed,— the depth of effect produced by the resonance of the chest, the force and firmness imparted by the due compression of the throat, the clear, ringing property, caused by the due proportion of nasal effect, and the softening and sweetening influence of the head and mouth.

All voices, trained to this appropriate union of qualities, become pleasing to the ear, and produce dignity of effect. Genuine cultivation secures these properties, as habits of the voice, from childhood upward, or restores them when, through inadvertency, they have been lost. But to preserve, or recover them, much training and much preparatory discipline become necessary. Exercises, such as form the preliminary steps in the study of vocal music, are among the readiest and surest means of attaining that skill in the management and control of the organs and the breath, which is indispensable to purity of tone. See, for this purpose, the exercises and directions by Professor Webb, at the close of this volume

"Pure tone" exists in two forms, "subdued," and "moderate" force: the former implying the repressing power of an emotion which quiets utterance; the latter being, as its name implies, a medium of style.

The elocutionary practice best adapted to the formation of pure and smooth quality of voice, in the "subdued" form, consists principally in careful repetition of the tabular exercises on the "tonic" elements of the language, and the utterance of syllables and words, containing long vowels, and in the reading and recitation of passages of poetry marked by the prevalence of the expressive tones of *pathos*, *solemnity*, and *tranquillity*, as here exemplified.

The following exercises should be practised with the closest attention to the perfect purity of vocal sound, as associated with the spirit of deep-felt but gentle emotion. The perfect tranquillity and regularity of the breathing, and the cautious

---

[1] These terms are used not in strict propriety,—as the larynx is the immediate source of all vocal sounds, but for the description of *apparent* effects. The sound of the voice is made up of a *note*, or *tone*, and its *resonance*. The former comes directly from the *larynx*; the latter from the adjoining cavities of the *chest*, the *pharynx*, the *mouth*, the *nostrils*, and the interior of the *head*.

and sparing emission of the breath, are points of the utmost moment to the pure and perfectly liquid formation of voice. The mode of utterance required in the following exercises is "*effusion*,"—not "expulsion" or "explosion,"—a gentle, continuous emission of sound, articulate, but very soft; as it always is in the utterance of *subdued* and chastened emotion

EXAMPLES OF "PURE TONE."

I. "SUBDUED," OR SOFTENED FORCE.

*Example* 1.—*Pathos.*

FROM THE BURIAL OF ARNOLD.—*Willis.*

"Tread lightly, comrades! Ye have laid
His dark locks on his brow,—
Like life, save deeper light and shade,
We'll not disturb them now!

"Tread lightly! for 't is beautiful,
That blue-veined eyelid's sleep,
Hiding the eye death left so dull;—
Its slumber we will keep!"

2.—*Solemnity.*

SOLILOQUY OF DOUGLAS.—*Home.*

"This is the place,—the centre of the grove;—
Here stands the oak, the monarch of the wood:
How sweet and solemn is this midnight scene!
The silver moon unclouded holds her way
Through skies where I could count each little star;
The fanning west wind scarcely stirs the leaves;
The river, rushing o'er its pebbled bed,
Imposes silence with a stilly sound.
In such a place as this, at such an hour,—
If ancestry may be in aught believed,—
Descending spirits have conversed with man
And told the secrets of the world unknown.'

### 3.— *Tranquillity.*

FROM LINES WRITTEN IN A HIGHLAND GLEN.— *Wilson.*

'Oh! that this lovely vale were mine!'
Then, from glad youth to calm decline,
My years would gently glide,
Hope would rejoice in endless dreams,
And Memory's oft-returning gleams
    By peace be sanctified!"

### II. "MODERATE" FORCE.

Perfect purity of tone is indispensable not only to the effect of subdued" force, which corresponds to the gentle style of passages marked "*piano*" in music, and has been exemplified in the preceding exercises, but, likewise, to that degree of force which may be termed *moderate*, in contradistinction to the energetic style of declamation, the bold tones of impassioned recitation, or, on the other hand, the suppressed or softened utterance of subdued emotion. "Moderate force" is a convenient designation of the usual utterance of didactic sentiment, in the form of essays or scientific and literary discourses, doctrinal and practical sermons, and other forms of address, not distinguished by vivid narration, graphic description. or impassioned feeling.

The style of utterance in the "moderate" force of "pure tone," is gentle "expulsion," with a clear "radical movement," which keeps it from subsiding into mere "effusion," and yet does not extend to explosion." The degree of force implied in this technical use of the word "moderate," is merely that which audible utterance, distinct articulation, and intelligible expression, demand for the ordinary purposes of public speaking, in those forms which address themselves to the understanding rather than the heart, and in which the speaker's great object in communication, is to be *understood*, rather than to be felt. "Pure tone" is, in these circumstances, of the utmost value to easy, distinct, and appropriate utterance; and any departure from it not only jars upon the ear, but impairs the clearness of the speaker's articulation, and detracts from the proper dignity of public address,— an exercise usually implying culture and taste on the part of the speaker.

Another consideration of great moment, in connection with this branch of elocution. is the unspeakable advantage of "pure tone," as a relief to the organs of the reader or speaker. The voice which obeys the laws of "pure tone," easily fills a vast space. The organic act becomes, in such cases, a spontaneous emission of sound, — like the act of singing, when appropriately performed, — free from every jarring, agitating, irregular impulse, and therefore not attended with labor or fatigue. The skilful public speaker, like the skilful singer, gives forth his voice in those clear, smooth, and pure tones which make the function of utterance a pleasure and not a pain, and which make organic exertion a salutary instead of an unhealthful process. It is as true of speech as of any other muscular process, that appropriate practice gives "the sleight" of execution, in consequence of which, powerful and long-sustained exertion is rendered an easy task.

"Moderate force," as a technical designation in elocution, exhibits pure tone in the following gradations.

### 1. — "*Grave*" *Style*.

The "grave" style differs from the "solemn" in the fact that the former is not marked by "effusive" or "subdued" force, but on the contrary, assumes something of the "expulsive" tone of firmness and authority, although in a gentle and moderate style. The "grave" style differs farther from the 'solemn," in not descending to so low a pitch, — as *solemnity* is not so deep-toned in its utterance as *awe*, nor *awe* so deep as *horror*.

The disturbing cause which usually vitiates the purity of tone in "grave" style, is a false, hollow, pectoral voice, which merely murmurs in the chest, without coming forth impressively to the ear. The deep effect of *solemnity*, or the sepulchral tone of *horror*, is, in this way, sometimes produced instead of the moderate character of a merely "grave" utterance.

The learner, after having practised the example of "grave" style, should repeat, in that tone, all the "tonic" elements, — then, a selection from the tabular exercises on words; so as to acquire a perfect command of the force and pitch of "grave" style, as differing from the "solemn," on the one hand, and from the "serious," on the other.

*Example.*

ETERNITY OF GOD — *Greenwood.*

The Throne of Eternity is a throne of mercy and love

God has permitted and invited us to repose ourselves and our hopes on that which alone is everlasting and unchangeable. We shall shortly finish our allotted time on earth, even if it should be unusually prolonged. We shall leave behind us al. which is now familiar and beloved; and a world of other days and other men will be entirely ignorant that once we lived. But the same unalterable Being will still preside over the universe, through all its changes; and from his remembrance we shall never be blotted. We can never be where He is not, nor where he sees and loves and upholds us not. He is our Father and our God forever. He takes us from earth, that He may lead us to heaven, that He may refine our nature from all its principles of corruption, share with us His own immortality, admit us to His everlasting habitation, and crown us with His eternity."

### 2.—"*Serious*" *Style.*

This form of utterance differs from the preceding, in not possessing so low a pitch. It is a still milder form of the same general effect. The fault usually exhibited in "serious" style, is nearly the same with that mentioned above: it substitutes the deep and full-toned notes of the "grave" style for the moderate and less-marked character of the merely "serious." The purity of tone, in this style, is usually marred by the same cause as in the preceding instance of the "grave" utterance. The beauty and gentleness of the tone of serious feeling, are thus lost; and the "expression" is untrue to the intended effect.

The following example requires attention and careful practice, to preserve its exact pitch and appropriate force.

When the "serious" tone has come fully under the student's command, by practice on the exercise subjoined, the repetition of the elements, syllables, and words, will serve to fix it definitely in the memory.

### *Example.*

THE BEAUTY OF VIRTUE.—*Blair.*

"There is no virtue without a characteristic beauty to

make it particularly loved of the good, and to make the bad ashamed of their neglect of it. To do what is right, argues superior taste as well as morals; and those whose practice is evil, feel an inferiority of intellectual power and enjoyment, even where they take no concern for a principle.

"Doing well has something more in it than the fulfilling of a duty. It is the cause of a just sense of elevation of character; it clears and strengthens the spirits; it gives higher reaches of thought; it widens our benevolence, and makes the current of our peculiar affections swift and deep."

### 3.—"*Animated,*" or *Lively, Style.*

This mode of voice differs, in three respects, from the serious:" it has more force, a higher pitch, and a quicker movement; and the comparatively greater force renders the purity of the tone still more conspicuous.

The common fault, as regards this style, is a dull or deadened tone, instead of that of animation. The dulness of the objectionable tone, arises from keeping the pitch as low, perhaps, as that of the "serious" tone, from withholding the due force of animated utterance, and from allowing the voice to move too slowly. Along with these faults usually goes an impure, husky quality of voice, instead of the clear resonant sound which belongs to animation of manner.

It is unnecessary to expatiate on the effects of a style so obviously bad as that of dulness and monotony. In consequence of indulging this habit, the school-boy reads with the tone of apparent reluctance, indifference, or stupor, and the man speaks as if his intention were to lull his audience to sleep. The origin of this false tone is to be found in the fact that elementary teachers too generally permit reading to be dull work, and that reading-books abound in dull or unintelligible lessons. The tones of life and interest, are not cultivated and cherished at the period when the style of the voice is forming; and neglected habit is attended, here, as elsewhere, with every evil: the voice is killed; the spirits are quenched; and the reader or speaker has apparently neither will nor power to awaken his own soul to perception and feeling, nor to arouse the hearts of others.

The following example should be attentively practised with reference to lively and spirited effect.

The exercise in "animated" utterance should be extended, as a matter of practice, to the elementary sounds, and to the repetition of the tables of words as far and as often, as individuals or classes may seem to require.

## Example.

**ANIMAL HAPPINESS.**—*Paley.*

"The air, the earth, the water, teem with delighted existence. In a spring noon, or a summer evening, on whichever side we turn our eyes, myriads of happy beings crowd upon our view. 'The insect youth are on the wing. Swarms of new-born flies are trying their pinions in the air Their sportive motions, their gratuitous activity, their continual change of place, without use or purpose, testify their joy, and the exultation which they feel in their lately discovered faculties."

### 4.—"*Gay*," *or Brisk, Style.*

This mode of utterance has all the characteristics of the "animated" style, carried to a greater extent. The tone to which we now refer, being that of exhilarated feeling, its pitch is higher, its force is greater, and its "movement" quicker than that of an utterance, which, as in the preceding instance, does not go beyond the style of animation or liveliness, merely.

Gaiety and vividness of expression, are, in their proper sphere, as important to appropriate effect in reading, as any of the opposite qualities of seriousness and gravity are in theirs. We can never, without these properties of voice, give natural expression to many of the most pleasing forms of composition, — to such, in particular, as derive their power over sympathy, from their presenting to us what the poet has termed "the gayest, happiest attitude of things," or from the glowing and exhilarating colors in which language sometimes delights to invest the forms of thought. Dramatic scenes, sketches of life and manners, vivid delineations of character, all demand the utterance of exhilarated emotion. Unaided by the effect of such expression, the finest compositions fall flat and dead upon the ear, and leave our feelings unmoved or disappointed.

The lifeless routine of school habit, is too generally the early cause of the formation of such tones; and the chief expedient for removing them, is to enter, with full life and spirit, into the sentiments and emotions which we utter in reading.

The practice of the following and similar examples, should be carefully watched, with a view to this end; and the exercise of brisk and exhilarated utterance, should be repeatedly practised on the elements, syllables, and words contained in the tables, as a means of fixing definitely and permanently in the ear the requisite properties of voice. The learner is imperfect in practice, as long as there remains perceptible in his utterance, the least approach to the partial impurity of tone arising from the languid drawling usually connected with "nasal and guttural qualities," the feeble thinness of a mere "oral" tone, or the hollow murmur of the "pectoral" style. A clear and perfectly pure, ringing voice, corresponding to what the musician terms "head tone," is the standard of practice in this branch of elocution.

*Example.*

RURAL HOLIDAY.—*Milton.*

' Sometimes, with secure delight,
The upland hamlets will invite,
When the merry bells ring round,
And the jocund rebecs sound,
To many a youth and many a maid,
Dancing in the checkered shade,
When young and old come forth to play,
On a sunshine holiday,
Till the livelong daylight fail."

5.—*" Humorous," or Playful, Style.*

Perfect purity of tone is indispensable to the utterance of fanciful and humorous emotion, unless in the few instances in which, for mimetic or enhanced effect, a peculiar and characteristic voice is assumed, on purpose. Humor, in its genuine expression, not only enlivens and kindles tone, but seems as it were to melt it, and make it flow into the ear and the heart, as the full, clear, sparkling stream gushes into the reservoir. The playful and the mirthful style of utterance, seems to be voice let loose from all restraints which would impose upon it any rigidness, dryness, or hardness of sound.

Humor goes beyond mere gaiety or exhilaration, in the unbounded scope which it gives to the voice: its tones are higher, louder, and quicker in "movement."

Humor excels even gaiety, in effusive purity of tone, which seems to come ringing and full from the heart, with all the resonance of head and chest combined,—" flooding," as the poet says of the skylark, " the very air with sound."

Destitute of such utterance, the reading of some of the finest passages of Shakspeare, of Scott, or of Irving, becomes cold and torpid, or excites only aversion and disgust. The lighter strains of Cowper, and innumerable passages in all the truest and best of our poets, demand this highest form of mirthful utterance.

The faults usually exemplified in regard to this tone, are similar to those which were mentioned in speaking of the gay and brisk style of expression, and are owing principally to the causes then indicated. The remedy must also be of the same description with that which was then suggested. Humor demands, however, not a mere fulness but an actual exuberance and overflow of feeling, in order to give it expression. An approach to the style of laughter, should be perceptible in the quality with which it inspires the voice.

The following exercises should be practised with all the playful, half-laughing style of voice, which naturally belongs to this vivid effusion of blended humor and fancy. The practice of the elements, in the same style, in sounds, and words, will be of the greatest service for imparting the entire and free command of the appropriate tone of humor; and even a frequent repetition of the act of laughter will be found highly useful, as a preparative for this style of expression, by suggesting and infusing the perfect purity of tone which naturally belongs to hearty and joyous emotion.

*Example.*

MERCUTIO'S DESCRIPTION OF QUEEN MAB.— *Shakspeare.*

" Oh! then, I see queen Mab hath been with you.
     She comes
In shape no bigger than an agate stone,
On the forefinger of an alderman,
Drawn by a team of little atomies
Athwart men's noses, as they lie asleep;
Her wagon-spokes made of long spinners' legs,
The cover, of the wings of grasshoppers;
The traces, of the smallest spider's web,
The collars, of the moonshine's watery beams:
Her whip of cricket's bone; the lash of film;
Her wagoner, a small gray-coated gnat;
Her chariot is an empty hazel-nut,
Made by the joiner squirrel, or old grub,
Time out of mind the fairies' coachmakers.
And in this state she gallops, night by night,
Through lovers' brains, and then they dream of .ove•
O'er lawyers' fingers, who straight dream on fees;
O'er ladies' lips, who straight on kisses dream:

Sometimes she gallops o'er a courtier's nose,
And then dreams he of smelling out a suit;
And sometimes comes she with a tithe-pig's tail
Tickling a parson's nose, as 'a lies asleep,
Then dreams he of another benefice:
Sometimes she driveth o'er a soldier's neck,
And then dreams he of cutting foreign throats,
Of breaches, ambuscadoes, Spanish blades,
Of healths five fathom deep: and then anon
Drums in his ear; at which he starts and wakes;
And, being thus frighted, swears a prayer or two,
And sleeps again."

III. "SUSTAINED" FORCE.

*Calling.*

A call is the highest and intensest form of "pure tone," and, when extended to a vast distance, becomes, it is universally known, similar to music, in the style of its utterance.

A high note is required, in order to reach to remote distance; and perfect purity of tone, is also indispensable, as a condition of the easy emission of the prodigious force of voice which calling demands, and which, in continuous effort, it must sustain. It is the "*maximum,*" or highest degree, of vocal force. But if unaccompanied by perfectly pure quality of sound, it pains and injures the organs. Its true mode is a long-sustained and exceedingly powerful singing tone. In this form, its use in strengthening the organs, and giving firmness, compactness, and clearness to the voice, is very great.

The student, in practising the call, as a vocal exercise, must see to it that the utmost purity of tone is kept up; as the exercise will otherwise be injurious. The more attentive he is to *sing* his words, in such exercises, the more easy is the effort, and the more salutary the result. The style of utterance, in this exercise, is that of vigorous, sustained, and intense "*effusion,*" but should never become abruptly "*explosive.*"

The following example should be practised on the scale indicated, not on the stage, but in historical fact, as when the herald stood on the plain, at such a distance as to be out of bow-shot, and called out his message, so as to be fully audible and distinctly intelligible to the listeners on the distant city-wall.

The elementary tables of sounds, and words, should be repeatedly practised, in the form of calling, till the student can command a full, clear, ringing, and musical call, or any form of sound which admits this function of the voice.

*Example.*

THE HERALD'S CALL.— *Shakspeare.*

" Rejoice, you men of Angiers! ring your bells.
King John, your king and England's, doth approach —
Open your gates, and give the victors way!"

"OROTUND QUALITY."

" Pure tone " is properly the perfection of vocal sound executed by human organs, in the form of music or of speech, in unimpassioned expression. Purity, as a quality of voice in utterance, is, so to speak, the investing property of the sounds in which gentle and moderate emotions are conveyed to the ear. But this quality does not extend beyond the limits of solemnity, on the one hand, or of gaiety and humor, on the other. Its boldest effect is exhibited, as already mentioned, in the mechanical act of calling, which, although sometimes accompanied by intense emotion, is not, by any means, necessarily so attended. The call may be uttered, as among laborers at work, for a merely mechanical purpose of convenience.

But when we advance in the gradations of feeling, and come to the stage of impassioned utterance, and, more particularly, to that in which deep and forcible emotions are combined, mere purity of tone is not adequate to the effect which is to be produced on the ear. In the utterance of contemplative repose, nothing beyond pure quality of voice is needed, to give expression to feeling so gentle in its mood. Energy would, in such circumstances, seem violence: it would disturb the quiet of the scene.

Not so when passion rouses or inspires the soul. The intense excitement of feeling then demands that volume and force should predominate in expression. Purity of tone must, indeed, even in such cases, be preserved, to constitute that utterance which, while it assumes an intense energy, still indicates, in the pure quality of the vocal sound, the delight which the soul feels in the consciousness of powerful action. But the properties of voice which, in these circumstances, predominate in the utterance, and fall most impressively on the ear, are volume and energy, combined with ample resonance.

We have a striking example of the species of voice under consideration, in the imagined rallying-shout of Satan to his fallen host, while they lie weltering on the infernal lake, when, — in the colossal image of the poet — " he called so loud, that all the hollow deep of hell resounded :'

"Princes! potentates!"
"Awake! arise! or be forever fallen!"

The human voice, here superadding intense emotion to the mere physical act of shouting and calling, becomes, as it were, translated to a sphere of superhuman force and grandeur.

In the "orotund quality" of utterance, volume and purity of tone, to the greatest extent of the one, and the highest perfection of the other, are blended in one vast sphere of sound, expressive of the utmost depth, intensity, and sublimity of emotion, and attended by the fullest resonance of the pharynx and the chest, as well as the larynx.

The voice, in the above case, inspired, expanded, and impelled, by the huge conception of the poet's imagination, becomes gigantic in its utterance. The force of the mental associations, imparts the impulsive energy, — and their conscious sublimity the " pure tone," or the highest joy. Blend these two properties, and the result is what Dr. Rush has so appropriately termed " orotund "[1] utterance.

The quality of voice to which we now refer, is mentioned by Dr. Rush as the highest perfection of the cultivated utterance of the public speaker. It is also justly regarded by him as the natural language of the highest species of emotion. It characterizes the vivid utterance of children, in their tones of love, and joy, and ecstasy. It belongs to the audible expression of masculine courage, energy, delight, admiration, and to the deliberate language of vengeance, as distinguished from the aspirated and suffocated voice of anger and rage.

In the furious excitement of anger, however, which breathes a fiendish delight in the very consciousness of the destructive passion, the " orotund " will be found to return in the utterance, and predominate even in the scream or yell of the wildest frenzy of excitement.

The property of voice defined by the term " orotund " exists, also, in certain physical and mechanical relations of the corporeal organs. Thus, we hear it in the audible functions of yawning, coughing, and laughing; all of which, when forcibly performed, are attended with a sudden and powerful

[1] From the Latin phrase "*ore rotundo*," used by the poet Horace, in allusion to the round and full utterance and flowing eloquence of the Greeks.

expansion of the organic parts, and a ringing fulness, round ness, and smoothness of sound.[1]

"Orotund" quality may, in one of its forms, (the short,) be regarded as the maximum of "pure tone," united with the most powerful resonance of the pharynx. Like the pure tone, however, t admits of degrees; and we find it existing, according to the greater or less intensity of emotion, in the different forms of "effusive," "expulsive," and "explosive," force. In other cases, it partakes of "aspiration," being rendered "impure," by violence of emotion and force of breath. We proceed to the exemplification of the first of the above gradations.

### I. "EFFUSIVE OROTUND."

This designation is applied to that species of utterance in which the voice is not sent forth from the organs by any obvious voluntary *expulsion*, but is rather suffered to *effuse* itself from the mouth into the surrounding air. It resembles the insensible and unconscious act of tranquil breathing, as contrasted with the effort of panting. But though perfectly gentle in its formation, and passing but little beyond the limits of merely "pure tone," it still obviously extends beyond that form of voice, and assumes a somewhat different character. "Pure tone," in its "effusive" form, is executed principally by the full expansion of the chest, a large inhalation but a very gentle and limited expiration; whilst "effusive orotund" gives a very free egress to the breath, and, by its larger volume of sound, and greater emissive force, uses more breath, in the production of sound. "Effusive pure tone" is obtained chiefly by skilful withholding of the breath, and using the larynx so gently and so skilfully, that every particle of air passing through it, is converted into sound. "Effusive orotund" demands a wider opening of the organs, and a freer and firmer use of them, so as to produce a bolder and rounder tone. It resembles, however, in its style, the "effusive" function of "pure tone," in its gentle and sustained swell of utterance, as contrasted with the "expulsive" and "explosive" forms of the "orotund."

---

[1] For a more minute description orotund" quality, we refer to the work of Dr. Rush.

The modes of feeling or emotion which are expressed by "effusive orotund voice," are *pathos*,—when mingled with *grandeur* and *sublimity*,—and *solemnity* and *reverence*, when expressed in similar circumstances.—*Pathos*, divested of grandeur, subsides into "pure tone," merely. The same result takes place in the utterance of *solemnity*, if unaccompanied by sublimity. But *reverence*, always implying grandeur or elevation in its source, is uniformly uttered by the "orotund" voice, though from the *tranquillity*, and the part'u *awe*, with which it is attended, its force does not go beyond the "effusive" form,—as may be observed in the appropriate tone of *adoration*, uttered in the exercise of devotion.

Analysis thus shows us the value of the "orotund," as imputing dignity of effect to utterance, even in its gentler moods. It teaches us, moreover, the inefficacy or the inappropriateness of all utterance which, in giving forth the language of noble and inspiring emotion, falls short of "orotund" quality, and reduces the style of voice to that of ordinary or common-place topics. Gray's Elegy, for example, if read without "orotund," becomes feeble and trite, in its style; Milton's Paradise Lost, if so read, becomes dry and flat; and the language of devotion, uttered in the same defective style, in prayer, or in psalms and hymns, becomes irreverent in its effect.

The mode of securing the advantages of "orotund" utterance, is, in the first place, to give up the whole soul to the feeling of what is read or spoken in the language of grave and sublime emotion. The mere superficial impression of a sentiment, is not adequate to the effects of genuine and inspiring expression. The reader or speaker must be so deeply imbued with the spirit of what he utters, that his heart overflows with it, and thus inspires and attunes his organs to the full vividness of expressive action. The ample and noble effect of "*orotund*" utterance, can never be acquired through the clearest apprehension of a sentiment by the understanding merely: the heart must swell with the feeling; and the stream of emotion must gush over the whole man. Nor is it sufficient that the reader's feeling be commensurate with the mere personal impression of a sentiment: genuine expression demands such a surplus, as it were, of emotion that it is sufficient to overflow the reader's own being and impel and carry on with it the sympathies of his audience. The reader must himself feel the inspiration of number enkindling his personal emotion, and elevating and expanding his being, for the full outpouring of expression.

But few readers seem fully to feel the difference between the quiet and passive state in which we sit and give up our imagination to be impressed by the language of an author, and the communicative and active energy requisite to stamp even such an impression on the minds of others. In the former case, we are but involuntary, or a the most, consentaneous *recipients:* in the latter, we are the positive and voluntary *creators* of effect.

The deep and full feeling of an author's sentiment, then, is the natural preliminary to expressive effect and consequent "orotund.' But, from the imperfections of early culture, attention is, in most cases, demanded, at the same time, to the state and functions of the organs.

The effect of "effusive orotund," on the voice, is identical in its quality with the soft, but round and deep tone of a prolonged yawn, — a form of voice which comes, obviously, from the peculiarly wide and free position of the organs in that act. Hence arises the suggestion to repeat voluntarily the effort of loud and prolonged yawning, and watch its peculiar effect on the sound of the voice, and repeat and prolong the sound in the form of the yawn, till it can be executed at pleasure.

"Effusive orotund" is, in one view, nothing else than "pure tone" rendered intense and ample in volume, by vigorous emission of breath, and by laryngial quality, or the full deep ringing effect of a free use of the larynx, and an ample expansion of the pharynx. The same position and movements of the organs, therefore, are used in the one, as in the other.

The larynx operates in both with the consentaneous enlargement of the pharynx, the elevation of the veil of the palate, and the exactly balanced use of the nasal passage, — a style in which it is neither too much compressed, nor too widely opened, but exerted in the mode required to produce what musicians term "head tone."

The cultivation of vocal music, in the form of singing bass, is one of the most effectual means of securing the property of "effusive orotund" utterance, in reading and speaking. The following, and similar examples, together with the tabular elements, should be attentively and repeatedly practised, till the full, clear, deep and perfect resonance of the "orotund" quality of voice, is perfectly at command.

I. *Examples of "Effusive Orotund."*

1. *Pathos and Gloom, or Melancholy mingled with Grandeur.*[1]

*From Gray's Elegy.*

"The curfew tolls,—the knell of parting day;
The lowing herd winds slowly o'er the lea;

---

[1] *Pathetic, tranquil,* and *solemn* emotions, always pass from "pure tone" to "orotund quality," when *force* or *sublimity,* in any degree, marks the language in which these emotions are uttered.

The ploughman homeward plods his weary way,
And leaves the world to darkness and to me.

" Now fades the glimmering landscape on the sight,
And all the air a solemn stillness holds;
Save where the beetle wheels his drony flight,
And drowsy tinklings lull the distant folds.

" Save that, from yonder ivy-mantled tower,
The moping owl does to the moon complain
Of such as, wandering near her secret bower,
Molest her ancient, solitary reign.

' Beneath those rugged elms, that yew-tree's shade,
Where heaves the turf in many a mouldering heap —
Each in his narrow cell forever laid, —
The rude forefathers of the hamlet sleep.

For them no more the blazing hearth shall burn,
Or busy housewife ply her evening care;
No children run to lisp their sire's return,
Or climb his knees, the envied kiss to share."

2. *Solemnity and Sublimity combined.*

MILTON'S INVOCATION OF LIGHT.

' Hail! holy Light,—offspring of Heaven, first-born,
Or of the Eternal coeternal beam
May I express thee unblamed? since God is light,
And never but in unapproached light,
Dwelt from eternity,—dwelt then in thee,
Bright effluence of bright Essence increate !
Or hear'st thou, rather, pure ethereal stream,
Whose fountain who shall tell?— Before the sun
Before the heavens thou wert, and, at the voice
Of God, as with a mantle didst invest
The rising world of waters, dark and deep,
Won from the void and formless infinite."

### 3. *Reverence*

FROM THE BOOK OF PSALMS.

' Bless the Lord, O my soul! O Lord, my God, Thou art very great; Thou art clothed with honor and majesty; who coverest thyself with light as with a garment; who stretchest out the heavens like a curtain: who layeth the beams of His chambers in the waters: who maketh the clouds His chariot, who walketh upon the wings of the wind; who laid the foundations of the earth, that it should not be removed forever "

## II. "EXPULSIVE OROTUND."

This form of the "orotund," or full utterance of public reading and speaking, bears precisely the same relation to the preceding, that "expulsive" bears to "effusive" "pure tone."

It arises from the forcible action of the abdominal muscles, added to full expansion of chest, and deep inspiration. It has the same laryngial property which justifies the application of the term "orotund" to the "effusive" style of that form of utterance.

"Expulsive orotund" belongs appropriately to earnest or vehement *declamation*, to *impassioned* and poetic excitement of emotion, and consequently to whatever language is uttered in the form of *shouting*.

The first-mentioned of these styles,—the *declamatory*, is exemplified in public address or debate, on exciting occasions. The second is heard in the utterance of *passion*, when the reader or speaker passes beyond the mere voluntary and conscious force of "declamatory" utterance, and, in part, becomes himself,—in common with his audience,—an unconscious, involuntary subject of the impelling emotion which he expresses. The third form of "expulsive orotund," is at once the impassioned and the voluntary burst of emotion which transcends the customary forms and effects of speech and, in the spirit of enthusiastic excitement, utters itself in *shouts* and *exclamations*.

This form of utterance, — the "expulsive orotund," — is one of the noblest functions of the human voice. It is this which gives to the ear the full effect of the majesty of man, as a being of heart and will and imagination. Without the full command of this property of utterance, the public reader or speaker falls short of whatever effect naturally belongs, in human speech, to the union of depth, force, and grandeur of emotion. The language of the loftier feelings of the soul, unaided by this natural advantage, becomes familiar, low, and trivial.

The forcible and manly eloquence of Demosthenes or of Chatham, divested of the full "expulsive" utterance of deep and powerful emotion, would become ridiculous in its effect on the ear and the imagination. The same would be true of the style of our own eminent contemporary and countryman, Webster. Depth, weight, and fulness of tone, form one powerful assemblage of effects, in all his utterance on great and exciting occasions.

To form the voice to the extent of the full property of "expulsive orotund," care should be taken to maintain a perfectly erect attitude of body, the chest fully expanded, and projected, and the shoulders depressed, — to maintain, also, a vigorous play of the abdominal muscles, and to practise the organic act of prolonged coughing, in a moderate form, which is the natural mechanical function most nearly resembling "expulsive orotund." The elements of the language should be practised in a similar style; and to these exercises should be added the repeated and energetic practice of the following examples.

Practice on the "crying" voice, or weeping utterance of sorrow, is another expedient for rendering nature's processes conducive to culture. The act of crying, being, in its mechanism, a perfect "expulsive orotund."

*Examples of "Expulsive Orotund."*

1. — *"Declamatory" Style.*

FROM WEBSTER'S SPEECH OF JOHN ADAMS.

"Sink or swim, live or die, survive or perish, I give my hand and my heart to this vote!"

"Sir, before God, I believe the hour is come. My judgment approves this measure; and my whole heart is in it. All that I have, and all that I am, and all that I hope, in this life, I am now ready here to stake upon it; and I leave off, as I began, that, live or die, survive or perish, I am for the declaration. It is my living sentiment; and, by the blessing of God, it shall be my dying sentiment: — independence *now* AND INDEPENDENCE FOREVER!"

### 2.—"*Impassioned*" *Poetic Style.*
FROM CAREY'S ODE ON ELOQUENCE.

' Where rests the sword ?—where sleep the brave?
Awake! Cecropia's ally save
   From the fury of the blast!
Burst the storm on Phocis' walls,—
Rise! or Greece forever falls;
   Up. or Freedom breathes her last!

### 3.—*Weeping Utterance.* (" Crying " Voice.)

PRINCE ARTHUR, [TO HUBERT, WHOSE ATTENDANTS ARE BINDING THE PRINCE, FOR THE PURPOSE OF PUTTING OUT HIS EYES.]—*Shakspeare*

" Alas! what need you be so boisterous rough?
I will not struggle,—I will stand stone still.
For Heaven's sake, Hubert, let me not be bound!
Nay, hear me, Hubert! drive these men away,
And I will sit as quiet as a lamb:
I will not stir, nor wince, nor speak a word,
Nor look upon the irons angrily.
Thrust but these men away, and I'll forgive you,
Whatever torment you do put me to!"

### 4.—*Shouting.*

RICHMOND TO HIS TROOPS.—*Shakspeare.*

" Advance your standards, draw your willing swords!
Sound drums and trumpets, boldly and cheerfully!
God, and Saint George! Richmond and victory!"

### III. "EXPLOSIVE OROTUND."

The "explosive" form of the "orotund" utterance, bears the same relation to "effusive" and "expulsive orotund," that "explosion" in breathing or whispering, bears to · effusion" and "expulsion," in those forms. It implies an instantaneous burst of voice with a quick, clear, sharp, and cutting effect on the ear.

This mode of voice proceeds from a violent and abrupt exertion of the abdominal muscles, acting on the diaphragm, and thus discharging a large volume of air, previously inhaled. The breath, in this process, is, as it were, dashed against the glottis or lips of the larynx, causing a loud and instantaneous explosion. In the act of "explosion" the chink of the glottis is, for a moment, closed, and a resistance, at first, offered to the escape of the breath, by a firm compression of the lips of the larynx, and downward pressure of the epiglottis. After this instant pressure and resistance, follows the explosion caused by the appulsive act of the abdominal muscles and the diaphragm, propelling the breath, with powerful and irresistible volume, on the glottis, and epiglottis, which at length give way, and suffer the breath to escape, with a loud and sudden report, of a purely explosive character.

The preceding and accompanying state of the organs, in the act of "explosion," sufficiently indicates the propriety of this mode of utterance being termed "orotund;" as it possesses all the depth, roundness, and fulness of the other forms of that "quality," which have been already discussed; and implies farther, that these are now compacted and condensed, to an extraordinary degree, so as to make the sound of the voice resemble, in its effect on the ear, that of a firm and hard ball striking against the surface of the body.

"Explosive orotund" is the language of intense passion· it is heard when the violence of emotion is beyond the control of the will, and a sudden ecstasy of *terror, anger*, or any other form of *intensely excited feeling*, causes the voice to burst forth involuntarily from the organs, with all the sudden and startling effect that would arise from its sound being forced out, by a sudden blow, applied to the back of the speaker. It exists only in the extremes of *abrupt emotion*, as in the burst of *anger*, or the shout of *courage*, and admits of no gradations.

This form of the human voice is one of the most impressive in its effect. By a law of our constitution, it acts with an instantaneous shock on the sympathetic nerve, and rouses the sensibility of the whole frame; it summons to instant action all the senses; and in the thrill which it sends from nerve to brain, we feel its awakening and inciting power over the mind. With the rapidity of lightning it penetrates every faculty, and sets it instinctively on the alert. It seems designed by nature as the note of alarm to the whole citadel within the soul.

We hear the "explosive orotund quality" exemplified in the sudden *alarm of fire*, in the short and sharp cry of *terror* or of *warning*, at the approach of instant and great danger

in the eruptive *curse of furious anger*, in the abrupt *exclamation of high-wrought courage*, and in the *burst of frantic
grief*. In reading and recitation, it belongs appropriately to
*the highest ecstatic effects of lyric* and *dramatic poetry*, as the
language of intense passion.

Without the full command of this element, emotion becomes lifeless and ineffective in tone; and the inspired language of the poet dies upon the tongue.

To gain the full command of " explosive orotund " voice, the practice of the elements, of syllables, and words, in the tones of anger and terror, should be frequently repeated, along with the following and similar examples. A previous organic practice should also be repeatedly made, on the mechanical exercise of abrupt and loud *coughing*, which is the purest form of " explosive orotund." The vocal elements and syllabic combinations should be repeated in the form of a sudden cough, at the opening of each sound. *Laughing*, — in its strongest and fullest style, — is another natural form of " explosive orotund;" and the mechanical practice of the act is one of the most efficacious modes of imparting to the organs the power of instantaneous " explosion," required in the vivid expression of high-wrought feeling. These processes at once secure a vigorous state of the organs of voice, and a round and compacted form of sound. No exercise is so effectual for strengthening weak organs, or imparting energy to tone, as the " explosive orotund " utterance. Like all other powerful forms of exertion, it should not, at first, be carried very far: neither should it be practised without a due interspersing of the gentler and softer exercises of voice. Pursued exclusively, it would harden the voice, and render it dry and unpleasing in its quality. Intermingled with the other modes of practice, it secures thorough-going force and clearness of voice, and permanent vigor and elasticity of organs.

*Examples of "Explosive Orotund."*

1. *Courage.* (" Explosive " Shouting.)

ODE TO THE GREEKS.—*Anon.*

" Strike for the sires who left you free!
    Strike for their sakes who bore you!
    Strike for your homes and liberty,
        And the Heaven you worship, o'er you!"

2. *Anger.*

ANTONY, [TO THE CONSPIRATORS.]—*Shakspeare.*

" Villains! you did not threat, when your vile daggers
Hacked one another in the sides of Cæsar!

You showed your teeth like apes, and fawned like hounds
And bowed like bondmen, kissing Cæsar's feet;
Whilst damned Casca, like a cur, behind,
Struck Cæsar on the neck.—Oh! flatterers!"

### 3. *Terror.*

FROM HALLECK'S MARCO BOZZARIS.

" To arms!—they come!—the Greek, the Greek!"

### 4. *Hurry and Commotion.*

MACBETH TO HIS OFFICER.—*Shakspeare.*

" Send out more horses,—skirr the country round;
Hang those that talk of fear!—Give me mine armor."

#### "ASPIRATED QUALITY."

The " qualities " of voice which are most frequently exemplified in reading and speaking, are those which have been defined and exemplified, under the designations of " pure tone " and " orotund." Deviations from purity of tone, are usually to be regarded as faults of inadvertency or of personal habit. Still, there are some classes of emotions, which, from their peculiar nature, require, as one element in their " expression," an " aspirated quality," or that in which, from the forcible character of the feeling, operating with a corresponding effect on the organs, more breath is expelled from the trachea, in the act of utterance, than is converted into sound by the exertion of the larynx. The stream of air which the excited action of the expulsory muscles, throws out, under the influence of certain passions, becomes too wide and too powerful to be moulded by the glottis and controlled by the vocal chords, which, for the moment, become, as it were, either paralyzed or convulsed, and unable to act with effect. Hence a rushing sound of the breath escaping, unvocalized, is heard along with the partially vocalized sounds by which such passions are expressed. The half-whispering voice of *fear*, and the harsh, breathing sound of *anger*, are examples in point, in the extremes of " expression."

The agitating character of these and similar emotions, disturbs the play of the organs, and not only prevents, in utterance, the effect of purity of tone,—which is always connected with comparative tranquillity of feeling,—but causes, by " aspirated quality," or redundant breath superadded to vocal sound, a positive *impurity* of tone, which has a grating effect on the ear,—somewhat as takes place when we hear a person attempting to play on a wind instrument which has been cracked, and which allows a hissing sound of the breath to escape along with the musical notes.

The emotions which are naturally expressed by the strongest form of "aspirated quality," are principally of that class which an eminent writer on the passions has denominated "malignant," from their peculiar character and effect, as contrasted with those of others which he denominates "genial." The former class includes *fear, hatred, aversion, horror, anger*, and all similar feelings: the latter, *love, joy, serenity, tenderness, pity*, &c.

"Aspirated quality," like other forms of utterance, may exist, according to the force of emotion, in the three gradations of "effusive," "expulsive," and "explosive" voice. The muscular action attending utterance in the form of "aspirated quality," is usually such as to blend with the "aspiration" either a "pectoral" or a "guttural" resonance, very strongly marked. Hence these properties of voice, which would, in the expression of other emotions, be mere organic faults, now become requisites to effect, and are, therefore, comparative excellences. They require, accordingly, special study and practice as modes of "expressive" utterance.

The "aspirated quality," in the "*pectoral*" form, belongs usually to *despair, deep-seated anger, revenge, excessive fear, horror*, and other deep and powerful emotions.

Other emotions, however, besides those which may be designated as "malignant," partake of "aspirated quality." *Awe*, may be mentioned as an example, which, when profound, is always marked by a slight aspiration, and a "pectoral quality." *Joy* and *grief*, too, become "aspirated" when highly characterized. *Ardor* and *intense earnestness* of emotion, are always "aspirated." The *fervent* expression of *love*, and even of *devotion*, admits, accordingly, of "aspirated" utterance. "Aspiration," like "tremor," thus becomes a natural sign of extremes in feeling; and these two properties united, form the *acmé* or highest point of "expression."

The 'aspirated quality," in the "guttural" form, belongs in various degrees, to all *malignant* emotions. In its stronger expression, it gives a harsh, animal, and sometimes even fiend-like character to human utterance, as in the malice and revenge of Shylock. In a reduced, though still highly impassioned degree, it gives its peculiar choking effect to the utterance of *anger*.

In the *yell* of *rage* and *fury*, "aspiration" is displaced by perfectly "pure tone" of the loudest sound, — by a law of man's organization, which it is unnecessary here to analyze, but which seems to make all the extremes, or utmost reaches of human feeling, musical in their effect. *Joy*, and the extremes of both *grief* and *anger*, may be mentioned as illustrations.

*Aversion, disgust, displeasure, impatience, dissatisfaction,* and *discontent*, all, in various degrees, combine "aspirated" utterance and "guttural quality."

The due "aspiration" of the voice, in all the emotions which have been enumerated as requiring that property, is a point indispensable to the natural and appropriate "expression" of emotion, and consequently an important accomplishment of good elocution, whether in reading or speaking.

To learners who have practised the exercises in whispering, which is the extreme of "aspiration" this quality will not prove difficult of acquisition. It will be of great service, however, to power of "expression," to render the command of "aspiration" easy by frequent repetition on elements, syllables, and words, selected for the purpose, and on the examples contained in the "exercises on aspirated quality," in the Appendix.

## CHAPTER IV.

### FORCE.

A PRIMARY characteristic of utterance, as expressive of emotion, is the degree of its energy, or force. The effect of any feeling on sympathy, is naturally inferred from the degree of force with which the sound of voice, in the utterance of that feeling, falls upon the ear of the hearer. The cause of this impression upon the mind, is, obviously, the law of organic sympathy, by which one part of the human frame naturally responds to another. A powerful emotion not only affects the heart and the lungs, and the other involuntary agents of life and of expression, but starts the expulsory muscles into voluntary action, and produces voice, the natural indication and language of feeling. The degree of force, therefore, in a vocal sound, is intuitively taken as the measure of the emotion which causes it. Except, only, those cases in which the force of feeling paralyzes, as it were the organs of the voice, and suggests the opposite measure of infer ence, by which a choked and struggling utterance, a suppressed or inarticulate voice, or even absolute silence, becomes the index to the heart.

The command of all degrees of force of voice, must evidently be essential to true and natural expression, whether in reading or speaking. Appropriate utterance ranges through all stages of vocal sound, from the whisper of fear and the murmur of repose, to the boldest swell of vehement declamation, and the shout of triumphant courage. But to give forth any one of these or the intermediate tones, with just and impressive effect, the organs must be disciplined by appropriate exercise and frequent practice. For every day's observation proves to us, that mere natural instinct and animal health, with all the aids of informing intellect, and inspiring emotion, and exciting circumstances, are not sufficient to produce the effects of eloquence, or even of adequate utterance.

The overwhelming power of undisciplined feeling, may not only impede but actually prevent the right action of the instruments of speech; and the novice who has fondly dreamed, in his closet, that nothing more is required for effective expression, than a genuine feeling, finds, to his discomfiture, that it is, perhaps, the very intensity of his feeling that hinders his utterance; and it is not till experience and practice have done their work, that he learns the primary lesson, that force of emotion needs a practised force of will, to balance and regulate it, and a disciplined control over the organs, to give it appropriate utterance.

The want of due training for the exercise of public reading or speaking, is evinced in the habitual undue loudness of some speakers, and the inadequate force of others the former subjecting their hearers to unnecessary pain, and the latter to disappointment and uneasiness.

Force of utterance, however, has other claims on the attention of students of elocution, besides those which are involved in correct expression. It is, in its various gradations, the chief means of imparting strength to the vocal organs, and power to the voice itself. The due practice of exercises in force of utterance, does for the voice what athletic exercise does for the muscles of the body: it imparts the two great conditions of power, — vigor and pliancy.

"Vocal gymnastics" afford no discipline more useful than that which accompanies the daily practice of the various gradations of force. Exercises of this description, enable the public speaker to retain perpetually at command the main element of vivid and impressive utterance; and they furnish to young persons of studious and sedentary habit the means of thorough invigoration for the energetic use of the voice, required in professional exertions.

Vocal exercises of the kind now suggested, are also invaluable aids to health, and cheerfulness, and mental activity, in all who practise them, and are not less useful in training the voice for the gentle utterance required in the practice of reading in the domestic or the social circle, than in invigorating it for public performances.

The effect of vocal training in the department of force, is greatly augmented when the bolder exercises are performed in the open air or in a large hall. A voice trained on this scale of practice, easily accommodates itself to a more limited space; while it is equally true, that a voice habituated to parlor reading only, usually fails in the attempt to practise in a room more spacious. Farther, the fact is familiar to instructors in elocution, that persons commencing practice with a very weak and inadequate voice, attain, in a few weeks, a perfect command of the utmost degrees of force, by performing their exercises out of doors, or in a hall of ample dimensions.

It is a matter of great moment, in practising the exercises in force, to observe, at first, with the utmost strictness, the rule of commencing with the slightest and advancing to the most energetic forms of utterance. When practice has imparted due vigor and facility, it will be a useful variation of order, to commence with the more powerful exertions of the voice, and descend to the more gentle. It is a valuable attainment, also, to be able to strike at once, and with perfect ease and precision, into any degree of force, from whispering to shouting.

As the exercises in the various "qualities" of the voice, have already led us over the ground of "force," in all its gradations, it will be sufficient to present them once in succession, without farther explanation. (See "exercises on force," in the appendix.)

## DEGREES OF FORCE.

The perfect command of every degree of force, and an exact discrimination of its stages, as classified by degree and character of emotion, are indispensable to correct and impressive elocution. Extensive and varied practice on force, in all its gradations, becomes, therefore, an important point, in the vocal culture connected with elocution. Nor is it less valuable as the chief means of imparting power of voice and vigor of organ, — as was formerly intimated.

The student's attention is again directed to the importance of this element, for the purpose of securing a patient and persevering practice on elementary sounds, with an exclusive view, at present, to the mechanical exertion of the organs in the successive stages of mere loudness of voice. It will be found a useful practice to repeat the first line of each example in succession.

After having completed the practice on force, as prescribed ir the preceding exercises, — in which its degrees are indicated by the feeling expressed in each example, — the various component elements of the language, the "tonics," "subtonics," and "atonics," and examples of their combination in syllables and words, may be repeated successively, (1.) in forms corresponding to the style of each exercise; (2.) in the musical gradations of " pianissimo," (very soft;) " piano," (soft;) " mezzo piano," (moderately soft;) " mezzo," (moderate;) " mezzo forte," (moderately loud;) " forte,' (loud;) and " fortissimo," (very loud;") (3.) in successive stages, commmencing with the slightest and most delicate sound that can be uttered in " pure tone," and extending to the most vehement force of shouting and calling in the open air, and with all the power that the voice can yield.

Persons who practise such exercises several times a day,[1] for ten or fifteen minutes at a time, will find a daily gain in vocal power and organic vigor to be the invariable result: every day will enable them to add a degree to their scale of force. To young persons whose organs are yet fully susceptible of the benefits of training, to students and sedentary individuals, in general, whose mode of life is deficient in muscular exercise, and consequently in power of voice, and to professional men whose exercises in public speaking are at comparatively distant intervals, (in which case, the organs need the aid of invigorating daily practice more than in any other,) the mechanical practice of graduated force, is the most effective aid that can be found.

The kind of exercise now recommended, if presented in a form addressed to the eye, might be marked thus:

· • • • ● ● ● ● ● ● ● ●

Each dot represents, in this scale, one and the same sound, or word, repeated with a gradually increasing force. The repetition of the same sound, for at least a dozen times, is preferred to a change of elements, because, by repetition, the ear becomes, as it were, a more exact judge of the successive degrees of force, when not distracted by attention to anything else than the one point of mere loudness.

This exercise can never injure, but will always strengthen, even weak organs, if the gradation of voice be duly observed, and the note of the scale kept rigorously the same, throughout, and not pitched, — at first, — either very high or very low on the scale.

## CHAPTER V.

### "STRESS."

Force, as a property of voice, may be regarded either as it exists in consecutive or in single sounds. Thus, the force of utterance, in a sentence or a clause, may be on one phrase, or even on a single word. In the pronunciation of a word, it may be exclusively on one

[1] It may not be improper to remark here, that vocal exercise should be practised at *a point of time as nearly as may be* INTERMEDIATE *to the hours assigned for meal-times;* as the organs are then in their best condition, — neither embarrassed nor exhausted, as regards the state of the circulation. The rule of the Italian vocal training, which prescribes powerful and continued exertion of voice, *before breakfast,* with a view to deepen the "register," implies a state of organs already inured to fatigue; and the stereotype direction of the old physicians, to declaim *after dinner,* with a view to promote digestion, implies either a meal in the poet's style of "spare fast, that oft with gods doth diet," or a strength of the digestive organ, that can render it callous to the powerful shocks which energetic declamation always imparts by impassioned emotion, to that chief "local habitation" of the "sympathetic" nerve.

syllable In the enunciation of a syllable, the organic force may lie chiefly on a single letter. In the sound of a letter, the force of the voice may lie conspicuously on the first, or on the last part of the sound, on the middle, or on both extremes; or it may be distributed, with an approach to equalizing force, over all parts of the sound.

The term "stress," as used by Dr. Rush, is applied to the mode in which force is rendered perceptible or impressive, in *single sounds*. Stress includes two elements of vocal effect: — 1st, mere *force* of sound; 2d, the *time* which it occupies. To these may be added, not improperly, a third element, which is the result of the union or combination of the other two, viz., *abrupt* or *gradual* emission.

The classification of the forms of stress is as follows:

1st, "*Radical stress*," or that in which the force of utterance is, usually, more or less "explosive," and falls on the "radical" (initial, or first) part of a sound.

2d, "*Median stress*," that in which the force is "expulsive" or "effusive," and swells out whether slowly or rapidly, at the middle of a sound.

3d, "*Vanishing stress*," or that which withholds the "expulsive" or "explosive" force till the "vanish," or last moment of the sound.

4th, "*Compound stress*," or that in which the voice, with more or less of "explosive" force, touches forcefully and distinctly on both the initial and the final points of a sound, but passes slightly and almost imperceptibly over the middle part.

5th, "*Thorough stress*," in which the initial, middle, and final portions of a sound, are all distinctively and impressively marked by special "expulsive force" of voice.

6th, "*Tremor*," tremulous, or intermittent "stress."

### I. "RADICAL STRESS."

This form of vocal force is exemplified in the mechanical act of abrupt coughing.[1] In speech, its highest form exists

---

- "There are so few speakers able to give a radical stress to syllabic utterance, with this momentary burst, which I here mean to describe, that I must draw an illustration from the effort of coughing. '␣t will be perceived that a single impulse of coughing, is not, in all points, exactly like the abrupt voice on syllables: for that single impulse is a forcing out of almost all the breath; yet if the tonic element a-we be emp ␣␣␣d as the vocality of cough ␣g. its in the utterance of all sounds which embody startling and abrupt emotions; as *fear, anger*, &c. It exists, also, although in a reduced form, in the tones of *determined will, earnest argument, emphatic* and *distinct* or *exact communication*, and other unimpassioned modes of expression.

In the latter shape, "radical" stress does little more than impart to speech an additional degree of that clear, distinct, and energetic character of utterance, which is marked by the decision of its "radical movement," — the phrase, (it will be recollected,) by which Dr Rush has designated the opening, or initial part, of articulate sounds. But, even in this reduced degree, it forms one of the most valuable accomplishments of elocution ; for, although it does not, in this mode, aim at a sympathetic effect on passion or imagination, it subserves the substantially useful purpose of addressing, in clear, distinct style, the ear and the understanding. The definiteness and decision of the speaker's intention, the clear conviction of his judgment, the distinctness of his perceptions, and the energy of his will, are all indicated in this natural language of voice.

A due "radical stress," farther, imparts point and spirit to articulation : it gives an edge and a life to utterance, and hinders emotion from rendering the voice confused and indistinct. Vehemence, without "radical stress," becomes vociferation and bawling.

The energy of the "radical movement," may, indeed, be justly termed the salt and the relish of oral communication, as it preserves the pungency and penetrating effect of articulate utterance. Without due "radical stress," reading or speaking becomes insipid and ineffective. The argumentative speaker who has not this quality at command, seems to strike with the flat rather than the edge of the rhetorical weapon.[1] Carried to excess, it becomes, of course, a fault : it savors of dogmatical arrogance and assumption, of selfish wilful-

---

acrub: opening will truly represent the function of radical stress when used in discourse.

"The clear and forcible radical stress can take place only after an interruption of the voice. It would seem as if there is some momentary occlusion in the larynx, by which the breath is barred and accumulated for the purpose of a full and sudden discharge. This occlusion is most under command, and the explosion is most powerful, on syllables beginning with a tonic element, or with an abrupt one preceding a tonic ; for, in this last case, an obstruction in the organs of articulation, is combined with the function of the larynx, above supposed." — *Dr. Rush.*

[1] " It is this," (radical stress,) " which draws the cutting edge of words across the ear, and startles even stupor into attention : — this which lessens the fatigue of listening, and outvoices the stir and rustle of an assembly : — and it is the sensibility to this, through a general instinct of the animal ear which gives authority to the groom and makes the horse submissive to his angry accent." — *Id*

ness, and self-conceit. Persuasion, not intimidation, is the soul of eloquence; argument, not assertion, the instrument of conviction; sympathy, not opposition, the avenue to the heart. A uniform, hard "radical stress," therefore, can effect none of the best purposes of speech, and must ever be regarded as allied to violence and vulgarity, or the slang of party invective.

The utter absence, however, of "radical stress," bespeaks timidity and indecision, confusion of thought, and feebleness of purpose. The speaker who fails in regard to the effect of the property of "radical stress," solicits our pity, rather than commands our respect. The right degree of this function indicates the manly, self-possessed, and impressive speaker. These remarks all apply, with corresponding force, to the exercise of reading. A feeble, vacillating, inexpressive utterance, kills, as it were, by a slow but sure death, the sentiments of the most impressive writer; and the hacking edge of a uniform, unmodified, "radical stress," turns the parlor or the classroom into the arena of a debating-club.

False taste and style in the practice of elocution, sometimes lead to the cultivation of an exclusive habit of "radical stress," in the utterance of young readers and speakers. The effect of this fault is very unfavorable. The decision of tone which it implies, belongs properly to years and to experience, on special occasions, or to the language of vehement excitement. It is utterly incompatible with the just diffidence and respectful tone appropriate in youth, and forever prevents the winning effect of nature's genuine eloquence, in the tones of feeling chastened and subdued by reverence for truth and respect for man.

The orator, however, and the reader, must still be regarded as, in their function, representing, for the moment, the sentiments of humanity, not merely the opinion or feeling of the individual. Hence, a just degree of firmness and force, (and the "radical stress" is the exponent of these qualities,) is a point indispensable to eloquent speaking and impressive reading.

The practice of the following examples should be accompanied by an extensive and thorough course of discipline on all degrees of "explosion," in elements, syllables, and words,—advancing from the very slightest to the intensest form, and occasionally reversing the order, so as to reduce the function of explosion from its most impassioned to its merely intellectual character and expression.

EXAMPLES OF "RADICAL STRESS."

I. "*Impassioned Radical.*"

*Example* 1. *Fear.*

("Explosive' Utterance: "Aspirated Guttural Quality.";
FROM BYRON'S LINES ON THE EVE OF WATERLOO.

[" While throng the citizens with terror dumb,
Or whispering with white lips,] ' The foe!—they come they come!'"

### 2. *Anger and Scorn.*

("Explosive" Utterance: "Aspirated Pectoral Quality,
Coriolanus, [to the People.]—*Shakspeare.*

"You common cry of curs! whose breath I hate
As reek o' the rotten fens,—whose loves I prize
As the dead carcasses of unburied men,
That do corrupt my air,—*I* banish *you!*"

### 3. *Courage.*

("Explosive" Utterance: "Pure Tone.")

"Up! comrades, up!—in Rokeby's halls
Ne'er be it said our courage falls!"

### II. "*Unimpassioned Radical.*"

*Example* 1. *Didactic Composition: Grave Style.*[1]
("Pure Tone:" "Moderate Force," "Grave" Style.—Usual Style of a *Sermon*, or of a *Moral* or *Political* Discourse.)

Immortality of the Soul.—*Addison.*

"How can it enter into the thoughts of man, that the soul, which is capable of such immense perfections, and of receiving new improvements to all eternity, shall fall away into nothing almost as soon as it is created? Are such abilities made for no purpose? A brute arives at a point of perfection that he can never pass: in a few years he has all the endowments he is capable of; and were he to live ten thousand more, would be the same thing he is at present. Were a human soul thus at a stand in her accomplishments, were her faculties to be full blown, and incapable of farther enlargement, I could imagine it might fall away insensibly, and drop at once into a state of annihilation. But can we believe that a thinking being which is in a perpetual progress of improvements, and travelling on from perfection to perfection,—after having just looked abroad into the works of its Creator, and made a few discoveries of His infinite goodness, wisdom, and power,—

[1] See foot note on next page.

must perish at her first setting out, and in the very beginning of her inquiries?'

2. *Didactic Composition: Serious Style.*[1]

("Pure Tone:" "Moderate" Force, "Serious" Style.—The usual form of utterance, in the reading of an *Essay*, or of a *Literary*, or *Scientific* Discourse.)

MORAL INFLUENCE OF LITERATURE.—*Frisbie.*

" The essay, the drama, the novel, have a most extensive and powerful influence upon the moral feelings and character of the age. Even descriptions of natural scenery owe much of their beauty and interest to the moral associations which they awaken.

" In like manner, fine turns of expression or thought, often operate more by suggestion than enumeration. But when feelings and passions are directly described, or imbodied in the hero, and called forth by the incidents of a story, it is then that the magic of fiction and poetry is complete,—that they enter in and dwell in the secret chambers of the soul, moulding it at will. In these moments of deep excitement, must not a bias be given to the character,—and much be done to elevate and refine, or degrade and pollute, those sympathies and sentiments which are the sources of much of o virtue and happiness, or of our guilt and misery?"

3. *Poetic Composition: Animated Style.*[1]

(' Pure Tone:" " Moderate " Force, " Lively " Style.)

SPRING.—*Bryant.*

" Is this a time to be gloomy and sad,
When our mother Nature laughs around;
When even the deep blue heavens look glad,
And gladness breathes from the blossoming ground?

---

[1] In these examples the "radical stress" is merely of that gentle kind which gives distinctness and life to articulation, by a firm and clear "radical movement," and preserves the *serious* style from verging on the *solemn*, by "swell" and prolongation, or by drawling. The slightest form of a clear cough, is the mechanical standard of organic action, in this degree of "stress;" and this distinction should be carefully observed; for, when strong feeling is expressed in "grave," or in "serious," or in "animated" style especially in poetry, the ' stress" changes to "median," for greater "expressive effect."

"The clouds are at play, in the azure space,
 And their shadows at play on the bright green vale,
And here they stretch to the frolic chase,
 And there they roll on the easy gale.

"And look at the broad-faced sun how he smiles
 On the dewy earth that smiles on his ray,
On the leaping waters and gay young isles,—
 Ay, look, and he 'll smile thy gloom away."

### 4. *Poetic Composition: Gay Style.*

("Pure Tone:" Moderately Strong Force, "Brisk" Style.)

VOICE OF SPRING. — *Mrs. Hemans.*

"Ye of the rose lip and the dew-bright eye
 And the bounding footstep, to meet me fly!
With the lyre and the wreath and the joyous lay,
 Come forth to the sunshine,—I may not stay."

SPRING.— *Bryant.*

"There 's a dance of leaves in that aspen bower,
 There 's a titter of winds in that beechen tree,
There 's a smile on the fruit, and a smile on the flower
 And a laugh from the brook that runs to the sea!"

## II. "MEDIAN STRESS."

This form of "stress" Dr. Rush describes as "a gradual strengthening and subsequent reduction of the voice, similar to what is called a swell, (swell and diminish,) in the language of musical expression."

"Radical stress," with its abrupt explosion, is the irrepressible burst of forcible utterance, in the language of unconscious and involuntary emotion. It is the expression of passion rather than of will

Median stress," on the contrary, is more or less a conscious and intentional effect, prompted and sustained and enforced by the will. It is the natural utterance of those emotions which allow the intermingling of reflection and sentiment with expression, and which purposely dwell on sound, as a means of enhancing their effect. The swell of "median stress" is, accordingly, more or less ample and prolonged, as the feeling which it utters is moderate, or deep and lofty and awful.

"Median stress" has the form of "effusive" utterance in *sublime, solemn,* and *pathetic* emotions: it becomes "expulsive," in those which combine *force* with *grandeur,* as in *admiration, courage, authoritative command, indignation, and similar feelings.* But its effect is utterly incompatible with the abruptness of "explosion." Its comparatively musical character adapts it, with special felicity of effect, to the melody of *verse,* and the natural "swell" of poetic expression.

This mode of "stress," is one of the most important in its effect on language, whether in the form of speaking or of reading. Destitute of its ennobling and expansive sound, the recitation of poetry sinks into the style of dry prose, the language of devotion loses its sacredness, the tones of oratory lose their power over the heart.

There is great danger, however, of this natural beauty of vocal expression being converted into a fault by being overdone. The habit recognized under the name of "mouthing," has an excessively increased and prolonged "median swell" for one of its chief characteristics. In this shape, it becomes a great deformity in utterance, — particularly when combined with what is no infrequent concomitant, the faulty mode of voice, known as "chanting" or "singing." Like sweetness among savors, this truly agreeably quality of sound, becomes distasteful or disgusting, when in the least degree excessive.

The practice of "median stress," therefore, requires very close attention. The spirit of poetry and the language of eloquence, — the highest effects of human utterance, — render it indispensable as an accomplishment in elocution. But a chaste and discriminating ear is requisite to decide the just degree of its extent.

"Median stress" is found in conjunction with most of the emotions which are uttered in the forms of "pure tone" and "orotund:" it exists also, though less perceptible in its effect, in union with "aspirated quality." It accompanies, likewise, all stages of force, from the slightest to the most vehement.

EXAMPLES OF "MEDIAN STRESS."

I. *"Effusive" Utterance.*

*"Pure Tone:" "Subdued" Force.*

1. *Pathos.* Gentlest form of "median stress," — a barely perceptible "swell.")

DEATH OF THE INFANT. — *Mrs. Hemans.*

" Calm on its leaf-strewn bier,
Unlike a gift of Nature to Decay —

Too rose-like still, too beautiful, too dear,—
The child at rest before its mother lay:—
　　Even so to pass away,
With its bright smile!—Elysium what wert thou
To her that wept o'er that young slumberer's brow?

2 *Solemnity.*　("Swell" moderately increased.)

### THE PAST.—*Bryant.*

"Thou unrelenting Past!
Strong are the barriers round thy dark domain;
　　And fetters, sure and fast,
Hold all that enter thy unbreathing reign.

"Far in thy realm withdrawn
Old empires sit in sullenness and gloom;
　　And glorious ages gone
Lie deep within the shadow of thy womb.

"Childhood, with all its mirth,
Youth, Manhood, Age, that draws us to the ground,
　　And last, Man's Life on earth,
Glide to thy dim dominions, and are bound."

3. *Tranquillity.*

### DEATH OF THE GOOD MAN.—*Bryant.*

Why weep ye, then, for him, who, having won
　　The bound of man's appointed years,—at last,
Life's blessings all enjoyed, life's labors done,
　　Serenely to his final rest has passed;
While the soft memory of his virtues, yet,
Lingers like twilight hues, when the bright sun is set?

"His youth was innocent; his riper age,
　　Marked with some act of goodness, every day;
And, watched by eyes that loved him, calm and sage,
　　Faded his late declining years away.
Cheerful he gave his being up, and went
To share the holy rest that waits a life well spent."

4. *Reverence.* (Fuller " swell.')

"*Effusive orotund quality.*"

FROM THE FOREST HYMN.—*Bryant.*

" Father! Thy hand
Hath reared these venerable columns; Thou
Didst weave this verdant roof. Thou didst look down
Upon the naked earth; and, forthwith, rose
All these fair ranks of trees. They in Thy sun
Budded, and shook their green leaves in Thy breeze,
And shot towards heaven. The century-living crow,
Whose birth was in their tops, grew old and died
Among their branches, till, at last, they stood,
As now they stand, massy and tall, and dark,—
Fit shrine for humble worshipper to hold
Communion with his Maker!"

5. *Pathos and Sublimity.* (Full and prolonged " swell.")

FROM DAVID'S LAMENTATION OVER SAUL AND JONATHAN.

———" How are the mighty fallen!—Saul and Jonathan were lovely and pleasant in their lives; and in their death they were not divided; they were swifter than eagles, they were stronger than lions.—Ye daughters of Israel, weep over Saul, who clothed you in scarlet, with other delights; who put on ornaments of gold upon your apparel!—How are the mighty fallen in the midst of the battle! O Jonathan! thou wast slain in thy high places!—How are the mighty fallen, and the weapons of war perished!"

6 *Solemnity, Sublimity, and Fervor.* (" Fullest swell.")

FROM THE BOOK OF PSALMS.

" Oh! sing unto the Lord a new song; for he hath done marvellous things: his right hand and his holy arm hath gotten him the victory.—Make a joyful noise unto the Lord, all the earth: make a loud noise, and rejoice, and sing praise. Sing unto the Lord with the harp; with the harp, and the voice of a psalm. With trumpets and sound of cornet, make a joyful noise before the Lord the King. Let the sea roar and the fulness thereof; the world, and they that dwell therein. Let the floods clap their hands: let the hills be joyful together."

II. *"Expulsive" Utterance.*

*'Pure Tone:" "Moderate" Force.*

1. *Grave Style.*[1]

(Gentle and pure " median stress," without prolongation.)

THE NEGLECT OF RELIGION.— *Alison.*

" The excuses of youth, for the neglect of religion, are those which are most frequently offered, and most easily admitted. The restrictions of religion, though proper enough for maturer age, are too severe, it is said, for this frolicsome and gladsome period. Its consolations, too, they do not want Leave these to prop the feeble limbs of old age, or to cheer the sinking spirits of adversity.—False and pernicious maxim! As if, at the end of a stated number of years, a man could become religious in a moment! As if the husbandman, at the end of a summer, could call up a harvest from the soil which he had never tilled! As if manhood, too. would have no excuses! And what are they? That he has grown too old to amend. That his parents took no pains with his religious education, and therefore his ignorance is not his own fault. That he must be making provision for old age; and the pressure of cares will allow him no time to attend to the evidences, or learn the rules of religion. Thus life is spent in framing apologies, in making and breaking resolutions, and deferring amendment, till death places his cold hand on the mouth open to make its last excuse, and one more is added to the crowded congregation of the dead.'

[1] This example furnishes an instance of the "grave" style assuming the 'median stress," for impressive effect, as formerly mentioned

## 2. Serious Style.[1]

"Median stress," still shorter in *duration*, but increased in *force* )

PLEASURES OF THE NATURALIST. — *Wood.*

"Whether the naturalist be at home or abroad, in every different clime, and in every season of the year, universal nature is before him, and invites to a banquet richly replenished with whatever can invigorate his understanding, or gratify his mental taste. The earth on which he treads, the air in which he moves, the sea along the margin of which he walks, all teem with objects that keep his attention perpetually awake, excite him to healthful activity, and charm him with an ever-varying succession of the beautiful, the wonderful, the useful, and the new."

## 3. Animated Style.[1]

(The approach to *poetic* description renders the "swell" still more forcible and full, but also allows the voice to dwell comparatively longer upon it.)

EARLY RISING. — *Robinson.*

" He who rises early, is met by the domestic animals, with peculiar pleasure : one winds and purs about him, another frisks and capers, and does everything but speak. The stern mastiff, the plodding ox, the noble horse, the harmless sheep, the prating poultry, each in its own way expresses joy when he first appears. Then how incomparably fine is the dawning of the day, when the soft light comes stealing on, at first glimmers with the stars, but gradually outshines them all. How beautiful are the folding and parting of the gray clouds, drawn back like a curtain, to give us a sight of the most magnificent of all appearances, the rising of the sun ! How rich is the dew, decking every spire of grass with colored

---

[1] These examples illustrate the application of the "median stress" to "serious" and "animated" style, from fulness of feeling and effect. Had the composition been of a lower tone, the utterance would have exemplified the application of the "unimpassioned radical."

spangles of endless variety, and of inexpressible beauty! Larks mount, and fill the air with a cheap and perfect music; and every tree, every steeple, and every hovel, emits a cooing or a twittering, a warbling or a chirping,—a hailing of the returning day.'

## 4. *Declamatory Force.*

RESISTANCE TO OPPRESSION.—*Sheridan.*

"Shall we be told that the exasperated feelings of a whole people, goaded and spurred on to clamor and resistance, were excited by the poor and feeble influence of their secluded princesses? or that *they* could inspire this enthusiasm and this despair into the breasts of a people who felt no grievance, and had suffered no torture?—What motive, then, could have such influence in their bosoms? What motive!—That which Nature, the common parent, plants in the bosom of man, and which is congenial with, and makes part of his being,—that feeling which tells him that man was never made to be the property of man; but that, when through pride and insolence of power, one human creature dares to tyrannize over another, it is a power usurped, and resistance is a duty,—that principle which tells him, that resistance to power usurped is not merely a duty which he owes to himself and to his neighbor, but a duty which he owes to his God, in asserting and maintaining the rank which He gave him in the creation!—to that common God, who, where he gives the form of man, whatever may be the complexion, gives also the feelings and the rights of man,—that principle which neither the rudeness of ignorance can stifle, nor the enervation of refinement extinguish,—that principle which makes it base for a man to suffer when he ought to act; which, tending to preserve to the species the original designations of Providence, spurns at the arrogant distinctions of man and vindicates the independent quality of his race."

## 5. Impassioned Force.

(A full and gushing "swell" of grief.)

ANTONY, [BEFORE THE CONSPIRATORS.] — *Shakspeare*

' That I did love thee, Cæsar, oh! 't is true.
If then thy spirit look upon us now,
Shall it not grieve thee, dearer than thy death,
To see thy Antony making his peace,
Shaking the bloody fingers of thy foes,
Most noble! in the presence of thy corse?
Had I as many eyes as thou hast wounds,
Weeping as fast as they stream forth thy blood,
It would become me better, than to close
In terms of friendship with thine enemies.
Pardon me, Julius!—Here wast thou bayed, brave hart,
Here didst thou fall; and here thy hunters stand,
Signed in thy spoil, and crimsoned in thy lethe.
O world! thou wast the forest to this hart;
And this, indeed, O world, the heart of thee!
How like a deer, stricken by many princes,
Dost thou here lie!"

## 6. Shouting and Calling.

The strongest " swell " of which the voice is capable, the note prolonged.)

CINNA, [AFTER THE ASSASSINATION OF CÆSAR.] — *Shakspeare.*

" Liberty! Freedom! Tyranny is dead!—
Run hence! proclaim, cry it about the streets!"

*Cassius.* " Some to the common pulpits! and cry out,
*Liberty, freedom, and enfranchisement!*"

### III. "VANISHING STRESS."

The word "vanishing," in this use of it, is divested entirely of its usual meaning. It has no reference whatever to an effect corresponding to the gradual disappearing of a visible object, withdrawing from the eye. It refers, as a technical term, merely to *the last audible moment of a vocal sound,*— as the word " vanish" was technically used in speaking of the " vanishing movement" in the utterance of a sound or the enunciation of a letter. The terms " radical" and " vanish,' used in elocution, with reference to the property of " stress," are always to be understood as exactly synonymous, the former, with the word *initial*, and the latter, with the word *final*.

We have observed, thus far, that some emotions, in their utterance, throw the " stress," or force of vocal sound, upon the *first* portion of an element, as in the " explosive radical " of *anger*, of *fear* of *scorn*, and similar passions; while others retain the " stress " for the effect of a " swell," or expulsive force, on the *middle* of a note, as in the " median " style of the shout of *triumph*, or the gentle, but full-swelling tone of *reverence*, or *adoration*. We proceed now to those emotions which express themselves by a jerking force, or " stress," thrown out at the " vanish " or *close* of a sound.

The force of utterance in the expression of emotions marked by " vanishing stress," begins with a light and gentle, and ends with a heavy and violent sound, which leaves off instantly and abruptly. But although the sound, in such cases, is obviously slight at its commencement, and powerful at its close, it is by no means a gradual formation and increase of force, easily followed by the ear or analyzed by the mind. On the contrary, the whole duration of such sounds is very brief and transient, and their effect on the ear excessively abrupt, as well as violent.

This form of " stress," being the natural expression of extreme emotion, does not admit of the gradations which may not unfrequently be traced in the " radical" and " median" modes. It exists only in the shape of a protracted or deferred " explosion." Its nature is incompatible with " expulsion," or any inferior force.

A pretty accurate impression of the character of the " vanishing stress," may be obtained by listening to the sound of a musket, when through negligent loading, or from damp powder, it " hangs fire, and a partially hissing, but growing sound precedes the final explosion. It is exhibited in the mechanical functions of the human organs of respiration and of voice, when the workman who is using a heavy sledge-hammer brings it down in coincidence with a groaning expiration, terminating at the moment of the blow, in the form familiarly termed a grunt. It is exemplified, in its moral effect, in the language of a child stung to a high pitch of impatient or peevish feeling, and uttering, in the tone of the most violent ill-temper, its appropriate "I won't!" or "You shan't!" In such circumstances the "explosion" of passion is deferred, or hangs, for a moment, on the ear, till the "vanish" or final part of the sound bursts out from the chest, throat, and mouth, with furious vehemence; leaving, in its abrupt termination, an effect directly contrary to the dying wail of *grief*, or the gentle vanish of the tone of *love*.

The obvious preparation of the organs for the vocal effect, in the expression of "vanishing stress," implies its comparative dependence on volition. Hence it is the natural utterance of *determined purpose*, of *earnest resolve*, of *stern rebuke*, of *contempt*, of *astonishment* and *horror*, of *fierce* and *obstinate will*, of *dogged sullenness of temper*, of *stubborn passion*, and all similar moods. It is the language, also, of *peevishness* and *impatience*, and, sometimes, of *excessive grief*.

Like all other forms of impassioned utterance which are strongly marked in the usages of natural habit, this property of voice is indispensable to appropriate elocution, whether in speaking or reading. Without "vanishing stress," declamation will sometimes lose its manly energy of determined will, and become feeble song to the ear. High-wrought resolution can never be expressed without it. Even the language of protest, though respectful in its form, needs the aid of the right degree of "vanishing stress," to intimate its sincerity and its firmness of determination, as well as its depth of conviction.

But when we extend our view to the demands of lyric and dramatic poetry, in which high-wrought emotion is so abundant an element of effect, the full command of this property of voice, as the natural utterance of extreme passion, becomes indispensable to true natural, and appropriate style.

EXAMPLES OF "VANISHING STRESS."

*Determined Purpose and Earnest Resolve.*

EXAMPLE 1. — [WEBSTER, ON FREEDOM OF DEBATE.]

("Pectoral quality:" "Declamatory" force: Bold "stress.")

"On such occasions, I will place myself on the extreme boundary of my right, and bid defiance to the arm that would push me from it."

2. [OTIS, AGAINST "WRITS OF ASSISTANCE."]
("Quality" and force, as in *Example* 1: "Stress" more deliberate.)

"Let the consequences be what they will, I am determined to proceed. The only principles of public conduct which are worthy of a gentleman or a man, are, to sacrifice estate, health, ease, applause, and even life, at the sacred call of his country."

3. [SWISS DEPUTY'S REPLY TO CHARLES OF BURGUNDY.]
("Aspirated Pectoral Quality:" "Impassioned" force: Increased "stress.")

"You may, if it be God's will, gain our barren and rugged mountains. But, like our ancestors of old, we will seek refuge in wilder and more distant solitudes; and when we have resisted to the last, we will starve in the icy wastes of the glaciers. Ay, men, women, and children, we will be frozen into annihilation together, ere one free Switzer will acknowledge a foreign master!"

4. [CAMPBELL'S WAR-SONG OF THE GREEKS.]
("Orotund Quality:" "Impassioned" force: "Stress" still more vehement.)

—— "We've sworn, by our country's assaulters,
By the virgins they've dragged from our altars,
By our massacred patriots, our children in chains,
By our heroes of old, and their blood in our veins,
 That living, we *will* be victorious,
 Or that dying, our deaths shall be glorious."

*Stern Rebuke.*

KING HENRY V. [TO LORD SCROOP, ON THE DETECTION OF HIS TREASON.
—*Shakspeare.*
("Aspirated Pectoral Quality:" "Impassioned" force: Vehement "stress.")

"But oh!
What shall I say to thee, Lord Scroop, thou cruel
Ungrateful, savage, and inhuman creature!

Thou that didst bear the keys of all my counsels,
That knew'st the very bottom of my soul,
That almost might'st have coined me into gold,
Wouldst thou have practised on me for thy use?"

### Contempt and Mockery.

QUEEN CONSTANCE, [TO THE ARCH-DUKE OF AUSTRIA.] —*Shakspeare.*

("Aspirated oral, and guttural Quality:" "Impassioned" force:
Violent "stress.")

"Thou slave! thou wretch! thou coward!
Thou little valiant, great in villany!
Thou ever strong upon the stronger side!
Thou Fortune's champion, that dost never fight
But when her humorous ladyship is by
To teach thee safety!"

### Astonishment and Horror.

MACDUFF, [ON DISCOVERING THE MURDER OF DUNCAN.] —*Shakspeare.*

(Extremely "Aspirated pectoral Quality:" "Impassioned" force:
Excessive "stress")

"Oh! horror! horror! horror!—Tongue nor heart,
Cannot conceive, nor name thee!

"Confusion now hath made his masterpiece!
Most sacrilegious murder hath broke ope
The Lord's anointed temple, and stole thence
The life o' the building.

"Approach the chamber, and destroy your sight
With a new Gorgon!"

### Fierce and Stubborn Will.

SHYLOCK, [REFUSING TO LISTEN TO ANTONIO.] —*Shakspeare.*

("Aspirated, pectoral and guttural Quality:" "Impassioned" vehemence: Excessive "stress.")

"I'll have my bond; I will not hear thee speak·
I'll have my bond; and therefore speak no more

I'll not be made a soft and dull-eyed fool,
To shake the head, relent, and sigh, and yield
To Christian intercessors. Follow not,
I'll have no speaking! I will have my bond"

*Peevish Impatience.*

HOTSPUR, [IRRITATED AGAINST HENRY IV.] —*Shakspeare.*

" Why, look you, I am whipped and scourged with rods,
Nettled, and stung with pismires, when I hear
Of this vile politician Bolingbroke!"

### IV. "COMPOUND STRESS."

This designation is applied to that form of "stress" which throws out the voice forcibly on the first and the last part of a sound, but slights, comparatively, the intermediate portion. It is, then, the application of a "radical" and a "vanishing" stress on the same sound, without an intervening "median."

It is the natural mode of "expression," in the utterance of *surprise*, and sometimes, though less frequently, of other emotions, as *contempt* and *mockery*, *sarcasm* and *raillery*.

In the instinctive uses of the voice, this function seems specially designed to give point and pungency to the " radical" and " vanish," or opening and closing portions of sounds which occupy a large space of time, and traverse a wide interval of the " scale." The " explosive" force at the commencement of such sounds, and the partial repetition of " explosive " utterance at their termination, seems to mark distinctly to the *ear* the space which they occupy, and thus intimate their significant value in feeling. We see an analogous proceeding which addresses itself to the *eye*, when the workman, desirous of obtaining a perfectly exact measure, makes a deep indentation with the end of his rule, at each end of a given line, or distance, upon the object which he is measuring. Such indentations may illustrate the design or the effect, of the pungent points of sound, in " compound stress:" they are distinct and impressive marks, and utter an important meaning.

The use of this form of " stress " belongs appropriately to feelings of peculiar force or acuteness. But on this very account, it becomes an indispensable means of natural expression and true effect, in many passages of reading and speaking. The difference between vivid and dull or flat utterance, will often turn on the exactness with which this expressive function of voice is exerted.

The careful and repeated practice of " compound stress," on elements, syllables, and words, should accompany the repetition of the following examples. To give these last, however, their true character and full effect, the imagination must be wholly given up to the supposed situation of the speaker; so as to receive a full sympathetic impression of the feeling to be uttered. Vivid emotion only, can prompt true expressive tone.

EXAMPLES OF "COMPOUND STRESS."

### 1. *Extreme Surprise.*

QUEEN CONSTANCE, [WHEN CONFOUNDED WITH THE INTELLIGENCE OF THE UNION OF LEWIS AND BLANCHE, AND THE CONSEQUENT INJURY TO HER SON, ARTHUR.]—*Shakspeare.*

("Aspirated, guttural, and oral Quality:" "Impassioned" force.)

"Gone to be married! Gone to swear a peace!
False blood to false blood joined! Gone to be friends!
Shall Lewis have Blanche, and Blanche these provinces?
It is not so; thou hast misspoke, misheard,—
Be well advised, tell o'er thy tale again:
It cannot be;—thou dost but say 't is so."

### 2. *Surprise, Perplexity, and Contempt.*

[THE EXAMPLES OF "COMPOUND STRESS" OCCUR IN THE WORDS WHICH THE SERVANT REPEATS AFTER CORIOLANUS. HE HAS ENTERED, POORLY CLAD, AND UNRECOGNIZED, THE MANSION OF AUFIDIUS, AND IS ILL RECEIVED BY THE DOMESTICS, WHOM HE TREATS WITH HARSHNESS AND DISDAIN ] *Shakspeare.*

*Servant.* "Where dwellest thou?
*Coriolanus.* ¹ Under the canopy.
*Serv.* Under the canopy!
*Cor.* Ay!
*Serv.* Where's that?
*Cor.* I' the city of kites and crows.
*Serv.* I' the city of kites and crows!—(What an ass it is!)
—Then thou dwellest with daws too?
*Cor.* No: I serve not thy master."

---

¹ The disdainful and repulsive manner of Coriolanus, causes all his replies to become striking examples of the most abrupt "*radical* stress." The short and snappish reply of petulance, always takes this form. It is not till provocation or irritation has stung its subject to the pitch of intolerable excitement, that utterance assumes the "vanishing stress."

## V. "THOROUGH STRESS."

This species of "stress" is produced by a marked force of utterance, placed distinctively on each part of a sound to which tne "radical," "median," and "vanishing" forms of stress, would apply separately. It exhibits all of these in succession, on one and the same sound.

The "thorough stress" is the natural mode of utterance in powerful emotion of that kind which seems as it were, to delight in full and swelling expression, and to dwell upon and amplify the sounds of the voice.

As far as vocal effect can be an exponent of feeling, this peculiarly characterized force, which omits no prominent portion of a sound, but pervades and obtrudes each one, would seem the appropriate language of all emotions which, in poetic phraseology, are said to "fill the soul," "swell the bosom," "fire the heart," or "delight and charm the fancy."

"Thorough stress," is accordingly, the characteristic mode of "expression" in the utterance of *rapture, joy, triumph*, and *exultation, lofty command, indignant emotion, disdain, excessive grief*, or whatever high-wrought feeling seems for the time to wreak itself on expressive sound. It is obviously the language of extreme or impassioned feeling only. It abounds, accordingly, in *lyric* and *dramatic poetry*. It is found, however, in all *vehement declamation* in which the emotion is sustained by reflective sentiment, as in the excitement of *virtuous indignation* and *high-souled contempt*.

"Thorough stress" is one of the most powerful weapons of oratory, as well as one of the most vivid effects of natural feeling. If indiscriminately used, it becomes ineffective, as savoring of the habit and mannerism of the individual, rather than of just and appropriate energy. In such circumstances, it becomes rant; and when joined, as it sometimes is, to the habit of " mouthing," it can excite nothing but disgust in a hearer of well-regulated taste.

Juvenile readers, however, in some instances, from diffidence, and students, from their enfeebling mode of life, are apt to fall far short of the requisite degree of this expressive function of the voice. To obtain the full command of it in all its applications, and to preserve it always from excess, much careful practice on appropriate examples, and on letters, syllables, and words, becomes indispensable, as a preparatory discipline in elocution

EXAMPLES OF "THOROUGH STRESS."

*Rapture, Joy, Triumph, Exultation.*

("Expulsive orotund;" "Impassioned" force: Powerful "stress.")

1.

FROM THE DYING CHRISTIAN. —*Pope.*

" Lend, lend your wings! I mount, I fly!
O Grave! where is thy victory?
O Death! where is thy sting!"

("Expulsive orotund:" Force of shouting: Vehement "stress")

2.

FROM MOORE'S LINES ON THE FATE OF NAPLES.

" Shout, Tyranny, shout
Through your dungeons and palaces, ' Freedom is o'er!'"

*Lofty Command.*

(" Expulsive orotund," and " sustained " force of calling, combined •
Powerful and prolonged " stress.")

FROM SATAN'S CALL TO HIS LEGIONS.—*Milton.*

" Princes! potentates!
Warriors, the flower of heaven! once yours, now lost
If such astonishment as this can seize
Eternal spirits,
Awake! arise! or be forever fallen!"

*Vehement Indignation.*

("Expulsive orotund:" " Declamatory" force: Vehement " stress.")

FROM CHATHAM'S REBUKE OF LORD SUFFOLK.

" These abominable principles, and this more abominable avowal of them, demand the most decisive indignation. I call upon that right reverend and this most learned Bench to vindicate the religion of their God, to defend and support the justice of their country. I call upon the bishops to interpose the unsullied sanctity of their lawn, upon the judges to inter• pose the purity of their ermine, to save us from this pollution.

ORTHOPHONY.

I call upon the honor of your-lordships, to reverence the dignity of your ancestors, and to maintain your own. I call upon the spirit and humanity of my country, to vindicate the national character."

## Disdain.

SATAN, [ı ı ITHURIEL AND ZEPHON.]—*Milton.*

(" Expulsive orotund :" " Impassioned " force : Powerful " stress.' ";

"Know ye not then," said Satan, filled with scorn,
"Know ye not me?—Ye knew me once no mate
For you; there sitting where ye durst not soar:
Not to know me argues yourselves unknown,—
The lowest of your throng."

## Violent Grief.

LADY CAPULET, [ON THE APPARENT DEATH OF JULIET.] —*Shakspeare.*

( ' Aspirated pectoral and oral Quality :" " Explosive " utterance: "Impassioned " force : Violent " stress.")

"Accurs'd, unhappy, wretched, hateful day!
Most miserable hour that e'er time saw,
In lasting labor of his pilgrimage!"

### TREMOR, OR "INTERMITTENT STRESS."

When, by the hysterical or excessive force of impassioned feeling, the breath is agitated into brief successive jets, instead of gushing forth in a continuous stream of unbroken sound, a tremor, or tremulous effect of voice, is produced which breaks its "stress" into tittles or points;—much in the same way that a row of dots may be substituted to the eye, for one continuous line. The human voice, in the case now in view, is as appropriately said to "tremble," as when we apply the term to the shivering motion of the muscular frame.

The "tremor' of the voice is the natural expression of al. emotions which, from their peculiar nature, are attended with a weakened condition of the bodily organs; such as extreme feebleness from *age, exhaustion, sickness, fatigue grief,* and even *joy,* and other feelings, in which *ardor* or *extreme tenderness* predominates.

In the reading or the recitation of lyric and dramatic poetry, this function of voice is often required for full, vivid, and touching expression. Without its appeals to sympathy, and, its peculiar power over the heart, many of the most beautiful, and touching passages of Shakspeare and Milton become dry and cold. Like the *tremula* of the accomplished vocalist, in operatic music, it has a charm, for the absence of which nothing can atone; since nature suggests it as the genuine utterance of the most delicate and thrilling emotion.

The perfect command of "tremor," requires often-repeated practice on elements, syllables, and words, as well as on appropriate passages of impassioned language.

EXAMPLES OF "TREMOR."

1. *The Tremor of Age and Feebleness.*

("Pure Tone:" "Subdued" force of Pathos: Tremulous utterance, throughout.)

STANZA FROM A POPULAR BALLAD.

"Pity the sorrows of a poor old man,
  Whose trembling limbs have borne him to your door,
Whose days are dwindled to the shortest span;—
  Oh! give relief; and Heaven will bless your store!'

2. *Exhaustion and Fatigue.*

("Aspirated pectoral and oral Quality:" "Suppressed" force: "Tremor" throughout.)

FROM "AS YOU LIKE IT."—*Shakspeare.*

Adam, [*to Orlando.*] "Dear master, I can go no farther: Oh! I die for food! Here lie I down, and measure out my grave. Farewell! kind master."

("Pure Tone:" "Subdued" force of Pathos: Occasional "tremor" of Tenderness.)

Orlando, [*to Adam.*] "Why, how now, Adam!—no greater heart in thee? Live a little; comfort a little; cheer thyself a little. For my sake be comfortable, hold death awhile at the arm's end: I will here be with thee presently

Well said! thou look'st cheerily: and I'll be with thee
quickly.—Yet thou liest in the bleak air: Come, I will bear
thee to some shelter. Cheerly, good Adam!"

### 3. *Sickness.*

KING JOHN, [ON THE EVE OF HIS DEATH, TO FAULCONBRIDGE ] —*Shakspear*

("Aspirated pectoral Quality:" 'Suppressed" force: Gasping and
tremulous utterance.)

"O cousin, thou art come to set mine eye:
My heart hath one poor string to stay it by,
Which holds but till thy news be uttered;
And then all this thou seest, is but a clod
And module of confounded royalty."

### 4. *Excessive Grief.*

EVE, [TO ADAM, AFTER THEIR FALL AND DOOM.]—*Milton.*

( Aspirated pectoral and oral Quality:" "Impassioned" force:
  Weeping utterance: "Tremor," throughout.)

"Forsake me not thus, Adam: witness heaven
What love sincere, and reverence in my heart
I bear thee, and unweeting have offended,
Unhappily deceived: thy suppliant,
I beg, and clasp thy knees; bereave me not,
Whereon I live, thy gentle looks, thy aid,
Thy counsel in this uttermost distress,
My only strength and stay: forlorn of thee
Whither shall I betake me, where subsist?"

### 5. *Extreme Pity.*

"Pure Tone:" "Impassioned" force: Weeping and tremulous
utterance.)

FROM THE TEMPEST.—*Shakspeare.*

*Miranda,* [*to her father.*] "Oh! I have suffered
With those that I saw suffer! a brave vessel,
Who had, no doubt, some noble creatures in her,
Dashed all to pieces. Oh! the cry did knock

Against my very heart! Poor souls! they perished.
Had I been any god of power, I would
Have sunk the sea within the earth, or ere
It should the good ship so have swallowed, and
The freighting souls within her!"

6. *Joy and Admiration.*

[ALONZO'S EXCLAMATION, ON BEHOLDING HIS SON FERDINAND, WHOM HE HAD SUPPOSED DROWNED.]—*Shakspeare*

("Pure Tone:" "Impassioned expulsive" force: "Tremor" of joy, throughout.)

" Now all the blessings
Of a glad father compass thee about!"

(" Pure Tone:" "Impassioned expulsive" force: Ecstatic "tremor" of joy, wonder, and love.)

*Miranda.* " Oh! wonder!
How many goodly creatures are there here!
How beauteous mankind is! Oh! brave new world,
That has such people in 't!"

---

The various modes of " stress " have been so copiously illustrated, that it seems unnecessary to add special exercises, at the close of this chapter. Before proceeding to the next subject, however, the student will derive much benefit from reviewing the examples of the different forms of " stress," and practising them in conjunction with the elementary sounds and combinations, and with the addition of the following words, as classified for this purpose.

"*Tonic Elements.*"

| Awe | Arm | An | Eve | Ooze | Err | End |
|---|---|---|---|---|---|---|
| all | ah! | add | eel | fool | erst | ebb |
| awful | art | as | ear | poor | earth | else |
| In | Air | Up | Or | On | Ale | Ice |
| ill | hair | us | orb | odd | ace | iss.e |
| is | lair | ugh! | order | off | aim | isles |
| Old | Out | | Oil | | Use | |
| own | owl | | oyster | | Ural | |
| ore | out | | oily | | your | |

## "Subtonics."

| Maim | Nun | Rap | Far | Sing | Babe | Did | Gug |
|---|---|---|---|---|---|---|---|
| madam | nine | rip | bear | hang | bulb | died | gig |
| mime | noun | rock | hear | tongue | bib | lared | Gog |
| Valve | Zone | Azure | Ye | Woe | Lull | THine | Joy |
| revolve | zeal | measure | yon | way | loll | THey | judge |
| velvet | zest | pleasure | you | war | lily | THan | jar |

## "Atonics."

| Pipe | Tent | Cake | Fife | Cease | He | Thin | Push | Church |
|---|---|---|---|---|---|---|---|---|
| pulp | tat | cark | fief | assess | hail | thank | hush | chaste |
| pop | tut | casque | fitful | stocks | hand | thaw | harsh | chat |

*Words comprising elements of opposite character and formation.*

| Awe | An | Arm | End | Eve | In | Ooze | Up | Ice | In | Old | On |
|---|---|---|---|---|---|---|---|---|---|---|---|
| all | add | ah! | ebb | eel | if | fool | us | isle | if | own | odd |
| always | at | art | ell | ear | it | poor | ugh! | ides | it | ore | off |

| Lull | Cake | Maim | Tent | Rap | Far |
|---|---|---|---|---|---|
| loll | cark | madam | tat | rip | bear |
| lily | kick | mime | tut | rock | hear |
| Nun | Cease | Zone | Thin | Azure | Fife |
| nine | assess | disease | thinketh | measure | fief |
| noun | stocks | disowns | thanketh | pleasure | fitful |

---

Teachers who are instructing classes will find great aid in the use of the black board, for the purpose of visible illustration, in regard to the character and effect of the different species of "stress." Exercises such as the following, may be prescribed for simultaneous practice in classes.

("*Radical Stress.*") ▷ All, (Repeat six times in succession, with constantly increasing force.)

("*Vanishing Stress.*") ◁ " " " " " "

("*Median Stress.*") ◇ " " ' " " "

("*Compound Stress.*") ⋈ " " " " " "

("*Thorough Stress.*") ◯ " " " " " "

("*Tremor.*") ••••• ' " • " " "

To commence with a definite idea of the mode of stress in each instance, set out from the standard of a given emotion decidedly marked, and let the degree of emotion and the force of utterance be increased at every stage. Thus, let ▷ represent the "radical stress" on the sound of *a*, in the word *all*, in the following example of *authoritative command:* "*Attend* ALL!"—◁ the "vanishing stress" on the same element, in the following example of *impatience* and *displeasure:* "I said ALL,—not one or two."—◇ the 'median stress" on the same element, in *reverence* and *adoration:* Join ALL ye creatures in His praise'"—⋈ the "compound stress," in *astonishment* and *surprise:* "What! ALL! did they ALL fail!"— ◯ the "thorough stress," in *defiance:* "Come one—come ALL!" .— . . . . . the " tremor" of *sorrow :* " Oh! I have lost you ALL!"— The practice of the examples and the elements should extend to the utmost excitement of emotion and force of voice. Ocular references may seem, at first sight, to have little value in a subject which relates to the ear. But notes and characters, as used in *music*, serve to show how exactly the *ear* may be taught through the *eye;* and even if we admit the comparatively indefinite nature of all such relations, when transferred to the forms of speech and of reading, the suggestive power of visible forms has a great influence on the faculty of association, and aids clearness and precision of thought, and a corresponding definiteness and exactness in sound.

---

## CHAPTER VI.

### "MELODY."

THE word "melody" may be applied to speech in the same general sense as in the technical language of music, to designate the effect produced on the ear, by the *successive notes* of the voice, in a passage of music or of discourse.

The use of this term presupposes, both in music and in speech, a certain "pitch," or initial note, whether predominating in a passage, or merely commencing it, and to which the subsequent sounds stand in the relation of higher or lower or identical.

The term "melody," used as above, does not necessarily imply a *melodious* or pleasing succession of sounds, or the reverse. It has regard merely to the fact just mentioned, that the successive sounds to which this term is applied, are comparatively higher or lower on the musical scale, or in strict unison with the first sound of a series. In this technical sense, the word "melody" applies to speech as well as to music.

Regarded in connection with the sense of beauty or of pleasure however, we perceive at once a marked difference between the 'melody" of music and that of speech. The former, has, comparatively, the effect of poetry: beauty is its chief element; and it yields to the ear an exquisite sense of pleasure. The latter may, as in the recitation or the reading of verse, possess a degree of this charm, though comparatively an imperfect one. But it may, on the contrary, possess no such beauty: it may exhibit a succession of the most harsh and grating sounds, intended to jar and pain the ear, by the violence of discordant and disturbing passion; or it may, at least, be but a tame and insipid succession of articulation, in the utterance of a fact addressed exclusively to the understanding, as in the common relations of magnitude, shape, or number. The melody of speech, in such cases, intentionally divests itself of whatever quality in tone is adapted, whether to pleasure or to pain, and adheres to the customary intonation of dry fact and plain prose.

In the latter case, however, not less than in the former, the relations of sounds to each other, as measured by the musical scale, can be distinctly traced; and, on this account, the "melody of speech," or of "reading," is a phrase as truly significant as that of the "melody of a strain of music."

### PITCH.

The word "melody," used in its technical sense, occupies, then, the same ground in elocution as in music, and refers us, in the first instance, to an initial or commencing sound to which others in a series may be compared as high or low or neither. To this sound the term "pitch" is applied, as designating the particular point of the scale, as high or low, on which the voice is thrown out. Thus, we speak of the deep tones or low notes of an organ, as contrasted with the shrill sound of a fife, of the grave tone of the voice of a man, or of the comparatively high pitch of that of a woman; or of the low voice of devotion, as contrasted with the high, shrill scream of excessive fear, or the piercing shriek of terror.

The correct practice of elocution, as in appropriate speaking, recitation, or reading, implies the power of easily and instantly shifting the "pitch" of the voice, according to the natural note of emotion required for every shade of expression depicted in the composition which is spoken, recited, or read. Nature, or, — more properly speaking, — the Author of the human constitution, has so contrived the organization of the corporeal frame, in conjunction with the sensibility of the soul, that certain notes of the voice are necessarily associated with certain emotions. Thus a repetition of low and subdued tones overheard from an adjoining apartment, suggests to us the thought that its occupant is employed in the exercise ot devotion; because solemn and reverential feeling is uniformly associated in voice with low notes of the scale. A succession of high and vivid tones, overheard, might suggest the idea of a lively conversation, or an earnest debate, or a fierce dispute, as the case might be; for the emotions implied in such communication, are all associated with high notes of the scale.

The study of "pitch," as an element of "melody," leads us accordingly in a classification of emotions as characterized by comparatively "high" or "low" notes. The science of music possesses, in the department of "pitch," a great advantage over that of elocution; as it refers, in all cases, to a perfectly exact measure of sound, as ascertained by reference to the invariable standard of certain notes, at given points of the scale, executed by musical instruments not liable to variation. The musician can thus apply, as his rule, a definite scale of vast extent, and of perfect precision in admeasurement. The elocutionist, on the contrary, derives his scale from feeling rather than from science or external rule. The natural pitch of human voices, varies immensely, not only with sex and age, but in the accustomed notes of one individual, as differing from those of another.

The musician, when speaking of a low strain of melody, can conveniently refer to a precise note of the scale, by the exact letter which designates it. The elocutionist, when referring to the low tone of *awe*, has no more definite measure in view than a note which lies low, in comparison even with the customary low notes of the voice of the reader or speaker.

Due attention, may, no doubt, enable the elocutionist to ascertain, in a given case, the precise note of the scale required according to the organic formation and the vocal habit of an individual. But such a note might prove too low for the compass of voice, in another person, or quite too high to be appropriate or impressive, in another still, whose voice is naturally low-pitched.

The language of elocution is accordingly limited to the familiar designations of "low," and "very low," "high," and "very high," when the scale is traced to any great extent beyond the "middle" or average pitch of utterance. This indefinite reference, however, is usually sufficient for the purposes of reading and speaking, which regard a general sympathetic effect, or feeling, rather than any which requires the precise measure of science.

## I. *"Middle" Pitch.*

The "middle" pitch of the voice is tha. of our habitual utterance, on all occasions of ordinary communication in conversation or address. It implies a medium or average state of feeling, or a condition of mind free from every strong or marked emotion. It is the natural note of unimpassioned utterance, seeking to find its way to the understanding rather than to the heart, and hence avoiding high or low pitch, as belonging to the language of feeling or of fancy. Common conversation, a literary or a scientific essay, a doctrinal sermon, or a plain practical discourse on any subject limited to purposes of mere utility, and demanding the action of judgment and reason, principally, may be mentioned as examples of "middle" pitch.

This form of "pitch" being that which is habitual, in comparison with others, becomes, in popular usage, the criterion of what is termed "natural" reading or speaking. It is, indeed, justly adopted as the standard of ordinary communication. The habit of observing this pitch on all common occasions of speech and of reading, becomes an important means of natural and true effect in elocution. Falling below this average of utterance, we drop necessarily into tones associated with grave and solemn effect; and, rising above it, we approach the style of light, gay, or humorous expression. Either of these extremes becomes not merely an error of taste in elocution, but of judgment and ear: it sets the voice at variance with the nature of the subject of communication, and defeats its proper effect.

Both of the extremes which have been mentioned, however, are current faults of usage. Some juvenile readers, in consequence of the *effort* which they usually make in their exercises, cause a slight overstrain of voice, which becomes apparent in the pitch rising above its appropriate level: others, from embarrassment, let the voice sink, as it were into the chest, with a partially hollow sound, and a note too grave. Students and sedentary persons, from their exhausting mode of life, incline habitually to the latter fault; and, when excited by unusual interest in public communication, perhaps unconsciously assume the opposite extreme, of a pitch too high for the free use of the voice.

The proper standard of middle pitch, for the purpose of vocal practice, is that of serious and earnest conversation in a numerous circle.

In selecting examples according to the rhetorical characteristics of style, the choice should be made from intermediate modes of writing, which are neither so deep-toned in their language, as those which are denominated "grave" or "solemn," nor yet so high-pitched as the "gay," or brisk, and the "humorous" or playful. The rhetorical styles intermediate to these, are the "serious" and the "animated." These are the fairest average representatives of plain expression, as it usually occurs in *conversation* and *discourse:* they serve also to exemplify the common forms of *narrative* and *descriptive* writing.

Close attention and a discriminating ear, are required, to keep the pitch exactly true, in such examples as the following. The least deviation of voice downward or upward on the scale, interferes with the appropriate utterance of sentiment; making the expression either too grave or too light. The practice of these examples should be accompanied by frequent repetition of the elements and of detached columns of words, with a view to fix permanently in the ear, the proper note of middle pitch, whether in " serious " or in " animated " utterance. The former is, of course, somewhat lower on the scale than the latter: the exact degree depends on the shades of expression in particular passages.

EXAMPLES OF " MIDDLE " PITCH.

*Serious Didactic Style.*

( • Pure Tone;" " Moderate " force : " Unimpassioned radical," and gentle " median stress."

PLEASURES OF KNOWLEDGE.—*Alison.*

" How different is the view of past life, in the man who is grown old in knowledge and wisdom, from that of him who is grown old in ignorance and folly! The latter is like the owner of a barren country, that fills his eye with the prospect of naked hills and plains, which produce nothing either profitable or ornamental: the former beholds a beautiful and spacious landscape, divided into delightful gardens, green meadows, and fruitful fields, and can scarce cast his eye on a single spot of his possessions, that is not covered with some beautiful plant or flower."

*Serious Narrative.*

(" Quality," " force," and " stress," as in the preceding example )

ANECDOTE.

" Raleigh's cheerfulness, during his last days, was so great, and his fearlessness of death so marked, that the dean of Westminster who attended him, wondering at his deportment, reprehended the lightness of his manner. But Raleigh gave God thanks that he had never feared death; for it was but an opinion and an imagination; and, as for the manner of death, he had rather die so than in a burning fever, that some might have made shows outwardly; but he felt the joy within."

### Serious Description.

("Quality," &c., as before.)

A SCENE OF ARAB LIFE. —*Anonymous.*

"All that has been related concerning the passion for tales which distinguishes the Arabs, is literally true. During the night which we passed on the shore of the Dead Sea, we observed our Bethlehemites seated around a large fire, with their guns laid near them on the ground, while their horses, fastened to stakes, formed a kind of circle about them. These Arabs, after having taken their coffee, and conversed for some time with great earnestness, and with their usual loquacity, observed a strict silence when the sheik began his tale. We could, by the light of the fire, distinguish his significant gestures, his black beard, his white teeth, and the various plaits and positions which he gave to his tunic, during the recital. His companions listened to him with the most profound attention; all of them with their bodies bent forward, and their faces over the flame, alternately sending forth shouts of admiration, and repeating, with great emphasis, the gestures of the historian. The heads of some few of their horses and camels, were occasionally seen elevated above the group, and shadowing, as it were, the picture. When to these was added a glimpse of the scenery about the Dead Sea and the mountains of Judea, the whole effect was striking and fanciful, in the highest degree."

### Serious Conversational Style.

IDLENESS.—*Addison.*

"An idle man is a kind of monster in the creation. All nature is busy about him: every animal he sees, reproaches him. Let such a man, who lies as a burden or dead weight upon the species, and contributes nothing either to the riches of the commonwealth, or to the maintenance of himself and family, consider that instinct with which Providence has endowed the an. And by which is exhibited an example of industry to rational creatures."

¹*Animated Narrative Style.*

("Pure Tone:" "Moderate" force: Vivid "radical stress.")

JULIUS CÆSAR.—*J. S. Knowles.*

"To form an idea of Cæsar's energy and activity, observe him when he is surprised by the Nervii. His soldiers are employed in pitching their camp.—The ferocious enemy sallies from his concealment, puts the Roman cavalry to the rout, and falls upon the foot. Everything is alarm, confusion, and disorder. Every one is doubtful what course to take,—every one but Cæsar! He causes the banner to be erected,—the charge to be sounded,—the soldiers at a distance to be recalled,—all in a moment. He runs from place to place;—his whole frame is in action;—his words, his looks, his motions, his gestures, exhort his men to remember their former valor. He draws them up, and causes the signal to be given,—all in a moment. The contest is doubtful and dreadful: two of his legions are entirely surrounded. He seizes a buckler from one of the private men,—puts himself at the head of his broken troops,—darts into the thick of the battle,—rescues his legions, and overthrows the enemy!"

*Animated Description.*

("Pure Tone:" "Moderate" force: Vivid "median stress.")

PHENOMENA OF THE UNIVERSE.—*Anonymous.*

"The physical universe may be regarded as exhibiting, at once, all its splendid varieties of events, and uniting, as it were, in a single moment, the wonders of eternity. Combine, by your imagination, all the fairest appearances of things. Suppose that you see, at once, all the hours of the day, and all the seasons of the year, a morning of spring and a morning of autumn, a night brilliant with stars, and a night obscure with clouds,—meadows, enamelled with flowers,— fields, waving with harvests,—woods, heavy with the frosts

---

. ¹ The vividness of effect in this style, raises the pitch above that of "serious" narrative: the prevailing note, however, is still as 'r conversation near the middle of the scale.

of winter;—you will then have a just notion of the spectacle of the universe. Is it not wondrous, that while *you* are admiring the sun plunging beneath the vault of the west, *another* observer is beholding him as he quits the region of the east,—in the same instant reposing, weary, from the dust of the evening, and awaking, fresh and youthful, in the dews of morn! There is not a moment of the day in which the same sun is not rising, shining in his zenith, and setting on the world! Or, rather, our senses abuse us: and there is no rising, nor setting, nor zenith, nor east, nor west; but all is one fixed point, at which every species of light is beaming, at once, from the unalterable orb of day."

### Animated Didactic Style, in Conversation.

("Pure Tone:" "Moderate" force: "Unimpassioned radical," and lively "median stress.")

IMAGINARY HAPPINESS.—*Anonymous.*

"People imagine they should be happy in circumstances which they would find insupportably burdensome in less than a week. A man that has been clothed in fine linen, and fared sumptuously every day, envies the peasant under a thatched hovel; who, in return, envies him as much his palace and his pleasure-grounds. Could they exchange situations, the fine gentleman would find his ceilings were too low, and that his casements admitted too much wind; that he had no cellar for his wine, and no wine to put in his cellar. These with a thousand other mortifying deficiencies would shatter his romantic project into innumerable fragments in a moment."

### Animated Didactic Style, in Public Discourse.

"Expulsive Orotund;" "Moderate" force: Energetic "radical" and "median stress.")

VIRTUE.—*Fawcett.*

Blood, says the pride of life, is more honorable than money. Indigent nobility looks down upon untitled opu ence. This sentiment pushed a little farther, leads to the point I am pursuing. Mind is the noblest part of man; and of mind, virtue is the noblest distinction.

"*Honest man*, in the ear of Wisdom, is a grander name, is a more high-sounding title, than peer of the realm, or prince of the blood. According to the eternal rules of celestial precedency, in the immortal heraldry of Nature and of Heaven, Virtue takes place of all things. It is the nobility of angels! It is the majesty of God!"

## II. "*Low*" *Pitch*.

This designation applies to the utterance of those feelings which we are accustomed to speak of as " deeper " than ordinary. Low notes seem the only natural language of grave emotions, such as accompany *deeply serious and impressive thoughts, grave authority*, or *austere manner*.

The transition in the voice, from " middle " to " low " pitch would be exemplified in passing from the utterance of a thought which is merely *serious*,—and so termed in contradistinction, rather to one of an animated and sprightly character,—to that of one still deeper in its shade of feeling, and which would be appropriately termed *grave*. At the stage of voice expressive of the latter, we should perceive an obvious though not very strikingly marked deepening of tone, or descent on the scale.

It is to this degree of depression of voice, properly, that the word 'low,'' in its connection with pitch, is applied, in elocution, as a technical designation; there being still lower notes of the scale implied in the expression of those emotions which are still deeper in character and deeper in utterance.

The full and impressive effect of a sentiment, particularly in circumstances of a grave character, as on the occasion of an address on topics of politics, morals, or religion, must often be dependent on appropriate gravity of tone. A uniformly grave tone, even in public reading or speaking, becomes, it is true, dull and uninteresting. But the absence of a due degree and application of it, divests public speaking of dignity and authoritative effect, and deprives deep sentiment of its impressive power over the mind. The " grave " style carried too low, becomes " solemn,"—a fault in consequence of which the lawyer and the popular orator sometimes seem to usurp the tone of the pulpit, and the preacher to lose the vocal and the moral power which comes from touching distinctly all the chords of sacred eloquence, and not dwelling exclusively upon one. There is more than a mere music to the ear, in the skill with which a practised elocutionist leads his own voice and the sympathies of his audience, as they glide gradually but perceptibly down the successive stages of emotion, from serious attention, to grave listening, and solemn impression.

The attainment of a perfect control over "pitch," renders the practice of all its gradations highly important. The following examples require attentive practice in conjunction with the repetition of the elements and of words selected from the exercises in enunciation

### EXAMPLES OF "LOW" PITCH.

*Grave and Impressive Thought.*

("Pure tone:" "Moderate" force: "Unimpassioned radical" and moderate "median stress.")

AGE.—*Godman.*

"Now comes the autumn of life,—the season of 'the sere and yellow leaf.' The suppleness and mobility of the limbs diminish; the senses are less acute; and the impressions of external objects are less remarked. The fibres of the body grow more rigid; the emotions of the mind are more calm and uniform; the eye loses its lustrous keenness of expression. The mind no longer roams abroad with its original excursiveness: the power of imagination is, in great degree lost. Experience has robbed external objects of their illusiveness: the thoughts come home: it is the age of reflection.—It is the period in which we receive the just tribute of veneration and confidence from our fellow-men, if we have so lived as to deserve it, and are entitled to the respect and confidence of the younger part of mankind, in exact proportion to the manner in which our own youth has been spent, and our maturity improved."

*Grave, Austere, Authoritative Manner.*

("Expulsive orotund:" "Declamatory" force: Firm "median stress.")

CATO [IN REPLY TO CÆSAR'S MESSAGE THROUGH DECIUS.]—*Addison.*

"My life is grafted on the fate of Rome.
Would he save Cato, bid him spare his country
Bid him disband his legions,

Restore the commonwealth to liberty,
Submit his actions to the public censure,
And stand the judgment of a Roman senate.—
Bid him do this, and Cato is his friend."

### III. *"Very Low"* Pitch.

This designation applies to the notes of those emotions which are of the deepest character, and which are accordingly associated with the deepest utterance. These are, chiefly, the following: *deep solemnity, awe, amazement, horror, despair, melancholy,* and *deep grief.*

The exceedingly "low pitch" of these and similar states of feeling, is one of those universal facts which necessarily become laws of vocal expression, and, consequently, indispensable rules of elocution. Any passage, strongly marked by the language of one of these emotions, becomes utterly inexpressive without its appropriate deep notes. Yet this fault is one of the most prevalent in reading, especially with youth. That absence of deep and powerful emotion of an expressive character and active tendency, which usually characterizes the habits of the student's life, often leaves a great deficiency in this element of vocal effect, even in individuals who habitually drop into the fault of a slackness of organic action which causes too low a pitch in serious or in grave style. The "very low" pitch is not a mere accidental or mechanical result: it requires the aid of the will, and a special exertion of organ, to produce it.

This lowest form of pitch is one of the most impressive means of powerful natural effect, in the utterance of all deep and impressive emotions. The pervading and absorbing effect of *awe, amazement, horror,* or any similar feeling, can never be produced without low pitch and deep successive notes; and the depth and reality of such emotions are always in proportion to the depth of voice with which they are uttered. The grandest descriptions in the Paradise Lost, and the profoundest meditations in the Night Thoughts, become trivial in their effect on the ear, when read with the ineffectual expression inseparable from the pitch of ordinary conversation or discourse.

The vocal deficiency which limits the range of expression to the middle and higher notes of the scale, is not, by any means, the unavoidable and necessary fault of organization, as it is so generally supposed to be. Habit is in this, as in so many other things, the cause of defect. There is truth, no doubt, in the remark so often made in defence of a high and feeble voice, that it is natural to the individual, or that it is difficult for some readers to attain to depth of voice without incurring a false and forced style of utterance. But, in most cases, it is habit, not organization, that has made certain notes natural or unnatural,— in other words, familiar to the ear or the reverse. The neglect of the lower notes of the sca e, and, consequently, of the organic action by which they are produced, may render a deep-toned utterance less easy than it would otherwise be. But most teachers of elocution are, from day to day, witnesses to the fact, that students, from the neglect of muscular action, and from al' the other enfeebling causes involved in sedentary habits and intellectual application, sometimes commence a course of practice, with a high-pitched, thin, and feminine voice, which seems at first incapable of expressing a grave or manly sentiment, and, in some instances, appears to forbid the individual from ever attempting the utterance of a solemn thought, lest his treble tone should make the effect ridiculous; but that a few weeks' practice of vocal exercise on bass notes and deep emotions, as embodied in rightly selected exercises, often enables such readers to acquire a round and deep-toned utterance, adequate to the fullest effects of impressive eloquence.

The exercise of singing bass, if cultivated as an habitual practice, has a great effect in imparting command of deep-toned expression, in reading and speaking. Reading and reciting passages from Milton and from Young, and particularly from the Book of Psalms, or from hymns of a deeply solemn character, are exercises of great value for securing the command of the lower notes of the voice.

The practice of the following examples should be accompanied by copious exercises on the elements, and on words selected for the purpose. These exercises should be repeated till the student can, at any moment, strike the appropriate note of *awe* or *solemnity*, with as much certainty as the vocalist can execute any note of the scale

### EXAMPLES OF "VERY LOW" PITCH.

*Deep Solemnity, Sublimity, and Awe*

CATO, [IN SOLILOQUY.] —*Addison.*

(' Effusive and Expulsive orotund :" " Subdued and Suppressoc force : " Median stress.")

" It must be so;—Plato, thou reasonest well!
Else, whence this pleasing hope, this fond desire
This longing after immortality?
Or whence this secret dread, and inward horror,
Of falling into nought? Why shrinks the soul
Back on herself, and startles at destruction?
'T is the Divinity that stirs within us:
'T is Heaven itself that points out an hereafter,
And intimates Eternity to man.
Eternity!—thou pleasing,—dreadful thought!
Through what variety of untried being,

Through what new scenes and changes must we pass!
The wide, the unbounded prospect lies before me;
But shadows, clouds, and darkness, rest upon it."

*Awe, Dismay, and Despair.*

("Aspirated pectoral Quality:" "Suppressed" force: "Median stress.")

THE PESTILENCE.—*Porteous*

" At dead of night,
In sullen silence stalks forth PESTILENCE:
CONTAGION, close behind, taints all her steps
With poisonous dew: no smiting hand is seen;
No sound is heard; but soon her secret path
Is marked with desolation: heaps on heaps
Promiscuous drop. No friend, no refuge, near:
All, all is false and treacherous around,
All that they touch, or taste, or breathe, is DEATH!'"

*Deep Grief.*

AFFLICTION AND DESOLATION.—*Young.*

( Effusive and expulsive orotund:" "Impassioned" and "subdued" force: "Vanishing" and "median stress.")

" In every varied posture, place, and hour,
How widowed every thought of every joy!
Thought, busy thought! too busy for my peace!
Through the dark postern of time long elapsed,
Led softly, by the stillness of the night,
Led like a murderer, (and such it proves!)
Strays, (wretched rover!) o'er the pleasing past:
In quest of wretchedness perversely strays,
And finds all desert now!"

IV. *" High" Pitch.*

The analysis of vocal expression, as regards the effect of " pitch," leads us now to the study of those modes of utterance which lie *above* the middle, or ordinary, level of the voice.

The higher portion of the musical scale is associated with

the notes of *brisk*, *gay*, and *joyous* emotions, with the exception of the *extremes* of *pain*, *grief*, and *fear*, which, from their preternaturally exciting power, compress and render rigid the organic parts that produce vocal sound, and cause the peculiarly shrill, convulsive cries and shrieks which express those passions.

Tracing the voice upward, as it ascends from the usual pitch of "serious" or of "animated expression," we observe it obviously rise, when it passes from the "animated," or lively, to the "gay" or brisk style, which implies a positive *exhilaration*, or vivid excitement of the animal spirits. *Cheerfulness* will suffice to produce "*animation;*" but *joy* is requisite to cause "*gaiety.*" The properties of voice, in the utterance of these feelings, are correspondent to their gradations of sensibility. "Animation" is expressed by "pure tone," "unimpassioned radical stress," and "middle pitch:" gaiety, by "expulsive orotund," vivid "radical and median stress," and "high pitch."

The command over "pitch," in its application to *joyous* emotions is not, it is true, of so much importance to the public speaker, as the power of adopting the appropriate tone of *serious*, *grave*, and *solemn* feeling. It is, however, an indispensable accomplishment in elocution, for the purposes of private and social reading; as much of the pleasure, as well as the true effect, of expression, in the reading of pieces adapted to the parlor, and the family or the social circle, depends on the vivid utterance and comparatively high pitch which occasionally prevail in the appropriate style of such reading; since it is not unfrequently marked by gay delineation and high-wrought graphic effect of incident, description, and sentiment.

A "pitch" too low for the natural effect of gay and exhilarated feeling deadens the effect of wit and vivacity, and renders, perhaps, a most expressive strain of composition, tame and dull, when it should abound in the tones of life and brilliancy.

Juvenile readers, from diffidence, often withhold the true effect of the voice in the reading of scenes of gaiety and joyousness, by allowing the pitch to remain too low. The gravity and austerity of the student's life, incline him to the same mode of utterance, as a habit, and hence impair that freshness of effect, even in serious communication, which comes from the frequent practice of utterance in strains of joy and gaiety. The proverbial dulness arising from "all work and no play," is felt nowhere more deeply than in the habits of the voice. Long-continued, intense mental application, betrays itself uniformly, in a tendency to hollow, "pectoral" tone; and the uniform "drowsy bass" of some public speakers, is but the unconscious yielding to this natural effect.

To give the voice suppleness, pliancy, and mobility, much attention must be bestowed on practice for the regulation of pitch. The following examples should be carefully repeated in conjunction with the elements and detached words, till the "high pitch" of *joy* is perfectly at command.

### EXAMPLES OF "HIGH" PITCH.

*Gay, or brisk, style.*
*Joy.*

FROM THE VOICE OF SPRING.—*Mrs. Hemans.*

("Expulsive orotund:" "Impassioned" force: "Median stress.")

" I come! I come!—ye have called me long:
I come o'er the mountains with light and song!
Ye may trace my step o'er the wakening earth,
By the winds which tell of the violet's birth,
By the primrose stars in the shadowy grass,
By the green leaves opening as I pass.

" From the streams and founts I have loosed the chain
They are sweeping on to the silvery main,—
They are flashing down from the mountain brows,—
They are flinging spray o'er the forest-boughs,—
They are bursting fresh from their sparry caves;—
And the earth resounds with the joy of waves!"

*Exultation.*

FROM THE HYMN OF THE STARS. —*Bryant.*

( Quality," force, and " stress," as before, but more fully given.)

" Away, away! through the wide, wide sky,—
The fair blue fields that before us lie,—
Each sun with the worlds that round him roll,
Each planet, poised on her turning pole,
With her isles of green, and her clouds of white,
And her waters that lie like fluid light!

" For the source of glory uncovers his face,
And the brightness o'erflows unbounded space;
And we drink, as we go, the luminous tides
In our ruddy air and our blooming sides·
Lo! yonder the living splendors play!
Away! on our joyous path away!

"Away, away!—In our blossoming bowers,
In the soft air wrapping these spheres of ours,
In the seas and fountains that shine with morn,
See Love is brooding, and Life is born;
And breathing myriads are breaking from night,
To rejoice like us, in motion and light!"

## V. *"Very High"* Pitch.

The extreme of the upper part of the musical scale, as far as it is practicable to individuals, in the management of the voice, is the natural range of pitch for the utterance of *ecstatic* and *rapturous* or *uncontrollable emotion*. It belongs, accordingly, to *high-wrought lyric* and *dramatic passages*, in strains of *joy, grief, astonishment, delight, tenderness*, and the *hysterical* extremes of passionate emotion generally.

As the appropriate utterance of excessive feeling, the "extremely high pitch" is not so important for the general purposes of elocution, as the "middle" or the "high." Passages requiring this mode of expression must obviously be of comparatively rare occurrence. It is not less true, however, that the peculiar beauty, or power, or natural effect, of a strain of poetry, may depend, for its true expression, on the command which the reader or reciter possesses over this element of voice. It is equally certain that practice and discipline on the uppermost notes of the scale, give the voice great pliancy, on the range immediately below; and that the frequent repetition of the highest note which the student can command, is one of the most efficacious means of imparting firm, clear, and well-compacted tone.

The following examples, together with the elements and selected words, should be repeated, as daily exercises, for the purpose of training the organs to easy execution on high notes.

EXAMPLES OF "VERY HIGH" PITCH.

*Ecstatic Joy.*

[SONG OF THE VALKYRIUR, OR FATAL SISTERS, TO THE DOOMED WARRIOR.]—*Mrs. Hemans.*

(" Expulsive Orotund:" " Sustained " force of calling and shouting ( " Median stress.")

"Lo! the mighty sun looks forth!—
Arm! thou leader of the north!

Lo! the mists of twilight fly—
We must vanish, thou must die!
" By the sword, and by the spear,
By the hand that knows not fear,
Sea-king! nobly shalt thou fall!
There is joy in Odin's hall!"

*Astonishment.*

DROMIO OF SYRACUSE, [ON HIS BEING MISTAKEN FOR HIS BROTHER.] — *Shakspeare.*

("Expulsive Orotund:" " Impassioned" force: "Thorough stress.")

" This drudge laid claim to me; called me Dromio; swore I was assured to her; told me what private marks I had about me, as the mark of my shoulder, the mole in my neck, the great wart on my left arm,—that I, amazed, ran from her as a witch; and I think, if my breast had not been made of faith, and my heart of steel, she had transformed me to a curtail-dog, and made me turn i' the wheel."

To attain a perfect command of " pitch," as an element of expression, it will be a useful exercise, to review, in close succession, all the examples of " pitch," and to add, at each stage, a repetition of the elements and of words. The student who can borrow the aid of the musical scale, will derive great benefit from the exactness which it will impart to his practice ; as it will enable him to observe and to remember certain notes as the appropriate pitch for natural and impressive reading, in passages characterized by given emotions. The habit of analyzing passages, so as to recognize readily their predominating feeling, and, consequently, their " pitch," is one which every earnest student of elocution will cultivate with persevering diligence, till he finds himself able, from a single glance at the first line of a piece, to determine its gradation of feeling, and its true note in utterance.

Besides practising the examples of " pitch," in the order in which they occur in the preceding pages, it will contribute much to facility in changing the " pitch " of the voice, if the student will vary the order of the examples, so as to become accustomed to pass easily from one point of the scale to another,—as from highest to lowest, and the reverse. The practice of the elements and of words, should always be added to the repetition of the examples.

## "TRANSITION" IN PITCH.

The paucity of terms in our language, for the various phenomena of voice, has laid writers on elocution under an imagined necessity of using some words, borrowed from other sciences or arts, in a manner not consistent with scientific accuracy of expression. Thus, the word "modulation," which has an exact meaning in music, has been used in elocution, in an irregular manner, to designate *the observance of the difference of pitch*, in the utterance of emotions, as they occur successively in reading or speaking. Popular, and even reputable usage, has sanctioned this application of the term. But as it tends to create confusion of ideas, when it is used in certain relations to elocution which regard the "melody" of the component parts of sentences, it would be better, perhaps, to regard the transitions of the voice from one strain to another, in consecutive reading, as merely the necessary assumption of a new "pitch," adapted to each successive emotion, and being nothing else, as a vocal accomplishment, than skill in instantly striking a given note of the scale.

A passage of composition, in prose or verse, used as an exercise in reading, may be marked to the ear by one prevalent tone of feeling, which allows or requires little or no variation of voice, and, consequently, as little transition from one note of the scale to another We find one piece, as Milton's Allegro, for example, pervaded by the expressive tones, and "high" notes, and consequent "high pitch," of *joy* throughout, — another, as the same author's Penseroso, marked by the prevalence of the style of *grave musing* and *poetic melancholy*, with their appropriate expression in "low" notes, and, therefore, "low pitch."

Other compositions are characterized by great and frequent transitions of feeling and of utterance, and consequently by corresponding high or low notes, and the frequent transition from one to the other. It is to these changes of voice that the term "modulation" has sometimes been arbitrarily applied; and it is to the department of elocution sometimes designated by this term, that we now proceed in our analysis.

This branch of our subject is one of the utmost importance to the student. Without the power of easy and exact accommodation of voice to the natural "pitch" of every successive emotion in a piece, there can be no such thing as natural or impressive reading. But variation of "pitch" is a topic on which we need not dwell; as it is, practically, but the consecutive application of the same functions of voice to which we have just been attending in detached and separate instances. Let the student read in close sequence, and with perfect exactness of "pitch," all the examples given under that head, and he will have necessarily executed, at the same time, an extensive practice in "transition" from one portion of the scale to another, as he shifted the pitch of his voice in passing from one example to another.

A piece of varied topics and style, in prose writing, or what has been termed a Pindaric ode, in lyric poetry, will furnish, by its changing character of thought and expression, appropriate occasions for frequent and great transitions on the scale, as the voice passes from the utterance of one strain of emotion to that of another

EXAMPLES OF "TRANSITION" IN PITCH.

1. *From Joy to Grave and Pathetic Emotion.*

(From " High " to " Low Pitch.")

THE VOICE OF SPRING.—*Mrs. Hemans.*

"*High.*"

" Away from the dwellings of care-worn men,
The waters are sparkling in grove and glen!
Away from the chamber and sullen hearth,
The young leaves are dancing in breezy mirth!
Their light stems thrill to the wild-wood strains;
And youth is abroad in my green domains!—

"*Low.*"

" But ye—ye are changed since ye met me last!
There is something bright from your features passed!
There is that come over your brow and eye,
Which speaks of a world where the flowers must die!—
Ye smile! but your smile hath a dimness yet:—
Oh! what have ye looked on since last we met?"

2. *From Horror to Tranquillity.*

(From " Very Low " to " Middle Pitch.")

STANZAS FROM A RUSSIAN POET.—*Bowring.*

"*Very Low.*"

" How frightful the grave! how deserted and drear!
With the howls of the storm-wind, the creaks of the bier
 And the white bones all clattering together!

"*Middle Pitch.*"

' How peaceful the grave! its quiet how deep:
Its zephyrs breathe calmly; and soft is its sleep·
 And flowrets perfume it with ether."

### 3. *From Rapture to Grief.*

(From " Very High " to " Low Pitch.")

STANZAS FROM MRS. HEMANS.

*"Very High."*

" Ring joyous chords!—ring out again!
A swifter still and a wilder strain!
And bring fresh wreaths!—we will banish all
Save the free in heart from our festive hall.
On through the maze of the fleet dance, on!"—

*"Low."*

" But where are the young and the lovely?—gone!
Where are the brows with the red rose crowned,
And the floating forms with the bright zone bound?
And the waving locks and the flying feet,
That still should be where the mirthful meet?—
They are gone!—they are fled, they are parted all:—
 Alas! the forsaken hall!"

4 *From Triumph and Exultation, to Grave, Pathetic, and Solemn feeling, and thence returning to Triumph and Exultation.*

(From " High " to " Low," and thence to " High Pitch.")

*"High."*

" Mark ye the flashing oars,
 And the spears that light the deep?
How the festal sunshine pours
 Where the lords of battle sweep!

" Each hath brought back his shield;—
 Maid, greet thy lover home!
Mother, from that proud field,
 Io! thy son is come!"

*"Low."*

" Who murmured of the dead?
Hush! boding voice. We know

"That many a shining head
Lies in its glory low.

" Breathe not those names to-day.
They shall have their praise ere long,
And a power all hearts to sway,
In ever-burning song."

"*High.*"

" But now shed flowers, pour wine,
To hail the conquerors home!
Bring wreaths for every shrine!—
Io! they come, they come!"

5. *From Tranquillity to Joy and Triumph, Awe, Scorn, Awe, Horror, Exultation, Defiance, Awe,—successively.*

ISRAEL'S TRIUMPH OVER THE KING OF BABYLON.]—*Isaiah.*

[*Tranquillity:* "*Middle Pitch:*"] "The whole earth is at rest, and is quiet:—[*Joy and Triumph:* "*High Pitch:*"] they break forth into singing. Yea, the fir-trees rejoice at thee, and the cedars of Lebanon, saying, ' Since thou art laid down, no feller is come up against us.'—[*Awe:* "*Low Pitch:*"] Hell from beneath is moved for thee, to meet thee at thy coming: it stirreth up the dead for thee, even all the chief ones of the earth: it hath raised up from their thrones all the kings of the nations.—[*Narrative:* "*Middle Pitch:*"] All they shall speak, and say unto thee,—[*Scorn:* "*High Pitch:*"] ' Art thou also become weak as we? Art thou become like unto us?'—[*Awe:* "*Low Pitch:*"] ' Thy pomp is brought down to the grave, and the noise of thy viols:'— [*Horror:* "*Very Low Pitch:*"] ' the worm is spread under thee, and the worms cover thee.'—[*Exultation:* "*Middle Pitch:*"] ' How art thou fallen from heaven, O Lucifer, son of the morning! how art thou cut down to the ground, which didst weaken the nations!'—[*Defiance:* " *High Pitch:*"] ' For thou hast said in thy heart, " I will ascend into heaven, I will exalt my throne above the stars of God. I will ascend above the heights of the clouds; I will be like the Most High."—[*Awe:* "*Low Pitch:*"] 'Yet thou shalt be brought down to hell, to the sides of the pit.'"

The same "transitions" of "pitch" which occur in passing from one paragraph or stanza to another, may also take place within the limits of *a single sentence*, if the feeling obviously changes from *clause to clause*, — as in the following extract.

*Reverence and Awe.*

("Low pitch:" rising gradually to "middle," in the fourth line.)

ADORATION. — *Porteous.*

" O Thou! whose balance does the mountains weigh,
Whose will the wild tumultuous seas obey,
Whose breath can turn those watery worlds to flame,
That flame to tempest, and that tempest tame,"—

*Deepest Reverence and Awe.*

("Very low pitch.")

"Earth's meanest son, all trembling, prostrate falls,'

*Reverence and Adoration.*

("Low pitch.")

"And on the boundless of Thy goodness calls."

*Solemnity.*

(Pitch still lower.)

"May sea and land, and earth and heaven be joined,
To bring the eternal Author to my mind!"

*Awe.*

("Very low pitch.")

"When oceans roar, or thunders roll,
May thoughts of Thy dread vengeance shake my soul!"

THE "PHRASES" OF "SENTENTIAL MELODY."

If we bring our analysis of a sentence into still closer distinctions of melody and pitch, we pass from *clauses* to *phrases*. The "melody of phrases and their relative "pitch," involve topics too numerous and too intricate for discussion in an elementary work. These subjects will be found fully explained in the work of Dr. Rush. We will select a few points of practical application and of primary importance. The "phrases of melody," in a sentence, admit of being arranged in two classes:—1st, those which prevail in the body of a sentence; 2d, that which occupies the last three syllables of a sentence, and forms the cadence. The former is termed the "current melody;" the latter, the "melody of the cadence."

The investigation of melody and pitch, in phrases, requires attention to the important distinction of "discrete" and "concrete" sounds. "Discrete" sounds consist of notes produced at intervals, or in close succession, but in *detached* and *distinct* forms, as in running up or down the keys of a piano, or the chords of a harp; or producing similar sounds on a violin, by twitching the strings with the finger, instead of gliding over them with the bow; or in the laughing utterance of *delighted surprise*, as when we laugh a "fifth" or an "octave" up the scale, on the interrogatory interjection "*eh?*" or when, in the laughing utterance of *derision*, we run down the scale, in the same way, in the long-drawn sound of the word "*no!*" In these last-mentioned instances, every note is executed by a distinct and separate little jet, or tittle, of voice. To such sounds, then, the word "discrete" in its proper etymological sense, may be justly applied, as intimating that they exist *apart*.

"Concrete" sounds, on the other hand, are produced by a succession of notes gliding into each other so imperceptibly to the ear, that they cannot be detached from each other; as when the violinist, in playful execution, sometimes makes his instrument seem to hold dialogue, in the tones of question and answer, by drawing the bow across the strings, while he slips his left hand, upward and downward, so as to shorten or lengthen the strings, and thus cause the sounds to glide up or down the scale, in one continuous stream of "mewing" sound. A parallel illustration may be drawn from the natural use of the voice, when we pronounce the interrogatory "*eh?*" of surprise, in a serious mood, but with great earnestness,—merely causing the voice to slide smoothly up the scale, through the interval of a "fifth" or an "octave," or when we utter the word "*no!*" in the tone of full and bold denial, and make the voice sweep continuously down the scale, through a similar interval.

In the "current melody," of a sentence, every syllable includes a "radical" and a "vanishing movement," united, which, in unimpassioned expression, occupy the space, on the scale, of one tone, or pass from one note to the next above it on the scale. The succession of "concrete" tones, is uniformly at the interval of a tone, upward or downward on the scale, as the case may be. The rise of voice within each syllable may therefore be called its "concrete pitch;" and the place that each syllable takes above or below another, the "radical pitch."

The "melody of phrases," prescribes no fixed succession of radical pitch, although it usually avoids a repetition of the same "radical pitch," unless for special effect, in extreme cases; and it forbids the see-saw tone of exact alternation, or measured recurrence, o. "radical pitch."

The convenience of using specific and exact terms, in relation to "melody" and "pitch," as they exist in speech, renders the following distinctions important to the student of elocution.

When two or more "concretes" occur in succession, on the same "radical pitch," they form a "monotone," or produce upon the ear the effect of unity or sameness of sound or tone. This concrete pitch is often used in conjunction with the low notes of *awe*, *sublimity*, and *solemnity*, for impressive effect, resembling that of the deep tolling of a large bell. "Monotone," however, is not to be confounded with *monotony*, the besetting fault of school reading, and which consists chiefly in omitting or slighting the "radical stress,' and sometimes abolishing even the "radical movement" of elements "Monotone" is the sublimest poetic effect of elocution: *monotony* one of the worst defects.

When the "radical pitch" is one note above or below that of the preceding tone, it is termed a "Rising" or a "Falling Ditone.' — When the radicals of three successive "concretes," rise or fall they become a "Rising" or a "Falling Tritone." — When there is a series of three or more, alternately a tone above and below each other, they form an "Alternate Phrase."

When three "concretes" gradually descend in their "radical pitch" at the close of a sentence, the "vanish" of the last, instead of ascending, descends; so as to give the peculiar closing effect to the cadence. This descent is, accordingly, for distinction's sake, termed the "Triad of the Cadence."

It is in this peculiar "phrase" of "sentential melody," that the very general fault, popularly called "a tone," exists. The common style of cadence, instead of being *spoken*, is usually such as causes it to be *sung*, more or less, by deviating from the melody of the "triad," and, at the same time, losing "radical," and assuming "median stress," accompanied by a half-musical wave or undulation of voice. A clear, distinct, and exact succession of "radical pitch," in the form of the "triad," would, in most cases, destroy the false tone, and impart to reading more resemblance than it often possesses to speech or to conversation.

The student will derive much assistance, in this branch of elocution, from repeating the "tonic elements," and appropriate words selected from the exercises in the chapter on enunciation, with a view, first, to observe the "concrete" character of the elementary sounds of speech in their initial "radical" and rising "vanish." Let letters, syllables, and words, then be practised, successively in the forms of the phrases of the "monotone," "falling" and "rising" "ditone," and "tritone," and the "triad of the cadence.'

The following illustration, selected from the work of Dr. Rush will suggest the idea how the exercises in this department may be practised in classes, by the use of the chart of exercises, or of the black-board.

The object in view, in the use of such diagrams as the following is not to exhibit the strict application of any rule or principle of elo e 1:ion, but merely to aid the mind in attaining an exact apprehension of the nature and character of the elements of vocal sound, in certain relations. It is not meant that either the couplet from Pope's Homer, which is introduced in the following illustration, or the lines which follow it, *must* be read with the precise melody exhibited in the diagram, or that they cannot be appropriately read with any other. The design of this exemplification, is merely to show the different forms of "radical pitch,' as they occur in the actual use of the voice, and to render the practice of them definite and exact. The repetition of the exercise will render the ear accurate and discriminating, and will preserve the student from inadvertently contracting the false intonation arising from the general neglect of this part of elocution, and from the impossibility of discussing or explaining its peculiarities till the means of instruction were furnished by exact analysis and precise nomenclature, — benefits for which science and education stand equally indebted to the discriminating genius and philosophic investigation of Dr. Rush.

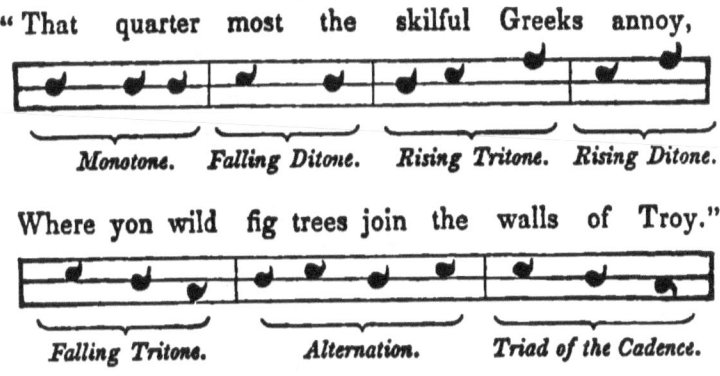

"That    quarter    most    the    skilful    Greeks    annoy,

*Monotone.*   *Falling Ditone.*   *Rising Tritone.*   *Rising Ditone.*

Where yon wild   fig trees join   the   walls   of   Troy."

*Falling Tritone.*       *Alternation.*       *Triad of the Cadence.*

To secure the full benefit of discrimination and of exact practice, it will be a useful exercise to repeat the phrases of melody in the diagram, on the "tonic" and other elements, on syllables, and on the following couplets.

1. — " Lo! the poor Indian, whose untutored mind
   Sees God in tempests, hears him in the wind."[1]

2. — " There, where a few torn shrubs the place disclose,
   The village preacher's modest mansion rose."

3. — " Thus every good his native wilds impart,
   Imprints the patriot passion on his heart."

[1] The above example is intentionally introduced as one of *cadence*, for the sake of contrast with the tone of *continuance*, which belongs to it in the original text.

4.—" The conscious swains, rejoicing in the sight,
Eye the blue vault, and bless the useful light "

THE " SLIDE."

We proceed to the examination of another function of the voice, connected with "melody," or the transition of vocal sound from one note to another of the musical scale.— The transit from the "radical" to the "vanish" of a sound, is, it will be recollected, limited, in "concrete pitch," to a single tone, or the distance measured to the ear, in passing from one note to the next above, on the scale. We should hear this transition exemplified in the sound of *a* in the word *arm*, in the following unimpassioned and incomplete phrase, if read as it would be in the case of a person suddenly interrupted, at the moment of uttering that word, in the act of reading a sentence; thus, " He raised his arm"— The broken or interrupted, progress of the voice, is here indicated by the fact that the sound of *a* in the word *arm* does not descend, but remains suspended by the effect of " concrete pitch," or the common difference between the " radical " and the " vanishing movement," in an unimpassioned or inexpressive sound.

But let us suppose the case of a person uttering the same element, in the vivid language of real or affected surprise, in the interjection " *ah!* " We shall now perceive, that the interval between the " radical" and the " vanish," is greatly enlarged, and that the voice has run *up* three, five, or perhaps, eight notes, according to the depth and earnestness of the feeling expressed in the utterance of the sound. The more slow and drawling the style of voice is made, in the repetition of the supposed example, the more distinct will be our perception of the transition of sound from note to note, as it glides up the scale. This vocal function is what, in elocution, is termed an " upward slide," or in the language of some elocutionists, a " rising inflection."

Let us suppose, once more, the sound of the same element falling on the ear, in the tone of the bold military command,

*Arm!*" We shall now perceive that, in the time which transpires from the first to the last moment of the sound, the voice glides *down* the scale, through an interval, greater or less, according to the boldness and fulness of the utterance. We have here an example of the "downward slide," or "falling inflection."

The extent of the "slide" depends, usually, on the intensity of a prompting emotion, as in the case of *surprise*, mentioned before. Let the student who has not yet trained his ear to discriminate the degrees of the "slide," and who wishes to attain a clear perception of its different forms, imagine a conversation going on between two persons, one of whom is relating to the other a series of events, each one successively more striking and more surprising than the preceding. Let the hearer be supposed to utter, at each stage in the narrative, the expressive interrogatory interjection of surprise, "*indeed!*" and with that marked increase of effect, which arises not only from the augmented intensity of force, but also from the wider interval of the scale, or the larger number of notes, which the voice traverses, in the "expressive melody" of speech.

The progressive change of feeling, which causes the progressive change of expression in the voice, may, for the sake of illustration, be supposed to rise from *surprise* to *wonder*, and from *wonder* to *astonishment*. In such circumstances, may be heard, 1st, the ordinary "slide" of *surprise*, — the interval occupied by the voice, from the moment of uttering the "radical" of the expressive sound, to that of uttering its "vanish," being a rising "third;" the voice gliding *upward*, with a continuous sound, terminating in the note which lies on the third degree of the scale above the "radical:"— 2d, the more expressive "slide" of *greater surprise*, or of *wonder*, — occupying the interval of an upward "fifth;" the gliding sound terminating on the note which is on the fifth degree of the scale above the "radical:" — 3d, *extreme surprise, excessive wonder*, or *astonishment*, whether real or affected, (and, particularly, if the latter,) will impel the voice with a slide which glides through a whole "octave," or interval of eight notes, from the "radical" to the "vanish."

Again, let it be supposed that the person who is listening to the narrator, is answering in *the derisive tone of mockery*. The voice, in this case, will utter the word "*indeed!*" in the downward "slide;" and if we suppose, farther, the tone of emotion increased in intensity of expression, at each stage, the effect may be to produce the same three intervals of the scale as before, but in the opposite direction: — 1st, the downward "third," — 2d, the downward "fifth," — 3d, the downward "octave;" the voice gliding down with a continuous sound, through each of these intervals, in succession, while uttering the last syllable of the expressive word "*indeed!*"

Similar illustrations might be drawn from the natural "expression" of other strong or distinctly marked emotions. But these will occur in subsequent examples. A clear and broad definition is all that is now requisite.

The "slides" of the voice have three important and distinct offices; and these produce the three principal forms of the 'slide:" 1st, the "slide of *passion* or *emotion*,"—2d, the "*distinctive* slide," or that which is addressed to the understanding and the judgment, as in *designation*, *comparison*, and *contrast*,—3d, the "mechanical slide," which belongs to the mechanism of a sentence, and the local position of phrases; as in the special instance of the *partial* cadence, which takes place when a distinct portion of the sense is completed, although the whole sentence is not finished; as in this instance: "Let your companions be select; let them be such as you can esteem for their good qualities, and whose virtuous example you may emulate." We have another example in the "triad" of the *full and final* cadence falling entirely within one syllable, as in the following emphatic negation:

"No; by the rood, not *so!*"

Another "slide" which serves a mechanical purpose, rather than one of thought or feeling, is the "penultimate slide" of most sentences, which serves the purpose of raising the voice deliberately and distinctly, previous to its final descent at the close of the sentence, and thus renders the cadence more perceptible and more impressive; as in the following example: "Let the young go out, under the descending sun of the *year*, into the fields of nature."

Few parts of elocution are more important to the practical teacher or to the earnest student, than the discrimination of the "partial" and the "final" cadence. The confounding of these two descents of voice, causes the two prevalent errors of school reading and popular oratory, as contradistinguished from true, natural, and appropriate expression. The school-boy, in attempting to give the "partial" cadence, when endeavoring to comply with his teacher's injunction, to "use a falling inflection," gives the full "triad" of the cadence, on the last three syllables, in the phrase of the preceding example, "*be select:*" which of course produces, at the colon, the proper effect of a period. The habitual tone of school reading, inclining, in didactic style, to a declamatory chant, the young reader, when he comes to the proper place of the cadence, at the close of the sentence, substitutes, for the proper "triad,"—on the last three syllables,—the "rising ditone," on the first and second, and a "concrete third" with a downward "vanish," on the third; and these are commonly rendered still more conspicuous by the unhappy effect, (intended, apparently, as a compensation for the want of true cadence,) of a superadded "wave." This "drift," or prevailing effect of false intonation, in the "melody of sentences," pervades the style of voice current in school reading, in academic declamation, and in public addresses, and substitutes something like the effects of song for those of speech.

The "triad" of the cadence derives its closing effect of repose and approaching cessation of voice, partly from its contrasting with the previous "penultimate upward slide," which usually occurs at the last comma, or similar pause, of a sentence, and terminates the penultimate clause; sometimes from a previous "falling tritone" preceding the penultimate rise; and always from its own regular descent, which resembles the effect of a gradual but distinct succession of downward steps. The "partial" cadence of complete sense, but incomplete period, on the contrary, preserves its more abrupt effect of imperfectly finished succession of sounds, by adopting, in the last three syllables of the clause to which it is applied, the "rising ditone" on the first and second, and the "concrete of the second," with downward "vanish," on the third. The effect of full cadence is thus entirely avoided, and yet that of partial completeness of sense, secured; the voice ending on a strain too high for the one, and yet, by the "concrete of the second" with the downward "vanish," preserving the indication of temporary cessation and slight repose.

## I. THE SLIDE OF EMOTION.

The "slide of emotion" extends through an interval corresponding, in every instance, to the intensity of feeling implied in "expressive" words, and may, accordingly, be measured, in most instances, by the "third," the "fifth," or the "octave."

Strong emotions are expressed by the "*downward* slide;" except *surprise*, and *earnest*, or *impassioned interrogation*, which usually adopt the "upward slide" of the "fifth" or the "octave."

### EXAMPLES.

1. *Impetuous Courage and Fierce Determination.*

RICHMOND TO HIS TROOPS.—*Shakspeare.*

("Orotund" and "aspirated pectoral quality:" Shouting: "Explosive radical" and "expulsive median stress:" "High pitch." The "downward slide" of the "third," takes place on every emphatic word in the first four lines, and the "downward fifth" on the remainder, as indicated by the grave accent, the usual mark for this "slide.")

"Fìght, gentlemen of Ènglând! fìght, bold yeòmen,
Dràw, archers, draw your arrows to the hèad:
Spur your proud horses hàrd, and ride in blòod,
Amaze the wèlkin with your broken stàves.—
A thòusand hearts are grèat within my bòsom:
Advance our stàndards, set upon our fòes!
Our ancient word of courage, fair Saint George,
Inspire us with the spleen of fiery dràgons!
Upòn them! Victory sits on our hèlms."

### 2. Impassioned burst of Scorn.

FROM CORIOLANUS.—*Shakspeare.*

("A spirated pectoral and guttural quality:" Violent force: "Explosive radical stress:" "High pitch." The exemplification occurs in the reply of Coriolanus, which contains the "downward slide' of the "octave," in the words "Measureless liar!" and "Boy!' and the "downward fifth" on the other emphatic words.)

*Aufidius.* "Name not the god,
Thou boy of tears.

*Coriolanus.* Mèasureless liar! thou hast made my heart
Too great for what contains it.
Bòy! Cut me to pìeces, Volscians: men and làds,
Stain àll your edges on me. Bòy!—
If you have writ your annals true, 't is there
That, like an eagle in a dovecot, I
Fluttered your Volscians in Corioli:
Alòne I did it.—Bòy!"

### 3. Indignant Rebuke.

MARULLUS TO THE PEOPLE.—*Shakspeare.*

(' Orotund and aspirated pectoral quality:" "Impassioned" force: "Explosive radical stress:" "Low pitch:" "Downward slide of the "fifth."

"Begòne! run to your hòuses, fall upon your knèes
Pray to the gòds to intermit the plàgues
That needs must light on this ingràtitude!"

THE "SLIDE." 135

4. *Excessive Grief.*

("Aspirated pectoral quality:" Weeping utterance: 'Impassioned" force: Violent "vanishing stress:" "High pitch:" "Downward slide" of the "fifth.")

DAVID, [BEWAILING THE DEATH OF ABSALOM.]

"Ò my son Àbsalom! my sòn, my son Àbsalom! Would Gòd I had died for thèe, Ò Àbsalom, my sòn, my sòn!"[1]

5. *Exception.*—*Surprise, Earnest and Impassioned Interrogation.*

EXTRACT FROM CHATHAM.

("Aspirated pectoral quality:" "Declamatory" force: "Compound stress:" "High pitch:" "Upward fifth.")

"Can ministers still presume to expect suppórt[2] in their infatuation? Can parliament be so dead to its dignity and its duty, as to give its support to measures thus obtruded and fórced upon it?"

FROM CICERO'S ACCUSATION OF VERRES.

"Is it come to thís? Shall an inferior mágistrate, a góvernor, who holds his whole power of the Roman péople, in a Roman próvince, within síght of Italy, bínd, scóurge, tórture with fíre and red hot plates of íron, and at last put to the infamous death of the cróss, a Roman cítizen?"

MARULLUS TO THE PEOPLE.—*Shakspeare.*

"O you hard hearts, you cruel men of Rome,
Knew ye not Pómpey? Many a time and oft
Have you climbed up to walls and battlements,
To towers and windows, yea, to chimney-tops,

---

[1] For fuller exemplification of the "slide," see "American Elocutionist" in which this and the other departments of sentential and rhetorical elocution, are fully discussed. The present volume, being designed merely as a manual for training in orthophony, and as an introduction to the Elocutionist, is limited to such an outline of the subject as might afford sufficient ground for the intelligent practice of a course of elementary exercises.

[2] The acute accent is the usual mark of the "upward slide," or "rising inflection."

Your infants in your arms, and there have sat
The live-long day, with patient expectation,
To see great Pompey pass the streets of Rome:
And when you saw his chariot but appear,
Have you not made a universal shout,
That Tiber trembled underneath her banks
To hear the replication of your sounds,
Made in her concave shores?[1]
And do you now put on your best attíre?
And do you now cull out a hóliday?
And do you now strew flowers in his way,
That comes in triumph over Pompey's blóod?"

II. THE "DISTINCTIVE" SLIDE.

This slide, it will be recollected, is used not for purposes of passion or emotion, but for suggestions connected with the understanding and judgment, — that which may be termed *intellectual*, not *impassioned*, expression.

The "downward distinctive slide" extends, usually, through the interval of a "third." It is used, first, for mere *designation*, as in *announcing a subject or topic*, in *didactic* style, in *introducing a person* or an *event* in *narrative*, or an *object*, in *descriptive* style; as in the following examples: "The duties of the citizens of a repùblic formed the subject of the orator's address." "Among the eminent men of the period of the American Revolution, Benjamin Frànklin held a conspicuous place." "From the date of the American Revolùtion, commenced a new era in the history of man." "The dazzling summits of the snow-capt mountains in the distance, threw an air of enchantment over the scene."

This slide is used also, for *distinction in contrasts*, as in the latter of two correspondent or antithetic words or phrases, in which the contrast is *exactly balanced;* thus, "I would neither be rích nor pòor," or when the antithesis is *unequal* and one word or phrase is intentionally made more expressive

---

[1] An interrogation of peculiar emphasis, or of great length, takes the downward slide; as, in such cases, the effect of interrogation is lost, in that of assertion.

than the other, in which case the more emphatic word or phrase takes the downward slide: thus, "I would rather be rich than poor."—The "distinctive upward slide" occurs in the word "*rich,*" in the former of these examples; and it may be given also in the word "*poor,*" in the latter, if pronounced with peculiar distinctive force, so as to authorize, in the sound of the word "*poor,*" an upward slide, instead of a cadence, at the close of the sentence,—an effect which often takes place in the unstudied and natural use of the voice, and which corresponds somewhat to the rebound of the ball, when it is thrown against the wall with sufficient force to produce that effect.

EXAMPLES OF " DISTINCTIVE SLIDES."

I. *Simple Designation.*

1. *Didactic Style.*

" The progress of the Italian òpera, in this country, will form the subject of this essay."

" The downfall of the Roman èmpire was the next great theme chosen by that eminent historian."

" The origin of the distinctions of rànk in society, forms one of the most interesting topics of historical investigation."

2. *Narrative Style.*

" The conspiracy of Càtiline, as related by Sallust, was one of the most atrocious designs ever plotted by desperate and heartless villany."

" From the time when the people enjoyed the right of electing their tribunes, they fondly deemed their liberty secured against future encroachments."

" The usurpation, as it has been termed, of Oliver Cròmwell, rightly interpreted, is one of the most memorable of lessons to monarchy, ever taught in the great school of history."

3. *Descriptive Style.*

" A sudden shòwer puts an end to the gaiety cf the revel

lers, and sends them scampering in all directions for shelter."

"The spots on the disc of the sùn, which, in some instances, are larger than a continent or an ocean, with us, are, it is believed, openings in the luminous àtmosphere of that body, exhibiting the dark surface beneath."

"The first primrose of the spring, was peeping through the shrivelled herbage at the roots of the hedge, along the side of the lane."

II. *Comparison and Antithesis, or Contrast.*

1. *Comparison of Single Objects.*

"As is the begínning, so is the ènd."

2. *Double Comparison.*

"As we cannot discern the moving of the shàdow over the ¹díal-plate; so we cannot trace the progress of the mínd in knòwledge."

3. *Contrast of Single Objects.*

"I mingled freely with all classes of society, and narrowly observed the life of the péasant, as well as that of the prince."

4. *Double Contrast, or Antithesis.*

"As it is the part of jùstice never to do víolence, it is that of módesty never to commit offènce."

III. THE "MECHANICAL SLIDE."

This form of the "slide" was defined as either "upward" or "downward;" the former occurring at the close of the penultimate clause of a sentence, in preparation for its cadence; the latter, when the cadence, from the absence of accent on preceding syllables, descends in the form of a

---

¹ In *double* contrasts, the full "distinctive slide of the third," falls only on the prominent parts of the contrast, the leading and determining words at the middle and the end of the sentence; the other pair of contrasted words are usually restricted to "falling" and "rising ditone," in their "radical pitch."

concrete downward slide" on a single sound, which includes, within itself, the whole interval otherwise occupied by a "discrete triad." Another form of the "mechanical slide," is used to indicate, as mentioned before, complete sense, or the finishing of an independent part of a sentence. Its effect, as a descent of voice, differs to the ear from that of the cadence, in the fact formerly stated, of its commencing and ceasing at a higher point of the scale, and from its not being preceded by the "penultimate slide," nor by a previous descent of voice which prepares the ear for the deliberate and full effect of cadence. It may be termed the "downward slide of complete sense" or "partial" cadence, as contrasted with its opposite, the "upward slide" of the "third," in incomplete sense, assumed, on purpose, in the middle of a sentence, to create expectation of farther expression, for the completion of a thought; or the "upward third" of unimpassioned interrogation, which also implies incomplete or undetermined sense. The "downward slide of complete sense," may be so denominated also, as contrasted with the mere effect of "concrete pitch," when a reader, as was formerly supposed, for the purpose of illustration, is suddenly interrupted in the act of reading, and breaks off at an incomplete phrase.

EXAMPLES.

1.—"*Penultimate Slide.*"

" The signification of our sentiments, made by tones and gestures, has this advantage above that made by wórds, that it is the language of nature."

" In epic poetry, the English have only to boast of Spenser and Milton, who neither of them wanted either genius or learning to have been perfect póets; and yet both of them are liable to many censures."

2.—"*Partial Cadence,*" *at the close of a clause which forms complete sense.*

" Greatness confers no exemption from the cares and sorrows of life: its share of them frequently bears a melancholy proportion to its exaltation."

"In man, we see a creature whose thoughts are not limited by any narrow bounds either of place or tìme, who carries his researches into the most distant regions of this globe, and beyond this globe, to the planets and heavenly bòdies; looks backward to consider the first origin of the human ràce; casts his eyes forward to see the influence of his actions upon posterity, and the judgments which will be formed of his character a thousand years hènce: a creature who traces causes and effects to great lengths and ìntricacy; extracts general principles from particular appèarances; improves upon his discòveries, corrects his mistákes,[1] and makes his very errors profitable."

3.—"*Upward Slide of incomplete or suspended sense.*"

"Were men entirely free from více, all would be uniformity, harmony, and order."

"The idea of that Divine Being, whose benevolence and wisdom have, from all eternity, contrived and conducted the immense machine of the universe, so as at all times to produce the greatest possible quantity of [2] háppiness, is certainly, of all objects of human contemplation, by far the most sublime."

"If a man is deeply impressed with the habitual and thorough conviction, that a benevolent and all-wise Being can admit into the system of His government no partial evil which is not necessary for the universal góod, he must consider all the misfortunes which may befall himself, his friends, his society, or his country, as necessary for the prosperity of the universe, and therefore as what he ought, not only to submit to with resignation, but as what he himself, if he had known all the connexions and dependences of things, ought sincerely and devoutly to have wished for."

4.—"*Upward Slide*" of "*unimpassioned interrogation.*"

"Have you heard the néws? Can we place any depén-

---

[1] "Penultimate upward slide"
[2] A "rising tritone" is sometimes the equivalent of the "upward slide of the third."

dence on the report? Is it probable that such an event could have bee a kept so long concealed?"

"Shall we adópt the measures proposed by this speaker? Are the arguments which he has advanced sufficient to produce convíction? Can we proceed with perfect confidence that we shall not have to retráce our steps?"

"Does the work relate to the interests of mankínd? Is its object useful, and its end móral? Will it inform the understanding, and amend the héart? Is it written with freedom and impartiálity? Does it bear the marks of honesty and sincérity? Does it attempt to ridicule anything that is good or gréat? Does a manly style of thinking predominate in it? Do réason, wít, húmor, and pléasantry, prevail in it? Does it contain new and useful trúths?"

## CHAPTER VII.

### "TIME."

THE chief characteristics of utterance, which are subjects of attention in vocal culture, are the "quality" of the voice, as sound, merely, and its "expression," as produced by "force," "stress," "melody," or "pitch," and "time,"—properties equivalent to those which are comprehended, in music, under the heads of "quality," "dynamics," (force,) "melody," and "rhythm," (the effect of the union of "accent," or comparative force, and "time," on the sequence of sounds.)

The subject of "time" is that which remains to be discussed, as the ground of practical exercises in elocution.

### "QUANTITY."

The study of *time*, as a measure of speech, will lead to the primary classification of *single* vowel sounds, as *long* or *short*, in duration, according to their character and expression, as elements of language. The contrast, in the duration of the "tonic element," or vowel sound, *a*, in the words *male* and *female*, will furnish examples; the *a* in the former being much longer, or, in other words, occupying a much larger space of time, in utterance, than the *a* in the latter. The technical designation of this property of vocal sounds, is "quantity,"—implying quantity of time, or duration. The *a* of *male*, is accordingly termed a "*long*," the *a* in *female*, a "*short quantity*."—Such is the usual distinction recognized in *prosody*, and applied to *versification*.

Syllables, when regarded in connexion with the "quantities" of their component elements, and classified for the purposes of elocution, have been arranged by Dr Rush, under the following denominations:

1st. "Immutable," or such as are, from the nature of their constituent sounds, incapable of prolongation. These are *immutably* fixed to the *shortest* "quantity" exhibited in an elementary sound, and cannot, even when accented, and uttered in solemn or in poetic expression, be prolonged, in any degree, without positive mispronunciation or destruction of the peculiar accent of the language; as the *i*, for example, in the word *sick*, or in the verb *convict*. "Immutable" syllables terminate with an abrupt, or "atonic" element, preceded by a short "tonic," as in the above examples.

The propriety of the designation "immutable" will be apparent, on referring to the following examples, in the utterance of which, although there is the utmost intensity of emotion, the elements *ic* oppose an insuperable resistance to any attempt to heighten the expression of passion by prolonging the sound of the syllable or word in which they predominate.

HOTSPUR, [EXCLAIMING ON HIS FATHER'S ILLNESS, AND CONSEQUENT ABSENCE FROM THE CAMP AT SHREWSBURY.]—*Shakspeare.*

"*Sick* now! droop now! This *sickness* doth infect
The very life-blood of our enterprise."

CATILINE, [INDIGNANTLY DEFYING THE ROMAN SENATE.]—*Croly.*

"Tried and conv*ict*ed traitor!—Who says this?
Who'll prove it, at his peril, on my head?"

2d. "Mutable" syllables are such as are constituted like the preceding, but are capable of a slight degree of prolongation. Their "time," therefore, is *mutable*, or admits of gradation, according to the length or shortness of sound, in their constituent elements, as pronounced with more or less emotion of a nature which requires slow, rapid, or moderate utterance of the words or phrases in which they occur. The monosyllable *yet*, or the accented syllable of the word *beset*, uttered in the tone of any vivid emotion, will furnish as example. An instance occurs in the scene of the combat between Fitz James and Roderic Dhu, when the latter makes the taunting exclamation, "Not *yet* prepared!"—and another in Blanche's dying warning.

" The path 's beset, by flood and fell!"

3d. "Indefinite" syllables, or those which contain, or terminate with, a "tonic" element, or with any "subtonic" but $b$, $d$, or $g$. The "quantity" of the predominating element in such syllables, even when it is not positively long, admits, without offence to the ear, of a comparatively *indefinite* prolongation; as the *a* in the words *man, unmannerly,* pronounced with emotion. The time occupied in the enunciation of such sounds, is properly determined by the degree of feeling which they are, for the moment, used to express; as we perceive in the different tones of the following examples: the first in Hamlet's admiring exclamation, "What a piece of work is a man!" and Lady Macbeth's indignant and reproachful interrogation addressed to her husband, when he stands horror-stricken at the vision of the ghost of Banquo, "Are you a man?"

The power and beauty of vocal "expression," are necessarily dependent, to a great extent, on the command which a reader or speaker possesses over the element of "quantity." Poetry and eloquence derive their audible character from this source, more than from any other. The music of verse is sacrificed, unless the nicest regard be paid to "quantity," as the basis of rhythm and of metre · and, with the exception of the most exquisite strains of well-executed music, the ear receives no pleasure comparable to that arising from poetic feeling, imbodied in the genuine melody of the heart, as it gushes from the expressive voice which has the power of

"Untwisting all the chains that tie
The hidden soul of harmony."

Milton, in his Paradise Lost, affords innumerable examples of the majestic grandeur of long "quantities" in epic verse; and without the just observance of these, the reading of the noblest passages in that poem, becomes flat and dry. The same is true, still more emphatically, of the magnificent language of the poetic passages of Scripture, in those strains of triumph and of adoration, which abound in the book of Psalms, and in the prophets.

The necessity, on the other hand, of obeying the law of "immutable quantity," even in the grandest and most emphatic expression, is an imperative rule of elocution. A false, bombastic swell of voice, never sounds so ridiculous as when the injudicious and unskilful reader or speaker attempts to interfere with the conditions of speech, and to prolong, under a false excitement of utterance, those sounds which nature has irrevocably determined short. We have this fault exemplified in the compound of bawling, drawling, and redoubled "wave," which some reciters contrive to crowd into the small space of the syllable *vic,* in the conclusion of Moloch's war-speech,

"Which if not *vic*tory is yet revenge."

The fierce intensity of emotion, in the true utterance of this syllable, brings it on the ear with an instantaneous *ictus,* and tingling effect, resembling that of the lash of a whip applied to the organ. A similar case occurs in Shylock's fiendish half-shriek, on the word *hip*, in his exclamation referring to Antonio,

"If I do catch him once upon the *hip*,
I will feed fat the ancient grudge I bear him!"

The sprawling, expanded utterance, which the style of rant preposterously endeavors to indulge, on this word, causes the voice, as it were, to fall in pieces in the attempt, and to betray the falsity of the style which it affects.

But it is in the chaste yet generous effect of the judicious prolongation and indulgence of "*mutable* quantities," that the skill of the elocutionist, and the power and truth of expression, are peculiarly felt. It is in these, that the watchful analyst can trace, at once, the full soul and the swelling heart, which would impel the speaker to prolong indefinitely the tones of passion, to give "ample scope and verge enough" to overflowing feeling, — but, not less surely, the manly force of judgment, and the disciplined good taste, which forbid any display of mere sound, in the utterance of earnest emotion.

A long-continued practice on the elements of the language, on syllables, words, and phrases, will be well bestowed in the endeavor to acquire a perfect command of "quantity."

### EXERCISES IN "QUANTITY."

The following exercises need close attention to the firmness, clearness, decision, and purity of the opening "radical," and the delicacy and distinctness of the "vanish." The latter should be occasionally practised in that long-protracted form, which, as Dr. Rush has expressively said, "knits sound to silence."[1] The elements may be practised in "effusive," "expulsive," and "explosive" utterance, on all the chief intervals of "slide" and "wave," commencing with the "second," and extending to the octave, both upward and downward, — and on the various degrees of "force" and modes of "stress," together with the distinctions of "pitch," and the "expression" of the chief characteristic emotions; as *awe, reverence, fear, horror, despair, anger, grief, joy, love,* &c.

1. *Examples of Long "Quantities," and "Indefinite" syllables.*

| *A*-ll | *A*-rm | *Ai*-r | *E*-ve | *Oo*-ze | *O*-r |
|---|---|---|---|---|---|
| *a*-we | *a*-h! | h-*ai*-r | ee-l | f-*oo*-l | m-*o*rn |
| b-*a*-ll | t-*a*-rn | d-*a*-re | ea-r | p-*oo*-r | f-*o*-rm |
| *aw*-ful | b-*a*-lmy | c-*a*-reless | e-vil | m-*oo*-nless | o-rder |

[1] The same thought is expressed, with inimitable beauty, in the lines of Sheridan Knowles:

"I hear a sound so fine, there 's nothing lives
'Twixt it and silence!"

"QUANTITY." 145

| | | | | | |
|---|---|---|---|---|---|
| a-ways | h-a-rmless | w-a-ry | ea-sy | s-oo-ner | o-rphan |
| au-gur | t-a-rnish | r-a-rely | fee-ble | c-oo-ling | o-rgan |
| app-a-ll | af-a-r | bew-a-re | rev-ea-l | rem-o-ve | ad-o-rn |
| bef-a-ll | dis-a-rm | ensn-a-re | conc-ea-l | unm-oo-r | acc-o-rd |
| rec-a-ll | lec-a-lm | decl-a-re | app-ea-l | repr-o-ve | forl-o-rn |
| A-le | I-ce | O-ld | Ou-r | Oi-l | U-se |
| ai-d | i-sle | ow-n | ow-l | j-oi-n | you |
| ai-m | d-ie | o-de | v-ow | b-oy | d-ew |
| b-a- eful | i-vy | o-ver | h-ow-ling | v-oi-celess | d-u-ly |
| h-ai-ling | dy-ing | o-nly | d-ow-nward | n-oi-sy | p-u-rer |
| w-ai-ling | h-i-ghly | h-o-ly | b-ou-ndless | p-oi-son | m-u-ral |
| unv-ei-l | repl-y | bel-ow | reb-ou-nd | enj-oy | ref-u-se |
| recl-ai-m | def-y | foreg-o | res-ou-nd | rej-oi-ce | am-u-se |
| lisd-ai-n | den-y | beh-o-ld | unh-ou-sed | empl-oy | den-u-de |

2.—*Short "Quantities," and "Immutable" Syllables.*[1]

| | | | | |
|---|---|---|---|---|
| B-a-ck | b-e-ck | p-i-ck | d-o-ck | d-u-ck |
| ı-a-ck | n-e-ck | s-i-ck | m-o-ck | t-u-ck |
| )-a-ckward | b-e-ckon | w-i-cked | s-o-cket | l-u-ckless |
| -a-ckey | sp-e-ckled | f-i-ckle | kn-o-cking | b-u-cket |
| ıtt-a-ck | bed-e-ck | unp-i-cked | bem-o-ck | rel-u-ct |

| | | |
|---|---|---|
| M-a-p | D-i-p | U-p |
| r-a-p | t-i-p | c-u-p |
| t-a-p | l-i-p | s-u-p |
| t-a-pster | s-i-pping | u-pper |
| str-a-pping | tr-i-pping | c-u-pful |
| B-a-t | B-i-t | B-u-t |
| c-a-t | p-i-t | c-u-t |
| p-a-t | f-i-t | n-u-t |
| b-a-tten | b-i-tter | m-u-tter |
| t-a-tter | f-i-ttest | c-u-tting |

3.—*Variable "Quantities," and "Mutable" Syllables.*

| | | | | | | |
|---|---|---|---|---|---|---|
| 4-pe | Wh-a-t | B-e-t | A-dd | B-i-g | O-dd | C-u-b |

"Immutable" syllables do not admit of "effusive" utterance. They are est adapted to the display of "explosive" style, although they occur also in expulsive" and "declamatory expression."

g-*ai*-t    n-*o*-t    d-*e*-bt    b-*a*-d    d-*i*-g    g-*o*-d    d-*u*-o
f-*a*-te    g-*o*-t    p-*e*-t    m-*a*-d    f-*i*-g    n-*o*-d    t-*u*-b
b-*a*-sely  d-*o*-tted b-*e*-tter s-*a*-dden g-*i*-ggle b-*o*-dy b-*u*-bble
w-*a*-keful c-*o*-ttage p-*e*-ttish m-*a*-ddest d-*i*-gger s-*o*-dden d-*o*-uble

EXAMPLES OF "QUANTITY," IN PHRASES AND SENTENCES.

1. — *Long* "*Quantities,*" *and* "*Indefinite*" *Syllables.*

[The object in view in these exercises, is, to enable the student to trace distinctly the wide scope of " expression " afforded by " indefinite " syllables, for the full prolongation of all elements which imbody the sounds of passion and emotion. " Time," in elocution, is the *opportunity* of effect, which inattention and rapidity throw away. Young readers, in particular, need much practice in this department; as they incline to haste and slight " expression." The mode of performing these exercises, should be regulated with a view, at first, to the fullest effect of expressive sound. Afterwards, the style may be reduced in effect, as the consecutive reading of whole pieces may require. In vocal training, as in athletic exercise, the object of practice is, sometimes, to execute a given feat, with a view to its effect on habit, — to gain the power of putting forth, on requisite occasions, a maximum of effort, in an easy, graceful, and appropriate manner.]

*Grief:*—"*Oh!* I have lost you *all!*
      Parents, and home, and friends."
*Courage:* —" Come one, come *all!*—this rock shall fly
      From its firm base as soon as I."
*Awe:*—" My heart is *awed* within me, when I think
      Of the great miracle that still goes on
      In silence round me."——
*Sublimity:*—" Hail! holy Light! offspring of Heaven first-
      born."
*Disdain:* —" None left but by submission; and that word
      Disdain forbids me."
*Shouting:*—"'To arms! to arms! to arms!' they cry."
*Regret:*—"*Ah!* why will kings forget that they are men,
      And men that they are brethren?"
*Delight:*—" The balmy breath of incense-breathing morn "—
      "*O* my soul's joy!"
*Fear:*—" While the deep thunder, peal on peal, a*far*"—
*Triumph:*——.    "*Io!* they come, they come!"

*Misery:* —" W*ai*ling and *wo*e, and grief, and f*ea*r, and p*ai*n."
*Horror:* ——" He woke—to d*ie*—midst flame and smoke·
And shout and groan and sabre stroke"—
*Calling:*— Awake! ar*i*se! or be forever fallen!"
*Defiance:*- " Thy threats, thy mercy, I def*y*!"
' I g*i*ve thee, in thy teeth, the l*ie*!"
*Denial:* —" The truth of his whole statement I do most peremptorily den*y*."
*Challenge:*—" Pal*e*, trembling coward! there I throw my gage."
" Dr*aw*, villain, dr*aw*, and defend thy life!"
*Exultation:*—" Poison, and Plague, and yelling Rage are fied!"
*Adoration:*—"A*ir*, earth, and s*ea*, res*ou*nd His pr*ai*se abr*oa*d!"
*Melancholy:*—"Old Ocean's gr*ay* and melancholy w*a*ste"—
*Grandeur:*—" Roll on, th*ou* deep and dark blue ocean, roll.'
Ten th*ou*sand fleets sweep over thee in v*ai*n!'
*Anger:*——" And d*ar*'st thou, then,
To beard the l*i*on in his d*e*n,
The Doūglas in his hall?
And hop'st thou hence unscathed to go?—
No! by Saint Bride of Bothwell, no!"
*Pathos:*——" For I am poor and miserably old!"
*Command:*—— " Chieftains forego!
The man who strikes makes me h*i*s toe.
" Hold, hold! for your lives!"
" Hold, hold! the general speaks to you;--
hold, for shame!"
*Earnest Entreaty:*—" Hear me! oh! hear me!"
*Despair:*——— —  " Farewell f*ea*r!
Farewell remorse!"
*Madness:*—— "*E*vil! be thou my good!'"
*Pity:*—— " Sic*k*ness, and want, and feeble, trembling age "—
*Distraction:*—" Bl*ow*, wind, and crack your cheeks! rage! bl*ow*!"

*Gloom:* — Thou drear and howling wilderness!'
*Vastness and Sublimity:* — " Boundless, endless, and sublime ! "
*Self-reproach:* — " O fool ! fool ! fool ! "
*Commiseration:* — ." Poor fool and knave, I have one part in my heart
That's sorry yet for thee *!* "
*Imprecation:* ——— " Strike her young bones,
You taking *a*irs, with lameness !
You nimble lightnings, dart your blinding flames
Into her scornful *e*yes ! "
*Accusation:* — " Nathan said unto David, ' Thou art the man ! ' "
" All the tr*e*asons, for these eighteen y*e*ars,
Complotted and concocted in this land,
Fetch from f*a*lse Mowbray their chief spring and head."
*Joy:* ——— " J*o*y, joy ! shout, shout aloud for j*o*y *!* "
*Fear:* — " With n*oi*seless foot she treads the marble floor."
*Grief:* — " The Ni*o*be of nations ! there she stands
Childless and crownless, in her voiceless woe *!* "
" Oh ! pardon me, thou bleeding piece of earth,
That I am meek and gentle with these butchers ! "
*Sorrow:* ——— " *A*h ! lady, n*o*w full well I kn*o*w
What 't is to be an *o*rphan b*o*y *!* "
*Delight:* ——— " Of p*u*re now p*u*rer air
Meets his approach,"
" Of bloom eth*e*real the light-footed D*e*ws."—-

2. — *Short* " *Quantities,*" *and* "*Immutable*" *Syllables.*

[The object in view, in the following examples, is to exhibit the "explosive" mode of utterance, and to impart the power of concentrating and condensing expression into the shortest sounds. *Instantaneous execution* is, in these examples, the point to be aimed at ; — the voice to be charged with the utmost impetuous force of utterance, on every expressive syllable ; and any approach to prolongation to be carefully avoided, as tending to weaken the proper effect The " explosion," in many of these instances, should resemble the startling abruptness of a sudden and violent blow.]

*Wrath:* — " Back to thy punishment! false fugitive."
*Maddened Resolve:* — " I 'll fight till from my bones my
     flesh be hacked!"
*Reproach:* ——" Up! sluggards, up!"
    " Wicked, remorseless wretch!"
    " O fickle fool!"
*Indignation:* — " Thou impious mocker, hence!"
   " Be ready, gods, with all your thunder
    bolts!
   Dash him in pieces!"
*Terror:* —— " Whence is that knocking?"
*Command:* —" Sound, tuckets!"
*Scorn:* —" You, wretch! you could enjoy yourself, like a butcher's dog in the shambles, battening on garbage, while the slaughter of the brave went on around you."
*Contempt:* —" Thou tattered starveling!"
   " The swaggering upstart reels!"
*Mirth:* —" Come, and trip it, as ye go,
  On the light fantastic toe!"
*Boasting:* —" I have seen the day, with my good biting
   falchion
  I would have made them skip!"
*Threatening:* —" This day 's the birth of sorrows: this
   hour's work
  Will breed proscriptions!"
*Scorn:* —" Faithful to whom? to thy rebellious crew!
  Army of fiends! — fit body to fit head!
*Amazement:* — " What! fifty of my followers at a clap!'
*Revenge:* —"Batter their walls down, raze them o the
   ground!"
*Shouting:* —" Victory! victory! Their columns give way! press them while they waver; and the day is ours!"
*Anger:* — " Thou muttering, malapert knave!"
*Derision:* —" Ay! sputter away, thou roasting apple Spit forth thy spleen! 't will ease thy heart."
*Horror:* ——— " I could not say, Amen,
  When they did say, God bless us

"Amen
Stuck in my throat!"
*Warning:* ——"Bitterly shall ye rue your folly!"
*Indignation:* ——" But this very day,
An honest man, my neighbor, — there he
stands, —
Was struck, — struck like a dog, — by one
who wore
The badge of Ursini,"—
*Remorse:* ——  " Whip me, ye devils!
From the possession of a sight like this."

### 3.—*Variable "Quantities," and "Mutable" Syllables.*

[The design of the following exercises, is to attract the student's attention to the partial *change* of " quantity," which emotion produces on " mutable " syllables, according to the characteristic tone, in each instance. True, natural, and full " expression," requires, for example, that *awe, solemnity, reverence,* and similar feelings, should be uttered with a comparative *prolongation* of " quantity," when the structure of syllables will admit the change, and that *hurry, agitation, alarm,* and other moods of mind tending to the same effects, should be expressed with a rapid enunciation, and " quantities " rendered as brief as possible.]

### 1.—*Impatience, and Revenge.*

[MACDUFF, AFTER HEARING OF THE MASSACRE OF HIS FAMILY BY THE ORDER OF MACBETH.]—*Shakspeare.*

" But gentle Heaven,

*Impatience:* (S. q.[1])

" Cut short all intermission: front to front,
Bring thou this fiend of Scotland and myself;

*Revenge:* (L. q.[2])

" Within my sword's length set him; — if he 'scape,
Heaven forgive him too!"

---

[1] Shorter quantity.  [2] Longer quantity.

## 2.—*Cheerfulness, and Scorn.*

*Cheerfulness:* (S. q.)

[THE BANISHED DUKE, IN THE FOREST, TO HIS FRIENDS.]—*Shakspear*

" Now my co-mates, and brothers in exile,
Hath not old custom made this life more sweet
Than that of painted pomp ? "

*Scorn:* (L. q.)

[SATAN TO ITHURIEL AND ZEPHON.]—*Milton.*

" Know ye not me ?   Ye knew me once no mate
For you; there sitting where ye durst not soar."

## 3 —*Reproachful Interrogation, and Indignant Surprise.*

*Reproachful Interrogation:* (S. q.)

[DEMOSTHENES TO THE ATHENIANS.]

" Will you forever, Athenians, do nothing but walk up and down the city, asking one another ' What news ?'

*Indignant Surprise:* (L. q.)

"' What news!'— Can anything be more new than that a man of Macedonia should lord it over Athens, and give laws to all Greece ? "

## 4.—*Surprise, and Contempt.*

*Surprise:* (S. q.)

[BANQUO, TO MACBETH, ON THE VANISHING OF THE WITCHES.]—*Shakspeare.*

" The earth hath bubbles, as the water has ,
And these are of them."

*Contempt:* (L. q.)

[FROM DRYDEN'S ODE FOR SAINT CECILIA'S DAY.]

" War, he sung, was toil and trouble,—
Honor but an empty bubble."

### 5.—*Impatience, and Awe.*

*Impatience:* (S. q.)

[CASSIUS, IN THE QUARREL WITH BRUTUS.]—*Shakspeare.*

' Ye gods! ye gods' must I endure all this?"

*Awe:* (L. q.)

[LEAR, IN THE THUNDER-STORM.]—*Ibid.*

" Let the great gods,
That keep this dreadful pother o'er our heads
Find out their enemies now."

### 6.—*Tranquillity, and Despair.*

*Tranquillity:* (M. q.[1])

ANONYMOUS LINES.

" He in his robe of virtue wraps himself,
And smiles at *Fate's* caprice!"

*Despair:* (L. q.)

" Fate! do thy worst!"

### PAUSES.

Time, when applied as a measure of speech, prescribes not only the length, or " quantity," of *sounds,* but also that of the *pauses,* or cessations of voice, which intervene between sentences and between their parts; as the intermissions of the voice are, *virtually,* though not nominally, constituents of " expression," whether we regard thought or feeling. Without distinct and appropriate pauses, we cannot understand oral communication; and without occasional impressive cessations of voice, there can be no true sympathy between speaker and hearer.

Pauses, as classified in elocution, are of two kinds: 1st, those which express *emotion;* 2d, those which modify *sense,* or meaning. Pausing, like utterance, is regulated by the character of the emotion, or the thought which is the subject of expression. The pauses used in the " expression" of all *grave, deep,* and *solemn* emotions, which incline to prolonged

---

[1] Moderate quantity.

" quantities," are comparatively *long*, and thus correspond, in character, to the vocal sounds between which they occur, and which they aid by their harmonious effect, as in the following instances:

Night,[1] ‖ sable goddess, ‖ from her ebon throne |
In rayless majesty | now stretches forth |
Her leaden sceptre | o'er a slumbering world.
Silence ‖ how dead! ‖‖ and darkness ‖ how profound!'

*Brisk*, *gay*, and *lively* feelings, are distinguished by brief " quantities," and corresponding short pauses, as in the following example:

" Haste thee | Nymph, | and bring with thee |
Mirth | and youthful jollity, |
Quips and cranks | and wanton wiles, |
Nods and becks | and wreathed smiles."

The pauses of *sense* or *meaning*, are of various lengths, according to the portions of speech which they are employed to separate; thus, we observe the long pauses between the principal parts of a discourse, the somewhat shorter pauses at its subdivisions, the shorter still at paragraphs, and the shorter than even these, at periods. Within a sentence itself, we can trace distinctly, in some instances, a principal pause at the middle, or the pause of compound clauses; and perhaps an inferior one, at or near the middle of each half, or the pause of simple clauses; and, on still closer examination, we find occasional shorter pauses in these subordinate portions, or the pause of phrases; and slight pauses even between words. The following sentence will exemplify these gradations of pausing.

" As we perceive the shadow | to have moved along the dialplate, | but did not perceive its moving; ‖ and it appears | that the grass has grown, | though nobody | ever saw it grow: ‖| so the advances we make in knowledge, | consist of minute

---

[1] The marks indicate the value or length of the pauses, from ‖‖| the longest within a sentence to ' the shortest.

successive steps; ‖ and we are unconscious of them. ǀ until we look back, | and thus become aware | of the distance | to which we have attained."

Pauses have sometimes been classified as follows: 1st, *Poetic* and *oratorical* pauses, or those which express *emotion*, and which are sometimes termed " impassioned " or " impressive ;" 2d, "*Rhetorical* pauses," or those which *divide* a *discourse* into its *heads* and *subdivisions*, and those which the *sense* and *structure* of a *sentence* demand, when taken in conjunction, as in the prose example preceding. These pauses are addressed to the *ear*, and, when they occur in a sentence, may, or may not, be indicated to the *eye*, by the ordinary punctuation; 3d, *Grammatical* pauses, — the *comma, semicolon, colon,* and *period,* — which are founded on the *syntactical structure* and *subdivision* of sentences. These pauses are addressed to the *eye,* and are always indicated by the usual points; 4th, *Prosodial* pauses, which are used only in *verse.*

1.—POETIC AND ORATORICAL PAUSES.

These pauses of emotion,—as they are sometimes termed, —are produced, for the most part, by feelings of *solemnity* and *pathos,* or by the affectation of these,—as in the style of *intentional exaggeration* and *bombast.* for the effect of *burlesque.*

Pauses of this description are sometimes superadded to the usual grammatical points, and sometimes are thrown in before or after, (sometimes both before and after,) an impassioned expression or emphatic word, in vivid passages of poetry or of declamatory prose,—without regard to the grammatical punctuation; and their length depends entirely on the feeling expressed in the passage in which they occur; they are *long* in *solemn,* and *short* in *lively* style.

Young readers, in particular, are often deficient in this most striking and impressive of all the effects of appropriate reading and recitation. It becomes, therefore, a matter of great moment, in practice, to cultivate the habit of watching the effect of full and long pauses, introduced at appropriate places. Without these the most solemn passages of Scripture, and the poetry of Milton and of Young, produce no effect, comparatively, on the mind; while reading, aided by their ' expressive silence," seems to be inspired with an unlimited power over the sympathies of the soul.

It will be useful, here, to review, once, on purpose, the examples prescribed for practice on long " quantities " and " indefinite " syllables, so as to trace the inseparable connection between the effect of these and of long pauses. The repetition of columns of words from the chapter on enunciation, will also be of great service, if the practice is varied occasionally, so as to produce the pauses of various moods of emotion, from the ordinary rate of "expression" to the most solemn and impressive.

### EXAMPLES OF POETIC AND ORATORICAL PAUSES

(Impassioned and Impressive Style.)

#### 1.— *Alarm, and Fear.*

[THE BALL AT BRUSSELS, ON THE EVE OF WATERLOO.]—*Byron.*

" And all went merry as a marriage bell:
But hush! || || hark! || || a deep sound || strikes like a rising knell!"

#### 2.— *Awe, and Terror.*

[SHIPWRECK.]—*Wilson.*

Many ports will exult at the gleam of her mast:
Hush! || hush! || thou vain dreamer! || this hour || || is her last. || ||
Her keel hath struck on a hidden rock; | [1]
And her planks are torn asunder; |
 And down come her masts with a reeling shock, |
And a hideous crash|| like thunder!"

#### 3.— *Horror.*

[BERNARDO DEL CARPIO, DISCOVERING THAT KING ALPHONSO HAS LED HIM FORTH TO SALUTE, NOT THE LIVING PERSON, BUT THE LIFELESS BODY, OF HIS FATHER.]—*Mrs. Hemans.*

" A lowly knee to earth he bent,—his father's hand he took— || ||
What was there in its touch, that all his fiery spirit shook? || ||
That hand was cold! || || a frozen thing:— || || it dropped from his like lead! || ||

He looked up to the face above— || the face was of the dead: || ||

A plume waved o'er the noble brow— || that brow was fixed and white: || ||
He met, at last, his father's eyes— || || but in them was no sight! ||'||
Up from the ground he sprang, and gazed— || || but who could paint that gaze? ||
They hushed their very hearts, || that saw its horror and amaze "

---

[1] Agitating emotions, such as those of *alarm hurry, terror,* and *confusion,* reduce the usual pauses to the shortest possible duration; so as to correspond to a rapid and breathless utterance inseparable from such feelings.

### 4.—*Stillness, and Awe.*

[NIGHT, FROM THE "NIGHT THOUGHTS."]—*Young.*

"Creation sleeps: |||| 't is as the general pulse of life | stood still! |
And nature made a pause, || an awful pause, || ||
Prophetic of her end!"

### 5.—*Solemnity, and Triumph.*

[CATO EXULTING IN THE CONTEMPLATION OF THE IMMORTALITY OF THE SOUL.]—*Addison.*

" The stars | shall fade away, || the sun ' himself |
Grow dim ' with age, || and Nature | sink ' in years,
But thou | shalt flourish ' in immortal youth, ||
Unhurt | amidst the war of elements, ||
The wreck of matter, || and the crush of worlds."

### 6.—*Grief.*

[ADAM'S LAMENTATION OVER THE FALL OF EVE.]—*Milton.*

" O fairest of creation! || last | and best |
Of all God's works, || creature in whom excelled
Whatever can to sight or thought be formed,
Holy, | divine, | good, | amiable, | or sweet! ||
How art thou lost, || || how on a sudden ' lost, ||
Defaced, || deflowered, || and how to death | devote!"

### 7.—*Contrition.*

[EVE IMPLORING FORGIVENESS OF ADAM.]—*Ibid.*

" On me | exercise not
Thy hatred | for this misery befallen,
On me | already lost, || me than thyself
More miserable! || || both | have sinned, || but thou |
Against God | only, I || against God | and thee; ||
And to the place of judgment ' will return, ||
There | with my cries ' importune Heaven, that all
The sentence | from thy head removed, may light
On me, || sole cause ' to thee | of all this woe. ||
Me, me only, || just object of His ire!"

## 8 —*Remorse, and Despair.*

[SATAN RECALLING THE BOAST WITH WHICH HE ARRAYED HIS LEGIONS, IN REBELLION.] —*Ibid.*

" Ay me! || they little know |
How dearly I abide that boast so vain, |
Under what torments | inwardly I groan, ||
While they adore me on the throne of hell! || ||
With diadem | and sceptre | high advanced |
The lower still I fall, || only supreme
In misery! || || Such joy | ambition finds."

## 9.—*Horror.*

[BURKE'S DESCRIPTION OF THE DESOLATION EFFECTED BY HYDER ALI AND HIS SON.] —*Burke.*

" So completely did these masters in their art, Hyder Ali, and his more ferocious son, absolve themselves of their impious vow, that when the British armies traversed, as they did, the Carnatic, for hundreds of miles, in all directions,— through the whole line of their march, | they did not see one man, | not one woman, || not one child, || || not one four-footed beast || of any description whatever. One | dead | uniform | silence || reigned | over the whole region."

## 10.—*Oratorical Interrogation.*

[BRUTUS'S HARANGUE TO THE PEOPLE, AFTER THE ASSASSINATION OF CÆSAR.] —*Shakspeare.*

' Who's here so base that would be a bondman? — || If any, speak; || for him have I offended. || || Who's here so rude, that would not be a Roman?— || If any, speak; || for him have I offended. || || Who's here so vile, that will not love his country?— || If any, speak; || for him have I offended.— || || I pause for a reply."

## II.—" RHETORICAL" PAUSES.

These are of great practical utility in reading; as, besides prescribing the indispensable long pauses at heads of discourse and paragraphs, they direct the voice to many cessations of utterance, which are not indicated by the usual punctuation of sentences. Their chief use is to supply the deficiency arising from the inadequacy of points, or grammatical punctuation, to mark all the places at which a pause necessarily occurs in reading.

The " rhetorical' pauses often coincide with the usual points; but they apply, also, in many cases in which no point is used. The common grammatical punctuation, (indicated by the comma, semicolon, colon, and period,) coincides, in most instances, with the cessations of voice which meaning requires. But this is not always the case; as they sometimes occur where the *syntax* of a sentence is interrupted or terminated, for the time, but where the *sense* requires no pause. "Rhetorical" pauses regard the *sense* of a sentence, and are intended for the *ear:* grammatical punctuation refers to the *syntactical structure* of a sentence, and is addressed to the *eye*. The "rhetorical" pauses are of indefinite length, and always vary, as to their duration, with the sentiment and the utterance, as brisk and animated, or slow and grave. Grammatical pauses have a fixed and uniform value, as representing the component parts of a sentence as such, and, in reading aloud, can seldom be appropriately used, as sometimes directed, by a process of counting, — " one, at a comma; two, at a semicolon;" &c., since the feelings which are expressed by the sentence, may, in one part of it, be lively and rapid, and in another solemn and slow; as in the following instance.

" Your house ' is finished, ' sir, | at last;
A narrower house, || || a house of clay."

"Rhetorical" pauses may be briefly classed in the manner before exemplified, in application to long and compound sentences, as dividing the whole, first, into two main parts, or *compound clauses,*— then, these into two minor portions, or *simple clauses,*—these again into *phrases,*—last of all, these *phrases* into *words*.

It is not meant that in every compound sentence all these divisions or subdivisions are invariably found, or that there may not be several successive principal and subordinate parts in one sentence. But in most compound sentences, and in many simple sentences, several of them will be found, and particularly the last two, — the rhetorical pause between *clauses* and *words,* — as in the following instances: " In a few days | the country was overrun." "They fled ' in haste." " The enemy ' approached."

The careful observance of the " rhetorical" pause, is one of the chief means of distinctness in the expression of thought. In *narration* and *description*, and in *plain didactic style*, it is equally important that the successive sounds of the voice should be relieved from each other, in portions best adapted to present the component parts of the whole in a clear, distinct, impressive manner, according to their comparative length and importance. The thought or sentiment which is thus communicated, falls on the ear with a definite and satisfactory succession of sounds, which the mind easily receives and appreciates. The parts being thus exactly given, each takes its own due weight, and at the same time, enhances the effect of the whole. The result is that the communication is fully understood and makes its just impression.

But young readers, especially, are apt to hasten on, in the act of reading till they come to a full stop; and even then to slight the due pause. This hurried mode of reading, renders it impossible to give a sentiment force or weight to the ear. Much time, therefore, should be spent in reading sentences of an unimpassioned character, such as usually require the most frequent application of the "rhetorical" pause. The following examples will serve to suggest the most important applications of this pause.

EXAMPLES OF THE "RHETORICAL" PAUSE.

### I.—*Between Phrases.*

*Phrases commencing with a Preposition.*

1. " Depart to the house which has | in this city | been prepared | for thy residence."

2. " My heart was wounded | with the arrow of affliction, and my eyes became dim | with sorrow."

3. " To increase the austerity of my life, I frequently watched all night, sitting at the entrance of the cave | with my face to the east, resigning myself | to the secret influences of the Prophet."

4. " When I awaked, I laid my forehead upon the ground, and blessed the Prophet | for the instruction of the morning."

5. " The king, whose doubts were now removed, looked up | with a smile that communicated the joy of his mind."

*Phrases commencing with an Adverb.*

1. " He has passed to that world | where the weary are at rest "

2. " The voice of Heaven summons you in these hours | when the leaves fall, and the winter is gathering."

3. " Be entreated to make the decisive effort | ere it be too late."

4. "He continued steadfast in his purpose | while others wavered."

*Phrases commencing with a Conjunction.*

1. "It is more blessed to give | than to receive."
2. "Yet I know not | whether my danger is a reality | or a dream."
3. "In the spirit of sympathy, we call on rocks | and streams | and forests || to witness | and share our emotions."
4. "The same sun which now marks the autumn of the year, will again arise in his brightness, and bring along with him the promise of the spring | and all the magnificence of summer."
5. "The voice of despair now whispers | that all exertion is in vain."
6. "We are often deceived | because we are willing to be deceived."

## II.—*Between Words.*

*The Nominative and the Verb.*

1. "The breeze | died away, as the sun | sank behind the hills."
2. "The smoke | rises not through the trees: for the honors of the grove | are fallen."
3. "Weeping | may endure for a night; but joy | cometh in the morning."

*Ellipsis.*

"Add to your faith virtue; and to virtue | knowledge; and to knowledge | temperance; and to temperance | patience.'

## III.—GRAMMATICAL PAUSES.

The due observance of the pauses indicated by grammatical punctuation, is one of the useful and effectual means of arresting the attention of young learners, and accustoming them to mark distinctly the component portions of a sentence. But the common fault of school reading, and, sometimes, of professional exercises,—a uniform

---

[1] For further statement and illustration of "rhetorical" pauses, see "American Elocutionist." The "prosodial pauses" will be found on a subsequent page of this manual, and, at greater length, in the "Elocutionist."

and mechanical style, — is, in part, owing to exact compliance with the direction to pause, invariably, for a given time at each point. A change of feeling, or a shade of meaning, may lengthen, shorten, or destroy the usual pause at a comma. The syntax of a sentence may demand a separating point, where oral expression glides on continuously, and allows no break. The converse is as true. The rule of syntax may forbid a comma where a sudden change of feeling may produce a pause longer than that usually made at a period.—A most instructive lesson in elocution is given by Sterne, in his satirical sketch of the literal critic, with stop-watch in his hand, taking note of Garrick's "ungrammatical" pause between the nominative and the verb.

The mistake, however, is too generally sanctioned by books and teachers, that the comma, semicolon, &c., are intended as guides to the *ear*. They do, no doubt, *incidentally*, serve this purpose,—but by no means uniformly. The design of grammatical punctuation is to aid the *eye* of the reader, in resolving a sentence into its *syntactical* portions. These often coincide, in phrases and clauses, with the natural cessations of voice, which mark the divisions and subdivisions of utterance that constitute the portions of the oral expression of a thought: they enable the reader to refer a given word or clause to another at a distance from it in place, but connected with it in sense, and thus aid his apprehension of its meaning. But, in many cases, this coincidence of grammatical and rhetorical pausing does not take place. Even the close punctuation adopted in modern typography, does not present all the pauses which feeling and sentiment, or abstract thought itself, require; as may be seen by running the eye over the rhetorical and other pauses marked in the exercises occurring in preceding pages. Nor is it possible to read correctly, in many instances, without omitting a pause at the grammatical points; as may be observed even in the familiar phrases, "Yes, sir,"—"no, sir." The comma, if followed as a guide, would here produce an awkward, limping gait of voice,—resembling that of a young child in its first lessons.

The exercise of reading aloud has but one true, safe, and uniform standard,—the *ear*,—or, rather the intuitive perception of the mind. The comma and other ocular points are, at best, but collateral and incidental aids,—not always to be depended on; and, sometimes, they are to be regarded as impediments which emotion is to put down in order to attain true expression.

The general rule of elocution, then, as regards the comma, semicolon, and colon, if we use them as guides to the voice, —must be, to follow them only so far as they coincide with the meaning, and to lengthen or shorten, or omit the pauses corresponding to them, as the sentiment or emotion expressed in a sentence may require, in slow or in lively utterance;— but especially to remember that there may be a long pause of feeling, where no grammatical point occurs.

## "MOVEMENT."

The application of "time" to speech, includes, in addition to points already discussed, the consideration of the rate of voice in *successive* sounds, — sometimes regulated by the predominating "quantities" of a passage, whether these be *long*, as in the *solemn* and *slow* utterance of "indefinite" syllables, or *short*, as in the *brisk* and *rapid* utterance of "immutable" syllables. "Movement," however, has its primary foundation on *emotion;* and although, in poetry, the "quantities" are often beautifully adapted, by the poet's natural ear and prosodial skill, to the expression of emotion, they are not uniformly so; and in prose, — which exhibits the effect of "movement" as distinctly as poetry, — less regard is usually paid to the effect of mere "quantity." "Movement," therefore, requires a distinct attention, as a separate element of expression in the voice, and of effect in elocution.

The term "movement," for which the word "*rate*" is sometimes substituted, has the same application in elocution as in music; and while "quantity" regards *single* sounds as *long* or *short*, "movement" regards *successive* or *consecutive* sounds as *fast* or *slow*. It unites, too, with "quantity" in regulating the length of pauses; as we find that *slow* "movement," as well as *long* "quantity," requires *long* pauses; and that *brisk*, or rapid "movement," and *brief* "quantity," equally require *short* pauses.

"Movement," in elocution, is not measured with the comparative exactness implied in the musical terms, *adagio, andante, mezzo, vivace, allegro, presto,* &c. It approaches however, to a considerable degree of definiteness in its use of the designations "slowest," or "very slow;" "slow;" "moderate;" "lively;" "brisk," or "quick;" and "rapid,' "quickest," or "very quick."

The "slowest," or "very slow movement," is exemplified in the expression of the *deepest emotions* of the soul; as *horror, awe, profound reverence* and *solemnity,* and *adoration.* — The "slow movement" characterizes the utterance of *gloom, melancholy, grief, pathos, sublimity, solemnity* and *reverence,* in their usual form, *profound repose, grandeur majesty, vastness, power,* and *splendor.* — "Moderate movement" is the usual rate of utterance in unimpassioned language. It belongs to common narration and description, and to didactic thought. The rhetorical modes of style to which it is applicable, are those which are denominated the " dry," the " plain," and the " neat."—" Lively movement" implies emotion in that gentle form which does not exceed *liveliness*, or *animation*. The lower degrees of all vivid feeling, are expressed by this style of " movement." A *slight* degree of *joy* is usually the under current of its effect.—" Quick" or " brisk movement," is characteristic of *gay*, *exhilarated*, and *glad* emotion : the *full* feeling of joy is implied in its " expression." It gives utterance to all *playful*, *humorous*, and *mirthful moods*. It sometimes, on the other hand, gives its characteristic effect to *fear*.—The "movement" designated as ' quickest," " very quick," or " rapid," is that of *haste, hurry, alarm, confusion*, and *fear*, when rising to *terror*.

It is evident from the very nature of " movement," that it must be an element of immense power, in expression. The funeral march suggests to the ear its effect, in music, as associated with *awe, gloom*, and *grief;* and the music of the dance reminds us of its power over the feelings of *gladness* and *exhilaration*. The grave psalm, and the song of serious sentiment, express, in their measured regularity, the adaptation of *gentle* and " *moderate movement* " to *tranquil* and *sedate* feeling.

Similar effects, in degree, characterize the use of the voice, in recitation and in reading. Appropriate elocution accommodates the movement of the voice to every mood of thought, — from the *slowest, prolonged*, and *lingering* utterance of *deep contemplation*, and *profound awe*, to the *swift* and *rapid* strains of *lyric rapture* and *ecstasy*. Every mood of mind has its appropriate " movement," or '' rate " of utterance, as definitely expressed as its " quality " of voice, its characteristic " force," or its peculiar " pitch," " slide," or " wave." Utterance, to be natural and effective, must have the genuine expression of its appropriate " movement." *Solemnity* cannot exist, to the ear, without *slowness*, nor *gaiety* without *briskness* of utterance, *gravity* without *sedate* style, nor *animation* without a *lively* " movement."

The power of " movement," in the elocution of a skilful reader or speaker, is indefinite ; as we may observe in the difference between a schoolboy gabbling through his task, in haste to get rid of it, and a great tragedian, whose whole soul is rapt in the part of Cato uttering the soliloquy on immortality, or Hamlet musing on the great themes of duty, life, and death.

A command over the " lively " and " brisk movements " of the voice, is not less important than the power of slow and solemn utterance. The style of reading which is most frequently introduced to enliven the evening circle at home, requires of the reader the power to "trip it as he goes," in the mood of *gay description, light satire, vivid dialogue,* and *droll humor.*

The three principal faults of " movement," which are exemplified in the common practice of reading, are *uniform slowness,* or, perhaps a *drawling* style ; *habitual rapidity,* which *prevents* all *deep* and *impressive* effect, and, perhaps, causes *indistinctness of enunciation;* a *uniform " moderate "* " movement," which never yields to any natural influence of emotion,—so as to become appropriately expressive, and pass from *grave* to *gay,* or the reverse, by a change in the gait of the voice,—but utters, automaton-like, all feelings in the same unmeaning and mechanical style; the voice marching on, with one uniform measured step, over all varieties of surface, as regards the tenor of language and the subject.

The following examples of " movement " should be assiduously practised, in conjunction with the elements and with tables of words, selected as exercises for this purpose, from the chapter on enunciation. The repetition of such exercises should be continued till the student can execute with perfect precision, and with the utmost readiness, all the " movements " enumerated in the classification.

EXAMPLES OF " MOVEMENT."

I.—"*Slowest Movement.*"

*Amazement, Awe, and Horror.*

[FROM BYRON'S DREAM OF DARKNESS.]

(' Aspirated pectoral quality :" " Suppressed " force : " Median stress :" " Lowest pitch :" Prevalent " monotone :" Extremely long pauses.)

" I had a dream which was not all a dream.
The bright sun was extinguished ; and the stars
Did wander darkling in the eternal space,
Rayless, and pathless ; and the icy earth
Swung blind and blackening in the moonless air;
Morn came, and went,—and came, and brought no day
    " The world was void .
The populous and the powerful was a lump,—
Seasonless herbless, treeless, manless, lifeless,—
A lump of death—a chaos of hard clay.
The rivers, lakes, and ocean, all stood still ;
And nothing stirred within their silent depths:
Ships, sailorless, lay rotting on the sea ;
And their masts fell down piecemeal: as they dropped

They slept on the abyss without a surge;—
The waves were dead; the tides were in their grave
The moon, their mistress, had expired before;
The winds were withered in the stagnant air;
And the clouds perished: Darkness had no need
Of aid from them,— She was the universe."

2.—*Profound Reverence, Solemnity, and Adoration.*

[DERZHAVIN'S HYMN.]—*Bowring.*

(" Effusive and expulsive orotund:" " Pectoral quality:" " Subdued" force: " Median stress:" " Low pitch:" Prevalent " downward slide," occasional " monotone:" Pauses extremely long.)

" Thou from primeval nothingness didst call
First chaos, then existence:— Lord! on thee
Eternity had its foundation;— all
Sprung forth from Thee,— of light, joy, harmony,
Sole origin:— all life, all beauty thine.
Thy word created all, and doth create;
Thy splendor fills all space with rays divine.
Thou art, and wert, and shalt be! Glorious! great!
Light-giving, life-sustaining Potentate!"

II.—"*Slow Movement.*'

1.—*Reverence, Gratitude, and Praise.*

[FROM THE BOOK OF PSALMS.]

(" Effusive orotund quality:" " Subdued " force: " Median stress:" " Low pitch:" Prevalent " downward slide:" Long pauses.)

" O Lord, our Lord, how excellent is Thy name in all the earth who hast set Thy glory above the heavens.

" When I consider Thy heavens, the work of Thy fingers; the moon and the stars, which Thou hast ordained; what is man that Thou art mindful of him? and the son of man, that Thou visitest him?

" For Thou hast made him a little lower than the angels, and hast crowned him with glory and honor. Thou madest him to have dominion over the works of Thy hands: Thou hast put all things under his feet.

"O Lord, our Lord, how excellent is Thy name in all the earth!"

### 2.—*Sublimity, Majesty, and Power.*

[FROM DAVID'S PSALM OF PRAISE, ON HIS DELIVERANCE FROM HIS ENEMIES.]

("Expulsive orotund:" "Impassioned" force: "Radical and Median stress:" "Low pitch:" Prevalent "downward slide," occasional "monotone:" Long pauses.)

"Then the earth shook and trembled: the foundations of heaven moved and shook, because he was wroth. There went up a smoke out of his nostrils; and fire out of his mouth devoured: coals were kindled by it. He bowed the heavens, also, and came down; and darkness was under his feet; and he rode upon a cherub, and did fly; and he was seen upon the wings of the wind; and he made darkness pavilions round about him, dark waters, and thick clouds of the skies. The Lord thundered from heaven, and the Most High uttered his voice; and he sent out arrows and scattered them; lightning, and discomfited them. And the channels of the sea appeared; the foundations of the world were discovered at the rebuking of the Lord, at the blast of the breath of his nostrils."

### 3.—*Splendor.*

[THE PALACE OF PANDEMONIUM.]—*Milton.*

('Effusive and expulsive orotund:" "Moderate" force: "Median stress:" "Low pitch:" Prevalent "monotone:" Pauses of moderate length.)

"Anon out of the earth a fabric huge
Rose like an exhalation, with the sound
Of dulcet symphonies, and voices sweet,
Built like a temple, where pilasters round
Were set, and Doric pillars, overlaid
With golden architrave; nor did there want

Cornice, or frieze, with bossy sculptures graven;
The roof was fretted gold. Not Babylon,
Nor great Alcairo, such magnificence
Equalled in all their glories, to enshrine
Belus, or Serapis, their gods ; or seat
Their kings, when Egypt with Assyria strove
In wealth and luxury. The ascending pile
Stood fixed her stately height: and straight the doors
Opening their brazen folds, discover wide
Within, her ample spaces, o'er the smooth
And level pavement: from the arched roof,
Pendent by subtle magic, many a row
Of starry lamps, and blazing cressets, fed
With naptha and asphaltus, yielded light
As from a sky."

III.—*"Moderate Movement."*

1.—*Narrative Style.*

[DESTRUCTION OF CARTHAGE.] —*Anonymous.*

("Pure tone:" "Moderate" force: "Unimpassioned radical stress:" "Middle pitch:" Varied "slides:" Moderate pauses.)

" The city and republic of Carthage were destroyed by the termination of the third Punic war, about one hundred and fifty years before Christ. The city was in flames during seventeen days ; and the news of its destruction caused the greatest joy at Rome. The Roman senate immediately appointed commissioners, not only to raze the walls of Carthage, but even to demolish and burn the very materials of which they were made ; and, in a few days, that city, which had once been the seat of commerce, the model of magnificence, the common storehouse of the wealth of nations, and one of the most powerful states in the world, left behind no trace of its splendor, of its power, or even of its existence.— The history of Carthage is one of the many proofs that we have of the transient nature of worldly glory ; for, of all her grandeur, not a wreck remains. Her own walls, like the calm ocean, that conceals forever the riches hid in its unsearchable abyss, now obscure all her magnificence."

### 2. — *Descriptive Style.*

[ASPECT OF EGYPT.] — *Addison.*

(" Pure tone:" " Moderate " force : " Unimpassioned radical " and gentle " median stress :" " Middle pitch :" Varied " slides :" Moderate pauses.)

" There cannot be a finer sight than Egypt, at two seasons of the year. For, if we ascend one of the pyramids, in the months of July and August, we behold, in the swollen waters of the Nile, a vast sea, in which numberless towns and villages appear, with several causeways leading from place to place; the whole interspersed with groves and fruit-trees, whose tops only are visible;—all which forms a delightful prospect. This view is bounded by mountains and woods, which terminate,—at the utmost distance the eye can discover,—the most beautiful horizon that can be imagined.—In winter, on the contrary, that is to say, in the months of January and February, the whole country is like one continuous scene of beautiful meadows, whose verdure, enamelled with flowers, charms the eye. The spectator beholds, on every side, flocks and herds dispersed over all the plains, with infinite numbers of husbandmen and gardeners. The air is then perfumed by the great quantity of blossoms on the orange, lemon, and other trees, and is so pure that a wholesomer or more agreeable is not to be found in the world; so that nature being then dead, as it were, in all other climates seems to be alive only for so delightful an abode.",

### 3. — *Didactic Style.*

[REASON AND INSTINCT.] — *Addison.*

" Pure tone :" " Moderate " force : " Unimpassioned radical stress :" " Middle pitch :" " Varied slides :" Moderate pauses.)

" One would wonder to hear skeptical men disputing for the reason of animals, and telling us it is only our pride and prejudices that will not allow them the use of that faculty.

"Reason shows itself in all occurrences of life; whereas the brute makes no discovery of such a talent but in what immediately regards his own preservation, or the continuance of his species. Animals, in their generation, are wiser than the sons of men; but their wisdom is confined to a few particulars, and lies in a very narrow compass. Take a brute out of his instinct, and you find him wholly deprived of understanding.— There is not, in my opinion, anything more mysterious in nature, than this instinct in animals, which thus rises above reason, and falls infinitely short of it. It cannot be accounted for by any properties in matter, and, at the same time, works after so odd a manner, that one cannot think it the faculty of an intellectual being. For my own part, I look upon it as upon the principle of gravitation in bodies, which is not to be explained by any known qualities inherent in the bodies themselves, nor from any laws of mechanism, but according to the best notions of the greatest philosophers, is an immediate impression from the **First Mover**, and the Divine energy acting in the creatures."

IV. —*"Animated, or Lively Movement."*

1. —*Narrative Style.*

[SUCCESSIVE DECLINE OF POPULAR FALLACIES.] —*Goldsmith.*

("Pure tone:" "Moderate" force: "Unimpassioned radical stress:" "Middle pitch:" Varied "slides:" Short pauses.)

"I have lived to see generals who once had crowds hallooing after them wherever they went, who were bepraised by newspapers and magazines,—those echoes of the voice of the vulgar; and yet they have long sunk into merited obscurity, with scarce even an epitaph left to flatter.— A few years ago, the herring-fishery employed all Grub street: it was the topic in every coffee-house, and the burden of every ballad. We were to drag up oceans of gold from the bottom of the sea: we were to supply all Europe with herrings, upon our own terms. At present, we hear no more of all this. We have fished up very little gold that *I* can learn nor do we furnish the world with herrings, as was expected. --Let us wait but a few years longer, and we shall fin l all our expectations a herring-fishery."

## 2.—*Descriptive Style.*

[RIDICULOUSNESS OF SELF-IMPORTANCE.] —*Goldsmith.*

("Pure tone:" "Moderate" force: "Expulsive median stress:' " Middle pitch:" Varied " slides:" Varied pauses.)

" There is scarce a village in Europe, and not one university, that is not furnished with its little great men. The head of a petty corporation, who opposes the designs of a prince who would tyrannically force his subjects to save their best clothes for Sundays; the puny pedant, who finds one undiscovered quality in the polypus, or describes an unheeded process in the skeleton of a mole, and whose mind, like his microscope, perceives nature only in detail; the rhymer, who makes smooth verses, and paints to our imagination, when he should only speak to our hearts; all equally fancy themselves walking forward to immortality, and desire the crowd behind them to look on. The crowd takes them at their word! ' Patriot philosopher, and poet!' are shouted in their train. ' Where was there ever so much merit seen? no times so important as our own! ages, yet unborn, shall gaze with wonder and applause!' To such music the important pigmy moves forward, bustling and swelling, and aptly compared to a puddle in a storm."

## 3.—*Didactic Style.*

[ABSURDITY AND IMPUDENCE.] —*Addison.*

("Pure tone:" "Moderate" force: " Unimpassioned radical stress." " Middle pitch:" Varied " slides:" Short pauses )

" If we would examine into the secret springs of action, in the impudent and the absurd, we shall find, though they bear a great resemblance in their behavior, that they move upon very different principles. The impudent are pressing though they know they are disagreeable; the absurd are importurate, because they think they are acceptable impudence is a vice, and absurdity a folly. Sir Francis Bacon talks very agreeably upon the subject of impudence. He takes notice, that the Orator being asked, what was the first, second, and third requisite to make a fine speaker? still answered, *Action*. This, said he, is the very outward form of speaking; and yet it is what, with the generality, has more force than the most consummate abilities. Impudence is, to the rest of mankind, of the same use which action is to orators "

### V.—"*Brisk, Gay, or Quick Movement.*"
### 1.—*Narrative Style.*

[LOCHINVAR'S EXPLOIT OF CARRYING OFF ELLEN OF NETHERBY.]—*Scott.*

(*Haste, Joy, Hurry.*— " Expulsive and explosive orotund :" " Impassioned " and shouting force : " Impassioned radical and median stress :" " High pitch :" Varied " slides :" Extremely short pauses.)

" One touch to her hand, and one word in her ear,—
When they reached the hall door, and the charger stood near ;
So light to the croupe the fair lady he swung,—
So light to the saddle before her he sprung !
' She is won !— we are gone, over bank, bush, and scaur,
They 'll have fleet steeds that follow,' quoth young Lochinvar.

" There was mounting 'mong Græmes of the Netherby clan ;
Forsters, Fenwicks, and Musgraves, they rode and they ran :-
There was racing, and chasing, on Cannobie Lee ;
But the lost bride of Netherby ne'er did they see.—
So daring in love, and so dauntless in war, .
Have ye e'er heard of gallant like young Lochinvar?"

### 2.—*Descriptive Style.*

[REPULSE OF THE ARCHERS :—BATTLE OF BEAL AN DHUINE. —*Scott*

(*Haste, Fear, Alarm.*— " Explosive orotund :" " Impassioned " force : " Radical stress :" " High pitch :" Extremely short pauses.)

" Forth from the pass in tumult driven,
Like chaff before the winds of heaven,
The archery appear ;

For life, for life their flight they ply;
While shriek and shout and battle cry,
And plaids and bonnets waving high,
And broadswords flashing to the sky,-
Are maddening in their rear."

### 3.—*Bold Address.*

[THE GHEBER TO HIS FOLLOWERS.]—*Moore.*

(*Courage, Revenge.*—" Explosive orotund, aspirated quality:"
"Impassioned" force : " Radical stress :" " High pitch ;" Varied
"slides :" Short pauses.)

"What! while our arms can wield these blades
Shall we die tamely? die alone?
Without one victim to our shades,
One Moslem heart, where, buried deep,
The sabre from its toil may sleep?
No—God of Iran's burning skies!
Thou scorn'st the inglorious sacrifice.
No—though of all earth's hope bereft,
Life, swords, and vengeance still are left.—
We'll make yon valley's reeking caves
Live in the awe-struck minds of men,
Till tyrants shudder, when their slaves
Tell of the Ghebers' bloody glen.
Follow, brave hearts!—this pile remains
Our refuge still from life and chains."

### 4.—*Playful and Humorous Description.*

[CARNIVAL SCENES IN VENICE.] — *Byron.*

(*Mirth and Exhilaration.*—" Pure tone :" " Moderate" force
" Radical stress :" " High pitch ;" " Monotone :" Extremely
short pauses.)

" And gaiety on restless tiptoe hovers,
Giggling with all the gallants who beset her;
And there are songs and quavers, roaring, humming
Guitars, and every other sort of strumming.

And there are dresses, splendid, but fantastical,
Masks of all times and nations, Turks and Jews,
And harlequins and clowns, with feats gymnastical,
Greeks, Romans, Yankee-doodles, and Hindoos."

5. — *Anger, Fierce and Stubborn Resolve.*

[CORIOLANUS, MADDENED AGAINST THE ROMAN POPULACE.] — *Shakspeare.*

("Aspirated quality:" Intensely "impassioned" force: "Explosive radical and vanishing stress:" "High pitch:" Downward "slide" of "fifth" and "octave." Extremely short pauses.)

"Let them pull all about mine ears; present me
Death on the wheel, or at wild horses' heels;
Or pile ten hills on the Tarpeian rock,
That the precipitation might down stretch
Below the beam of sight; yet will I still
Be thus to them."

VI. — *"Rapid, or Quickest Movement."*

*Lyric Style.*

[MAZEPPA, BOUND ON THE WILD HORSE.] — *Byron.*

("Aspirated quality:" "Impassioned" force: "Radical stress:" "High pitch:" Prevalent "monotone:" Extremely short pauses.)

"Away! — away! — and on we dash! - -
Torrents less rapid and less rash.
" Away, away, my steed and I,
 Upon the pinions of the wind,
 All human dwellings left behind:
 We sped like meteors through the sky,
 When with its crackling sound the night
 Is chequered with the northern light: —
" From out the forest prance
 A trampling troop, — I see them come!
 A thousand horse — and none to ride ' —
 With flowing tail, and flying mane,
 Wide nostrils, never stretched by pain,
 Mouths bloodless to the bit or rein,

And feet that iron never shod,
And flanks unscarred by spur or rod,—
A thousand horse,—the wild, the free,—
Like waves that follow o'er the sea,
  Came thickly thundering on:—
They stop,—they start—they snuff the air,
Gallop a moment here and there,
Approach, retire, wheel round and round,
Then plunging back with sudden bound,—
They snort,—they foam—neigh—swerve aside,
And backward to the forest fly,
By instinct, from a human eye."

### ACCENT.

#### 1.—"*Syllabic*" *Accent*.

The word "accent" has been usually considered as restricted to the designation of the comparative *force* of syllables, as they occur in the pronunciation of words. Dr. Rush, however, has, by the accustomed closeness and fidelity of his analysis, distinctly shown, that force is but *one* constituent, or form of accent; and that besides this mere comparative loudness, there are two other constituents of accent.

The modes of accent are determined as follows: 1st, " Immutable" syllables,—those which are constituted by fixed short quantities,"—are accented by "radical stress," "impassioned," "explosive,' or "unimpassioned," as the case may be, from the character of the utterance which marks the passage or the word in which such a syllable occurs. Thus, the word "*victory*," although consisting of three short syllables, has a decided and distinct accent on its first syllable, by means of "radical stress," whether we pronounce the word with impassioned "expression," or merely according to the rule of orthoëpical accent.

2d, "Mutable" syllables,—those which consist of "variable quantities," or such as admit of comparative prolongation,—may be accented by merely a louder sound, or greater force, pervading the given syllable, as compared with the others of the same word. Thus the word "*adjutant*" having a sufficient prolongation on its first *a*, to render the "radical stress" unnecessary, as a distinction,—may have its accent marked merely by comparative loudness of the "concrete" *ad-* although in impassioned utterance, it may be marked, also in part, by "radical stress," and a degree of prolongation. 3d, "Indefinite" syllables, or those which are constituted by prolonged "quantity," may be accented by their comparative long duration.

The distinctive element of such syllables being "time," Dr. Rush has designated them as possessing "temporal" accent. The *o*, in the word "*holy,*" is an instance. Syllables of this description may of course be executed with the additional accent arising from "loud concrete;" and, in impassioned utterance, they may be farther distinguished by abrupt "radical stress." But the "loud concrete," and "temporal accent," cannot be exhibited on "immutable" syllables.

The effect of all these modes of accent, is to impart prominence and impressiveness of sound to one syllable in most words, though, in some, to two syllables.

A syllable, in orthoëpy, consists, properly, of an entire "concrete," or the constituent radical and vanishing movement, requisite to constitute a sound in speech, as distinguished from one in music. Instances may be found in the simple element *a*, in *at;* in the compound *a*, in *ale;* in the consecutive "tonic" and "subtonic" *a* and *ll* in *all;* in the consecutive "tonic and subtonics" of the word *old;* or in the sequence of "aspiration," "tonic" "subtonic," and "atonic." in the word *halt.*

Correct accent is indispensable in reading and speaking,— not merely as a convenience of intelligible expression, and as a result of competent education, but as an indication of intelligence and of taste, in regard to language, and as an element of all distinct and spirited expression. The accented syllable of every expressive word, becomes the seat of life in utterance; and there can be no surer way to render the exercise of reading unmeaning and uninteresting, than to indulge the three prevalent faults of slighting the accent of words, unduly prolonging and forcing it, and distributing its effect over several syllables of a word instead of confining it to one

The single word "*promotion*" may suffice as an example of these faults. In the characteristic local accent of New England, the frequent use of the "wave," or "circumflex," and of consequent prolongation of sound, presents the word to the ear in the form of two separate words, or of systematic and formal syllabication in one; thus, "*pro motion*," or "*pro-motion*." The current usage of the Middle States, on the other hand, obscures the first *o* of the word, so as to reduce it nearly to a short *u*, and sinks the last *o* entirely. In this case, the word is pronounced *prŭmoshn*.

Few exercises would prove more useful for the purposes of education, in schools, or more serviceable to adult students, than the practice of reading aloud, daily, from the columns of a dictionary. Woids, when contemplated in this detached state, make a more distinct impression, both on the eye and the ear, — as far as regards their component elements of letters and sounds, than when they are read in connexion in sentences, in which case the attention is always prone to slight the sound, and dwell upon the sense. Preparatory training, and remedial discipline, require, first, a thorough course of enunciation for the definite and exact execution of every sound and syllable, and, subsequently, a special series of exercises including the union of sound and sense, in connected and consecutive expression.

The exercises which were prescribed under the head of "quantity," are so arranged as to admit of being converted into a systematic course of practice in accent, with a view to trace the constituent elements of syllables, in relation to accent, as always necessarily decided by the distinctions of "indefinite," "mutable," and "immutable." It is unnecessary, therefore, to repeat the syllabic exercises in the pages of the book. The teacher and the student can accomplish the object of practice, by reverting to them, and repeating such as best exemplify the different species of accent, — "radical," "concrete," and "temporal."

## II. — "*Rhythmical*" *Accent.*

The subject of accent is now to be considered in connexion not with single words, but *the sequence of phrases, in the utterance of successive sentences*, and as constituting an important part of the study of "time" applied to the current of the voice, in the continuous exercises of speech, reading, or recitation.

The first or lowest degree of musical accent, is called "rhythm;" the term, by its derivation, implying a comparison between the continuous *flow* of the voice in speech, and the motion of a stream, as contrasted with the still water of a lake. The voice, in the enunciation of a single sound or word, is comparatively stationary· in the utterance of successive sounds, it has something like progressive motion. This motion may be varied and irregular; or it may be uniform and measured; as the stream, when flowing over an uneven and rocky bed, may exhibit all varieties of motion, but when gliding along a smooth channel, may keep a regular rate of time, that may be exactly defined.

The " movement " of the voice in *conversation*, on light or ordinary subjects, is variable and irregular; on subjects of greater moment, it is more even and sedate; and, in the expression of deep and energetic sentiment, it becomes still more regular, and, perhaps to a certain degree, measured, in its rate of " movement." *Reading* is a mode of voice yet more distinctly marked in " movement," by its partial uniformity of utterance ; and *declamation* advances another degree, still, in " rhythm," by its deliberate and formal succession of sound. The reading or recitation of *poetry*, carries the " movement " to its highest degree of fixed and well marked " rhythm," as determined by the structure of *verse*, which derives its pleasing effect to the ear from the exact observance of a continued uniform, or correspondent " rhythm." The word " metre," or " measure," has accordingly its appropriate application to this species of " movement."

As " time " includes the duration of pauses as well as of " quantities," and of " movement," it necessarily comprehends under " rhythm " the exact proportion of pauses to sound, in the rate of utterance, when regulated by " rhythmical " accent. A part of the effect of " rhythm " on the ear, must arise, therefore, from the " time " of regularly recurring and exactly proportioned pauses. The full definition of " rhythm " would, accordingly, be, the effect of " time," in regularly returning " quantity," accent, and pause, in the successive sounds of the voice.

In the usual forms of familiar prose writing, little regard is paid to he placing of words, as respects the effect of accent Words, in plain, unpretending composition, follow each other, with but slight reference to the result in mere sound. Some writers, however, are distinguished by a style which is more or less measured and rhythmical to the ear. The stately and formal style of oratorical declamation, sometimes assumes this shape, as does also the language of sublime, pathetic, and beautiful description. Some writers, by high excellence of natural or of cultivated ear, succeed in imparting an exquisite but unobtrusive melody to their sentences, which forms one of the principal attractions of their style. We have instances of these various effects of the selection and arrangement of words, in the majestic and measured declamation of Chatham, or in the lofty and magnificent strains of Scripture. The cadences of Ossian exemplify, sometimes, the power and beauty of metrical arrangement, and, sometimes, the cloying effect of its too frequent and uniform recurrence. Every cultivated ear is familiar with the chaste and pleasing turn of the sentences of Addison, the easy flow of Goldsmith's, the ambitious swell of those of Johnson, the broken and capricious phrases of Sterne, the noble harmony of Burke, the abruptness of Swift, and the graceful smoothness of Irving.

The characteristic melody of each of these authors, is owing, as we find, on analysis, to more or less attention paid to the effect of "rhythmical" accent: it is, in fact, a species even of "metre" itself, or, at least, a close approach to it. Examined in detail, it will usually be found to consist in a skilful avoiding of "abrupt elements," in securing the coincidence of emphasis with "mutable" and "indefinite quantities," but, more particularly, an exact timing of the recurrence of accents at the end of clauses, and in the cadence of sentences; as these places are peculiarly adapted to sounds intended for effect on the ear, whether the design of the writer is to render them prominent and striking, or subdued and quiet. Such results tell, with equal power, on the hearer, whether they are studied or unconscious, on the part of the writer; and they demand equal attention on the part of the reader.

"Rhythm," then, the lowest gradation of "metrical movement," exists in prose as well as poetry; and good reading preserves it distinctly to the ear.

It is a useful exercise, therefore, to study the styles of different authors, with reference to this point, and to read aloud, from characteristic passages, so as to become familiar with their peculiarities of "rhythm," and to gain the power of giving these a distinct and perceptible existence in the voice, without carrying the effect so far that sense is in danger of being merged in sound, or the thought, of being lost in the language. Everything mechanical, in reading, is an offence to sound judgment and true taste.

The following examples of the notation of "rhythmical" accent will serve to suggest to the student the exercise of marking with a pencil the "rhythm," in passages of his own selection. The teacher may prescribe exercises of this sort to his pupils, by the use of the black board. The system of notation needs attention to the following explanatory statement.

The notation of "rhythm" is founded on the theory of Steele, that utterance, in speech and in reading, may, like music, be divided into regular portions by accent, and indicated by "bars," as in music, when written or printed; each "bar" commencing with an accented syllable, or an equivalent pause.

"Rhythm," however, it must be remembered, in the practice of all such exercises as the following, is like every other requisite of elocution, — an aid and an ornament, within due limits of effect, but a deformity when rendered prominent and obtrusive. The wavering and unsteady voice of juvenile readers, and the unsatisfactory current of utterance in the style of some professional speakers, is owing to the want of a firmly marked "rhythm," — a fault which necessarily produces to the ear of the hearer a wandering uncertainty of effect. "Time," to which "rhythm," is subordinate, demands precision and exactness, when applied as a measure of speech. Some readers, how:'er, err on the extreme of marking time too prominently, and with a jerking accent, which offends the ear by causing reading to resemble a *music* lesson in "accent," accompanied with a heavy 'beat,' for the sake of awakening the attention of a learner whose 'organ of time' is dull.

The style of practice in the first stages, must, of course, be char acterized by full and distinct effect, even at the hazard of seeming labored and forced, — if the reader's ear is not naturally susceptible, and requires powerful impressions. But much practice should be added, with a view to produce smoothness and delicacy; as the painter does not rest satisfied with the mere blocking out of light and shadow in his picture, but labors till he has secured that exquisite finish, which is the crowning grace, in every successful attempt of art; and art fails in its endeavors, if it does not present nature in the union of beauty and truth.

EXAMPLES OF "RHYTHM."

1. — *Declamatory Style.*

[FROM A SERMON OF ROBERT HALL.]

" It re- | mains with | you then | ⌐[1] to de- | cide | whether that | freedom | ⌐ at | whose | voice | ⌐ the | kingdoms of | Europe | ⌐ a- | woke from the | sleep of | ages, | ⌐ to | run a ca- | reer of | virtuous | [2] emu- | lation | ⌐ in | everything | great and | good ; | ⌐⌐ | ⌐ the | freedom | ⌐ which dis- | pelled the | mists of | [2] super- | stition, | ⌐ and in- | vited the | nations ¦ ⌐ to be- | hold their | God ; | ⌐⌐ | ⌐ whose | magic | touch ⌐ | kindled the | rays of | genius, | ⌐ the en- | thusi- asm of | poetry, | ⌐ and the | flame of | eloquence ; | ⌐⌐ | ⌐ the | freedom ¦ ⌐ which | poured into our | lap ⌐ | opulence | ⌐ and | arts, ¦ ⌐⌐ | ⌐ and em- | bellished | life | ⌐ with in- | numerable | [2] insti- | tutions | ⌐ and im- | provements, | ⌐⌐ | ⌐ till it be- | came a | theatre of | wonders ; | ⌐⌐ | ⌐ it is for | you | ⌐ to de- | cide ⌐ | ⌐ whether | this | freedom | ⌐ shall | yet sur- | vive, | ⌐ or | perish | ⌐ for- | ever."

[1] "Rhytnmical" pause.
[2] A "secondary" instead of the usual "primary" accent.

## 2.—*Poetic expression in Prose.*

[PASSAGES OF SCRIPTURE INTRODUCED IN THE BURIAL SERVICE.]

| "I | ⌣ am the | ¹ Resur- | rection | ⌣ and the | life, | ⌣⌣ | ⌣ saith the | Lord; | ⌣⌣ | he that be- | lieveth in | me, | ⌣⌣ | ⌣ though he were | dead, | ⌣⌣ | yet shall he | .ive: | ⌣⌣ | ⌣ and | whoso- | ever | liveth, | ⌣ and be- | lieveth in | me, | ⌣ shall | never | die. | ⌣⌣ | ⌣⌣ |

⌣ I | know | ⌣ that my Re- | deemer | liveth, | ⌣ ⌣ | and that he shall | stand | ⌣ at the | latter | day | ⌣ upon the | earth, | ⌣⌣ | ⌣ and though | worms de- | stroy this | body, | ⌣⌣ | yet in my | flesh | ⌣ shall I | see | God." | ⌣⌣ | ⌣⌣ |

## 3.—*Sentiment, in Didactic Style.* [GOLDSMITH.]

"Writers | ⌣ of | every | age | ⌣ have en- | deavored to | show | ⌣ that | pleasure | ⌣ is in | us, | ⌣ and | not in the | objects | ⌣⌣ | offered | ⌣ for our a- | musement. | ⌣⌣ | ⌣⌣ | ⌣ If the | soul be | happily dis- | posed, | ⌣ ⌣ | everything | ⌣ be- | comes | capable | ⌣ of af- | fording | enter- | tainment; | ⌣ ⌣ | ⌣ and dis- | tress | ⌣ will almost | want a | name. | ⌣⌣ | ⌣⌣ | Every oc- | currence | ⌣⌣ | passes in re- | view | ⌣ like the | figures | ⌣ of a pro- | cession ; | ⌣⌣ | some | ⌣ may be | awkward, | ⌣⌣ | others | ⌣ ill | dressed ; | ⌣ but none but a | fool | ⌣ is, for | this, | ⌣ en- | raged with the | master of the | ceremonies. | ⌣⌣ | ⌣⌣ |

## 4.—*Splendor and Pathos.*

[BURKE'S DESCRIPTION OF MARIE ANTOINETTE.]

"It is | now, ⌣ | sixteen or | seventeen | years | ⌣ since | saw the | Queen of | France, ⌣ | then the | Dauphiness, | ⌣ at Ver- | sailles : ⌣ | ⌣⌣ | ⌣ and | surely | never | .ighted on this | orb, ⌣ | ⌣ which she | hardly | seemed to | touch, ⌣ | ⌣ a | more de- | lightful | vision. | ⌣⌣ | ⌣⌣ | ⌣ I | saw her | just a- | bove the ho- | rizon, | ⌣⌣ | decorating | ⌣ and | cheering | ⌣ the | elevated , sphere | ⌣ she | just be- | gan to | move

---

¹ A "secondary," instead of the usual "primary," accent.

m: | ⌣⌣ | glittering, | ⌣ like the | morning | star : | ⌣⌣ | full
of | life, | ⌣ and | splendor, | ⌣ and | joy. ⌣ | ⌣⌣ | ⌣⌣ |

Oh! | what a | revo- | lution! | ⌣⌣ | ⌣ and | what a | heart
| ⌣ must I | have, | ⌣ to con- | template | ⌣ with- | out e- |
motion, ⌣⌣ | that ele- | vation | ⌣ and | that | fall." ⌣ | ⌣
⌣ | ⌣⌣ |

### 5. — *Oratorical Declamation.* [Lord Chatham.]

"I | cannot, | ⌣ my | Lords, ⌣ | ⌣ I | will not, | join | ⌣ in
con- | gratu- | lation | ⌣ on mis- | fortune | ⌣ and dis- | grace.
| ⌣⌣ | ⌣⌣ | This, | ⌣ my | lords, ⌣ | ⌣ is a | perilous | ⌣ and
tre- | mendous | moment; | ⌣⌣ | ⌣ it is | not a | time for |
adu- | lation: | ⌣⌣ | ⌣ the | smoothness of | flattery | ⌣⌣ |
cannot | save us | ⌣ in this | rugged and | awful | crisis. | ⌣
⌣ | ⌣⌣ | ⌣ It is | now | necessary | ⌣ to in- | struct the |
throne | ⌣ in the | language of | truth. | ⌣⌣ | ⌣⌣ | ⌣ We |
must, ⌣ | ⌣ if | possible, | ⌣ dis- | pel the de- | lusion and |
darkness | ⌣ which en- | velope it; | ⌣⌣ | ⌣ and dis- | play,
| ⌣ in its | full | danger | ⌣ and | genuine | colors, | ⌣ the
| ruin | ⌣ which is | brought to our | doors." | ⌣⌣ | ⌣⌣ |

### 6. — *Sentiment, in Didactic Style.* [Addison.]

"I | know but | one | way | ⌣ of | forti- | fying my | soul
| ⌣ a- | gainst | gloomy | presages and | terrors of | mind; |
⌣⌣ | ⌣ and | that is, | ⌣ by se- | curing to my- | self ⌣ | ⌣
the | friendship and pro- | tection | ⌣ of | that | Being | ⌣
who dis- | poses of e- | vents, | ⌣ and | governs fu- | turity.
| ⌣⌣ | ⌣⌣ | He ⌣ | sees, ⌣ | ⌣ at | one | view, | ⌣ the |
whole | thread of my ex- | istence, | ⌣⌣ | ⌣ not | only | that
| part of it | which I have al- | ready | passed | through, | ⌣
but | that | ⌣ which runs | forward | ⌣ into | all the | depths
| ⌣ of e- | ternity. | ⌣⌣ | ⌣⌣ | ⌣ When I | lay me | down to
| sleep, | ⌣ I recom- | mend myself | ⌣ to | his | care ; | ⌣⌣ |
⌣ when I a- | wake, | ⌣ I | give myself | up to | his di- | rec-
tion. | ⌣⌣ | ⌣⌣ | ⌣ Amidst | all the | evils that | threaten me
| I will look | up to | him for | help; | ⌣⌣ | ⌣ and | question
not | ⌣ but he will | either a- | vert them, | ⌣ or | turn them | to

my ad- | vantage | ⌒⌒ | ⌒⌒ | ⌒ Though I | know | neithei the | time nor the | manner | ⌒ of the | death | I am to | die, | ⌒ _ | am not at | all so- | licitous a- | bout it ; | ⌒⌒ | ⌒ be- | cause I am | sure | ⌒ that | he , knows them | both, | ⌒⌒ | ⌒ and that he | will not | fail to | comfort | ⌒ and sup- | port me ⌒ | under them." | ⌒⌒ | ⌒⌒ |

### 7.—*Sentiment, in Didactic Style.* [JOHNSON.]

" Kindness | ⌒ is pre- | served by a | constant re- | cip- ro- | cation of | benefits | ⌒ or | interchange of | pleasures ; | ⌒⌒ | ⌒ but | such | benefits | only | can be be- | stowed, | ⌒ as | others | ⌒ are | capable of re- | ceiving, | ⌒ and | such | pleasures im- | parted, | ⌒ as | others | ⌒ are | qualified to en- | joy. | ⌒⌒ | ⌒⌒ |

⌒ By | this de- | scent from the | pinnacles of | art | ⌒ no | honor | ⌒ will be | lost ; | ⌒⌒ | ⌒ for the | conde- | scensions of | learning | ⌒ are | always | over- | paid | ⌒ by | gratitude. | ⌒⌒ | ⌒⌒ | ⌒ An | elevated | genius | ⌒ em- | ployed in | little | things, | ⌒ ap- | pears, | ⌒ to | use the | simile of Lon- | ginus, | ⌒ like the | sun | ⌒ in his | evening | decli- | nation: | ⌒⌒ | ⌒ he re- | mits his | splendor, | ⌒ but re- | tains his | magnitude ; | ⌒⌒ | ⌒ and | pleases | more, | ⌒ though he | dazzles | less." | ⌒⌒ | ⌒⌒

The difference of effect in " rhythmical accent," it will be perceived, on closely examining the style of the preceding passages, is greatly dependent on the number of syllables included within each " bar," and, not less, on the pauses, which are also included in the " rhythm," and therefore enclosed within the bars ; since the " time " of the voice necessarily includes its rests and intermissions, as well as its sounds. " Rhythm " depends, farther, on the position of the accented syllable which takes on the emphasis of a phrase, as well as on the different species of accent, as " radical," " concrete," or " temporal." Compare, particularly, the contents of the " bars " in the last few lines of the last two examples. They will be found to imbody the expressive genius of each author, and " clothe his thought in fitting sound." The meek and quiet spirit of Addison, breathes in the plain, conversational, and comparatively uniform style of " rhythm," in the close of the paragraph quoted from him ; and the noble soul, but mechanical ear, of Johnson, are equally expressed in the sweeping " rhythm " of " quantity " and pause, and measured antiphony in the cadence of the last sentence extracted from the

Rambler The limits of an elementary work like the present, will not admit the details of analysis by which the peculiar character of each of the authors quoted might be verified by his peculiar " rhythm." But in the statements already made on " quantity," " pause," " movement," " accent," and ' rhythm," the implements of analysis have been furnished; and the exercise of applying them may be left to the teacher and the student.

## III.—*Prosodial Accent, or "Metre."*

The term " metre," or " measure," is applied, in prosody and in elocution, to that exact gauge of " rhythm," which is furnished in the process of prosodial analysis termed " scanning," by which a " verse," or line of poetry, is resolved into its constituent " quantities " and " accents."

" Metre," as a branch of prosody, comprehends, in our language, both " quantity " and " accent." The ancient languages, and those of modern Europe, generally, are less favorable than ours, to this union. The Greek and the Latin seem to have leaned chiefly on ·' quantity;" and we discern a similar tendency, though in an inferior degree, in the European continental languages, — particularly those of the South. A language abounding in long " quantities " of various sound, needs less aid from " accent," whether for distinctive enunciation or expression of feeling, than one redundant, like the English, in the number and force of its consonants. The racy energy of English enunciation, is owing to the comparative force, spirit, and brilliancy of its accent, which strikes so instantaneously on the ear, with a bold " radical movement " and absorbing power, that compel the attention to the determining syllable of every word. It bespeaks at once the practical and energetic character of the people with whom it originated. — Other modern languages seem to distribute the accent among all the syllables of a word, and to leave the ear doubtful to which it is meant to apply, — unless in the case of long vowels, in which they greatly excel, as regards the uses of music and of " expressive " speech, or impassioned modes of voice.

In emphatic utterance, however, the firm grasp which our numerous hard consonants allow to the organs, in the act of articulation, gives a peculiar percussive force of explosion to the vowels that follow them in accented syllables; and the comparatively short duration of our unaccented sounds, causes those which are accented, when they possess long " quantity," to display it with powerful effect in the utterance of " expressive " emotion. Our poets sometimes turn this capability of the language to great account; and none abounds more in examples than Milton, whose ear seems to have detected and explored every element of expressive effect which his native tongue could furnish.

Syllables have been classed, in prosody, as long or short, accented or unaccented; and the prosodial characters, ¯ (long,) and ˘ (short,) have been used to designate them to the eye. The same marks have been arbitrarily used to denote accented and unaccented syllables.

The " rhythm " of verse, as measured by " long and " short ' or by "heavy," (accented,) and "light," (unaccented,) syllables has the following metrical designations:

## I.—"*Iambic Metre.*"

This form of verse takes its name from the circumstance of its being constituted by the "foot," or sequence of syllables, called an "iambus." The words "foot" and "feet" are arbitrarily used in prosody, to express a group of syllables constituting a distinct and separable portion of verse. The "iambus" is a "foot" consisting of two syllables: the first, short, or unaccented, or both; the second long, or accented, or both; as in the word *repēal*.

"Iambic" metre is exemplified in "epic" or "heroic" poetry, whether in the form of "blank verse," — so called from its *not furnishing rhymes*, and its consequent *blank* effect on the ear, as in Milton's Paradise Lost, or of rhyming "couplets," — so called from the lines rhyming in *couples*, — as in Pope's translation of Homer. Each line, in "blank verse" and the "heroic couplet," contains five 'iambuses," or ten syllables, alternating from short to long, or from unaccented to accented; as in the following examples.

"*Blank*" *Verse.*

"Ădvāncĕd | ĭn vĭēw,| thĕy stănd, | ă hōr- | rĭd frōnt |
Ŏf drĕad- | fŭl lēngth, | ănd dāz- | zlĭng ārms, | ĭn guīse |
Ŏf wăr- | rĭŏrs ōld, | wĭth ōr- | dĕred spēar | ănd shĭeld. |

"*Heroic Couplet.*"

" Lĭke lĕaves | ŏn trēes |thĕ lĭfe | ŏf măn | ĭs fŏund ; |
(¹ 1.) Nŏw grēen | ĭn yŏuth, | (¹ 2.) nŏw wĭth- | (¹ 3.) ĕrĭng ŏn |
thĕ grōund ; |
Ănŏth- | ĕr răce |thĕ fŭl- | (¹ 4.) lŏwĭng sprĭng | sŭpplīes :
Thĕy făll | sŭccĕs- | (¹ 5.) sĭve, ănd | sŭccĕs- | sĭve rĭse."

"Iambic" verse is exemplified, also, in octosyllabic lines in rhyming "couplets," and in quatrain, or four-line "stanzas." The following are examples.

*Octosyllabic Couplet*

" Thĕ wăy | wăs lōng, | thĕ wĭnd | wăs cōld ; |
Thĕ mĭn- | strĕl wăs | ĭnfĭrm | ănd ōld :"

*Quatrain Stanza: Octosyllabic Couplets.*

" Thĕ spā- | cĭŏus fĭr- | măměnt | ŏn hĭgh |
Wĭth āll | thĕ blūe | ĕthĕ- | rĕāl skȳ, |

---

¹ Irregular feet used as substitutes for the "iambus," according to the "license" of versification. These feet are called, (1. and 2.) the "spondee, — *two long* syllables ; (3.) the "tribrach," *three short* syllables ; (4.) the "anapæst," *two short* syllables, and *one long;* (5.) the "pyrrhic," *two short* syllables.

"METRE."  185

And spa̤-  | glĕd hēavens, | ă shīn- | ĭng frāme, |
Thĕir grēat | Orĭg- | ĭnăl | prŏclāim." |

*Quatrain Stanza:  Octosyllabic Lines, rhyming alternately.*

"Thĕ hēavens | dĕclāre | thy̆ glō- | ry̆, Lōrd, |
In ēv- | ĕry̆ stār | thy̆ wĭs- | dŏm shīnes ; |
Bŭt whĕn | oŭr ēyes | bĕhōld | thy̆ wōrd, |
Wĕ rēad | thy̆ nāme | ĭn fāir- | ĕr līnes." |

'*Common Metre" Stanza:  Alternate Lines of Eight and Six
Syllables.*

"Thy̆ lŏve | thĕ pōwer | ŏf thōught | bĕstōwed; |
Tŏ Thēe | my̆ thōughts | wŏuld sōar : |
Thy̆ mĕr- | cy̆ ō'er | my̆ līfe | hăs flōwed ; |
Thăt mĕr- | cy̆ I | ădōre." |

'*Short Metre" Stanza: Two Lines of Six, one of Eight, and on
of Six Syllables.*

"Tŏ ēv- | ĕr frā- | grănt mēads, |
Whĕre rĭch | ăbŭn- | dănce grōws, |
Hĭs grā- | cĭŏus hānd | ĭndūl- | gĕnt lēads, |
And guārds | my̆ swēet | rĕpōse."

"Iambic" verse occurs, likewise, in the form of the "elegiac" stanza, — so called from the circumstance of its having been employed for he purposes of *elegy*.

*Elegiac Stanza: Lines of Ten Syllables, rhyming alternately*

"Fŭll măn- | y̆ ă gĕm, | ŏf pūr- | ĕst rāy | scrēne, |
Thĕ dārk, | ūnfāth- | ōmed cāves | ŏf ō- | ceăn bēar. |
Fŭll măn- | y̆ ă flōwer | ĭs bōrn | tŏ blŭsh | ūnsēen, |
And wāste | ĭts swēet- | nĕss ŏn | thĕ dĕs- | ĕrt āir." |

Another form of the "iambic" verse, of frequent occurrence in reading, is that of the "Spenserian" stanza, — so called from the poet Spenser, who was the first to use it, in a continuous poem o. considerable length.

*Spenserian" Stanza: Eight Lines of Ten Syllables and one of
Twelve: the Rhymes occurring as follows: on the 1st and 3d, — on
the 2d, 4th, 5th, and 7th, — and on the 6th, 8th, and 9th.*

"Whĕrē'er ' wĕ trēad, | 't ĭs hāunt- | ĕd hō- | ly̆ grōund ; |
Nŏ ēarth | ŏf thīne | ĭs lōst | ĭn vŭl- | găr mōuld ! |
Bŭt ōne | văs* rēalm | ŏf wŏn- | dĕr sprēads | ărōund ; |
And āll | thĕ Mūs- | ĕs' tāles | sĕem trū- | ly̆ tōld, |
Tĭll thĕ | sēnse āches | wĭth gāz- | ĭng, tŏ | bĕhōld }

Thḗ scēnes | ŏur ēar- | lĭĕ́st drēams | hăve dwĕlt | upŏn. |
Ĕach hĭll | ănd dāle, | ĕach dēep- | enīng glĕn | ănd wōld, |
Dĕfīes | thĕ pŏwer | whĭch crŭshed | thў tĕm- | plĕs gōne : |
Āge shăkes | Āthē- | nă's tōwer, | bŭt spāreṣ | grāy Mār- | ăthŏn.

There are many other forms of "iambic" verse; but they occur less frequently; and most of them can be easily analyzed after scanning the preceding specimens.[1]

## II.—"*Trochaic*" *Metre.*

This species of verse derives its name from its predominating foot he "trochee," which consists, as mentioned before, of a long syllable followed by a short, as in the word *fā́tăl*.

"Trochaic" verse is exemplified in the following lines from Dryden's Ode for St. Cecilia's Day.

"Sŏ́ftlў | swēet, ĭn | Lў́diăn | mēasŭres,
Sōon hĕ | sōothed hĭs | sōul tŏ́ | plēasŭres. — |
Wār, hĕ́ | sŭng, ĭs | tōil ănd | trōublĕ,
Hōnŏr,| bŭt ăn | ēmptў | bŭ́bblĕ."

This species of verse is seldom used in long or continuous poems but principally in occasional passages, for variety of effect. It is found usually in octosyllabic lines of rhyming "couplets," as above.

## III.— *Anapæstic Metre.*

This form of verse takes its name from its prevalent foot, the "anapæst," consisting of *two short* syllables followed by *one long*, as in the word *ĭntĕrvēne.*

"Anapæstic" verse is found usually in the two following forms:

### 1.

*Stanza of Four or Eight Lines of Three* "*anapæsts,*" *or equivalent feet.*

"Hŏw flēet[2] | ĭs ă glānce | ŏf thĕ mīnd !
Cŏmpāred | wĭth thĕ spēed | ŏf ĭts flīght, |
Thĕ tĕmp- | ĕst ĭtsĕ́lf | lăgs behīnd, |
And thĕ swīft | wĭngĕd ār- | rŏws ŏf līght."

### 2.

*Stanza of Four Lines of Four* "*anapæsts,*" *or equivalent feet.*

"Thĕ ēven- [2]| ĭng wăs glō- | riŏus; ănd līght | thrŏugh thĕ trēes
Plăyed thĕ sŭn- | shĭne ănd rāin- | drŏps, thĕ bīrds | ănd thĕ brēeze ;
Thĕ lănd- | scăpe, oŭtstrĕtch- | ĭng ĭn lōve- | lĭnĕss, lăy |
On thĕ lăp | ŏf thĕ yēar, | ĭn thĕ bēau-| tў ŏf Māy." |

---

[1] For farther examples, and a more extended statement, regarding the "reading of poetry," see "American Elocutionist."

[2] An "iambus" sometimes occurs as the first foot in an "anapæstic" line

## IV. — *Rhythmical and Prosodial Accent combined.*

The preceding examples of verse have all, it may now be perceived, been marked with the characters used in prosody But, for the purposes of elocution, it is important to the control of the voice, in the reading of verse, that the student should accustom himself to the practice of marking the accentuation of verse to the ear, — a process in which the actual "rhythm" of the voice is decided, as in prose, by the position of accent. The mere prosodial "quantities" must, in elocution, be regarded as but subordinate and tributary means of effect to "rhythmical accent," and as contributing to secure its perfect ascendency.

Metre, then, in reading, is to be considered as but precision of "rhythm" by which utterance is brought more perceptibly under the control of "time," than in prose. Verse, accordingly, is scored for accent, exactly as prose is. Here, also, the student may be reminded that, in practising on metre, whilst, for the sake of distinct impression, he indulges its effect to the full extent, at first, he must accustom himself to reduce it gradually within those limits which shall render it chaste and delicate. The peculiar effects of " measure " in music, do not exceed those of metre, in good reading and recitation; and they are indispensable in the reading of all forms of verse, but, particularly, in lyric strains. In these, — as even a slight attention will suffice to prove, — the poet often changes the mood of his metre along with that of his theme. The Ode on the Passions, and all similar pieces, require numerous changes of " rhythm " and prosodial effect, as the descriptive or expressive strain shifts from passion to passion, — and from measure to measure. — It is by no means desirable, however, that the metre should be marked in that overdone style of chanting excess, which offends the ear, by obtruding the syllabic structure of the verse, and forcing upon our notice the machinery of prosodial effect.

The subjoined example may serve to suggest, to the teacher and the student, the mode of marking on the black board, or with a pencil, similar exercises selected from the pages of this volume, or any other, at choice.

It was deemed preferable to use, for our present purpose, the same examples which have been analyzed for the study of the prosodial structure of verse, so as to show, as impressively as possible, the difference between the literal accent of the mere mechanism of verse as such, and the free, varied, and noble " rhythm," which it acquires when, in reading and recitation, the object in view is to render verse tributary to meaning and sentiment, or to vivid emotion. The servile style of reading verse which follows its sound rather than its sense, is no worse fault than a literal practising of prosody, a fair and honest but most gratuitous *scanning*, of the lines, rather than the reading of them. The strict metrical marking, however, and due practice on it, may be very useful to those students whose habit, in reading, is to turn verse into prose, through want of ear for metre

## NOTATION OF RHYTHMICAL AND PROSODIAL ACCENT COMBINED.

### I.—"Iambic" Metre.

*"Blank" Verse.*

⌣"Ad-| vanced in | view, | ⌣¹they | stand, | ⌣¹a | horrid | front ⌣
⌣ Of | dreadful | length, | ¹ ⌣ and dazzling | arms, | ⌣¹ in | guise |
⌣ Of | warriors | old | ⌣ ³ with | ordered | spear and | shield." | ⌣
⌣ | ⌣ ⌣ |

*"Heroic Couplet."*

⌣" Like | leaves on | trees | ⌣ the | life of | man | ⌣ is | found : | ⌣ ⌣
| Now ⌣ | green | ⌣ in | youth, | ⌣ ⌣ | now ⌣ | withering | ⌣ on
the | ground ; | ⌣ ⌣ |
⌣ An- | other | race | ⌣ the | following | spring | ⌣ sup- | plies : | ⌣ ⌣|
⌣ They | fall suc- | cessive, | ⌣ and suc- | cessive | rise." | ⌣ ⌣ |
⌣ ⌣ |

*"Octosyllabic Couplet."*

⌣ " The | way | ⌣ was | long, | ⌣ ⌣ | ⌣ the | wind | ⌣ was | cold
⌣ ⌣ |
⌣ The | minstrel | ⌣ was in- | firm | ⌣ and old." | ⌣ ⌣ | ⌣ ⌣ |

*"Quatrain" Stanza: "Octosyllabic Couplets."*

⌣ " The | spacious | firmament | ⌣ on high, | ⌣ ⌣ |
⌣ With | all the | blue e- | thereal | sky, | ⌣ ⌣ |
⌣ And | spangled | heavens, | ⌣ a | shining | frame, | ⌣ ⌣
⌣ Their | great O- | riginal | ⌣ pro- | claim." | ⌣ ⌣ | ⌣ ⌣ |

*Quatrain Stanza: Octosyllabic Lines, rhyming alternately.*

⌣' The | heavens | ⌣ de- | clare | ⌣ thy | glory, | Lord, | ⌣ ⌣ |
⌣ In | every | star | ⌣ thy | wisdom | shines ; | ⌣ ⌣ |
⌣ But | ⌣ when our | eyes be- | hold thy | word, | ⌣ ⌣ |
⌣ We | read thy | name | ⌣ in | fairer | lines." | ⌣ ⌣ | ⌣ ⌣

---

1 " Demi-cæsural" pause.  2 " Final" pause.  3 " Cæsural" pause. — The pauses marked with the figure 1, &c., are founded primarily and necessarily on the sense ; but the prosodial pauses, indispensable to the " rhythm" of every well-constructed verse, happen, in the present instance, to coincide with the pauses of the meaning. Every line of verse has a " final pause," which detaches it from the following line, and a " cæsural" pause, which divides it into two parts, equal or unequal, or two "demi-cæsural" pauses, which divide it into three parts. The "demi-cæsural" pauses are sometimes used in addition to the " cæsural," to subdivide the two parts which it separates.

## "*Common Metre*" Stanza.

Thy | love | ⌣the | power of | thought | ⌣be- | stowed ; | ⌣⌣|
⌣To | Thee | ⌣ my | thoughts | ⌣ would | soar : ⌣⌣ |
⌣Thy | mercy | ⌣ o'er my | life | ⌣ has | flowed ; | ⌣⌣ |
⌣That | mercy | ⌣ I a- | dore." | ⌣⌣ | ⌣⌣ |

## "*Short Metre*" Stanza.

⌣" To | ever | fragrant | meads, | ⌣⌣ |
⌣ Where | rich a- | bundance | grows, | ⌣⌣ |
⌣ His | gracious | hand | ⌣ in- | dulgent | leads, | ⌣⌣ |
⌣ And | guards my | sweet re- | pose." | ⌣⌣ | ⌣⌣ |

## *Elegiac Stanza.*

⌣" Full | many a | gem, | ⌣ of | purest | ray | ⌣se- | rene, | ⌣⌣ |
⌣ The | dark | ⌣ un- | fathomed | caves of | ocean | ⌣⌣ | bear :
| ⌣⌣ | ⌣⌣ |
⌣Full | many a | flower | ⌣ is | born to | blush un- | seen, | ⌣⌣ |
⌣And | waste | ⌣its | sweetness | ⌣on the | desert | air." | ⌣⌣
| ⌣⌣ |

## "*Spenserian*" Stanza.

⌣ " Wher- | e'er we | tread, | ⌣ 'tis | haunted, | ⌣⌣ | holy ⌣ |
      ground : | ⌣⌣ | ⌣⌣ |
| No | earth | ⌣ of | thine | ⌣⌣ | ⌣ is | lost | ⌣ in | vulgar |
      mould ! | ⌣⌣ |
⌣ But | one | vast | realm | ⌣ of | wonder | ⌣⌣ | spreads a- |
      round ; | ⌣⌣ |
⌣ And | all the | Muse's | tales | ⌣ seem | truly | told, | ⌣⌣ |
Till the | sense | aches with | gazing | ⌣ to be- | hold |
⌣ The | scenes | ⌣ our | earliest | dreams | ⌣ have | dwelt upon.
      | ⌣⌣ | ⌣⌣ |
| Each | hill | ⌣ and | dale, | ⌣⌣ | ⌣ each | deepening | glen | ⌣
      and | wold, | ⌣⌣ |
⌣ Do- | fies the | power | ⌣ which | crushed thy | temples | gone :
      | ⌣⌣ | ⌣⌣
| Age | shakes A- | thena's | tower, | ⌣but | spares | ⌣gray | Mar-
      athon." | ⌣⌣ | ⌣⌣ |

## II. — "*Trochaic*" Metre.

" Softly | sweet, | ⌣ in | Lydian | measures, | ⌣⌣ |
Soon | ⌣ he | soothed his | soul | ⌣ to | pleasures. — | ⌣⌣ !

War | ᴗ he | sung | ᴗ is | toil | ᴗ and | trouble | ᴗᴗ |
Honor, | ᴗ but an | empty | bubble." | ᴗᴗ | ᴗᴗ |

### III.—"*Anapæstic*" *Metre.*

#### 1. *Lines of Three "Anapæsts."*

ᴗ" How | fleet | ᴗ is a | glance of the | mind! | ᴗᴗ | ᴗᴗ |
ᴗ Com- | pared with the | speed of its | flight, | ᴗᴗ |
ᴗ The | tempest | ᴗ it- | self | ᴗᴗ | lags be- | hind, | ᴗᴗ |
ᴗ And the | swift-winged | arrows of | light." | ᴗᴗ | ᴗᴗ |

#### 2. *Lines of Four "Anapæsts."*

ᴗ" The | evening | ᴗ was | glorious; | ᴗ and | light | ᴗ through tne | trees | ᴗᴗ |
ᴗ Played the | sunshine | ᴗ and | raindrops, | ᴗ the birds | ᴗ and the | breeze; | ᴗᴗ ᴗᴗ |
ᴗ The | landscape | ᴗ out- | stretching | ᴗ in | loveliness, | lay | ᴗ ᴗ |
ᴗ On the | lap | ᴗ of the | year, | ᴗ in the | beauty | ᴗ of | May.' | ᴗᴗ | ᴗᴗ |

---

## CHAPTER VIII.

### EMPHASIS AND "EXPRESSION."

The analysis of elocution has, in the preceding chapters, been extended so far as to comprehend all the chief topics of practical elocution. The subjects of *emphasis* and "*expression*," have been reserved for the conclusion of this manual, as they properly comprise a virtual review of the whole subject.

### I.—*Impassioned Emphasis.*

Emphasis, in its usual acceptation, is limited to mere comparative force of utterance on an accented syllable. The term, properly defined, extends to whatever expedient the voice uses to render a sound specially significant or expressive. Thus, in the scornful challenge which Bolingbroke addresses to Mowbray.

"*Pale, rembling* coward! there I throw my gage:"—

The emphasis lies, doubtless, on the word *coward*, and is

concentrated in the syllable *cow-*, by peculiar force of utterance. But the mere force or loudness used, is only one of the many elements of expression, which the syllable is made to comprise, in the intensely excited passion implied in the words.

Attentive analysis will show that, in what is termed "emphasis," in this instance, there are included all of the following elements of vocal effect: 1st, the mere force or energy of the utterance, which produces the *loudness* of voice, that accompanies violent or vehement excitement of feeling; 2d, the *abrupt and explosive articulation* with which the accented syllable is shot from the mouth, in the expression of anger and scorn; 3d, the comparatively *low pitch* on which the syllable *cow-* is uttered, as contrasted with the high note on the opening word "*pale*," and which indicates the deep-seated contempt and indignation of the speaker; 4th, the comparatively *long duration of the accented syllable*, and the consequent effect of deliberate and voluntary emotion, as contrasted with the rapid rate of hasty and rash excitement; 5th, the *downward* "*slide*," the inseparable characteristic of all impetuous, violent, and angry emotion; 6th, the "*pectoral*," "*guttural*," and *strongly* "*aspirated quality*" of voice, with which the utterance seems to burst from the chest and throat, with a half-suffocated and hissing sound, peculiarly characteristic of fierce and contemptuous emotion.

It may appear, at first view, that this analysis extends beyond emphasis into "expression." But emphasis is, in fact, nothing else than "expression," concentrated and condensed into an accented syllable. For confirmation of this assertion we may refer to the result, in cases of acknowledged imperfect emphasis, that a failure, as regards the full effect of any one of the above elements, produces the fault. Let the student himself bring the matter to the test of his own observation, by uttering the word "*coward*," six times in succession, dropping, each time, one of the elements of "expression," enumerated in the preceding analysis; and he will perceive that he loses, in every instance, the emphasis of impassioned accent. — Similar illustrations might be drawn from all emotions, in turn. But the verification may be left for the practice of oral illustration, by the student or the teacher.

## II.—*Unimpassioned Emphasis.*

It may be thought, however, that, although the emphasis of passion does include many elements, the common emphasis of meaning, in unimpassioned intellectual communication, may be sufficiently expressed by mere comparative force of accent. This impression, too, will, on examination, be found erroneous. The simplest distinctive emphasis that can be given, comprises several points of effect, which are easily detected by analysis.

We may take, for an example of unimpassioned emphasis, the expressions in the moral of the fable of the Discontented Pendulum, 'Let any man resolve always to do right *now*, leaving *then* to do as can; and if he were to live to the age of Methuselah, he would never do wrong.'

The words "*now*" and "*then*," in this passage, are instances of distinctive emphasis: they are marked, 1st, by *the usual superior force of utterance*, which belongs to important and significant words; 2d, by a *jerking stress*, repeated at the beginning and end of each "tonic" element of sound in the two words, and constituting what, in elocution, is technically termed "compound stress;" 3d, by the comparatively *high pitch* on which each of these two words is set, relatively to the rest of the sentence; 4th, by a significant turn or "double slide" of voice, termed the "wave," or, perhaps, — in the spirit of very keen and peculiarly marked distinction, — by a double turn, constituting a quadruple "slide" and a "double wave," in the style peculiar to the prolonged utterance of acute verbal distinctions; 5th, by the *protracted sound* of the words, which is inseparable from the enunciation of significant expressions, in general, but particularly, as just mentioned, from the style of verbal distinctions and subtle discriminations; 6th, by the "oral quality" of voice, with which the words are uttered. — By "oral quality" is not meant that "pure" or "head tone," which always accompanies unimpassioned and merely intellectual communication, — an utterance addressed to the *understanding*, and not to the *passions*, and hence divested of deep "pectoral" or harsh "guttural" quality, — but that distinctly marked and exclusively *oral* tone, which causes the voice to sound as if it emanated from, or originated in, the mouth alone, and designedly threw the utterance into the shape of a mere process of articulation, dependent, for its whole effect, on the tongue, the palate, the teeth or the lips. All nice distinctions in grammar, in logic, and even in ethics, are given in this purely "oral" form. This mode of voice, is, as it were, the opposite pole to that of deep passion, which is not merely low-pitched, but designedly resounds in the thoracic cavity, and by its hollow "pectoral" effect, seems to emanate from the chest. It indicates, thus, to the ear the presence, as the "oral quality" does the absence, of a deep inward movement of feeling. — The effect of the "oral quality," as a part of the emphasis of intellectual distinctions, may be ascertained by the student for himself, if he will utter the words "*now*" and "*then*" in the preceding passage, first, with "low pitch," and deep "pectoral" murmur, and, afterwards, with "high pitch," and thin "oral" enunciation. A similar analysis may be made on all the constituent elements of unimpassioned emphasis, as enumerated in this paragraph.

The reason why, in our analysis of elocution, the consideration of emphasis was postponed to other topics, will now be distinctly perceived. The appropriate study of emphasis, requires a knowledge of its various constituents. But the previous discussion and exemplification of these, renders the separate practice of each, under the denomination of emphasis, unnecessary. It will be sufficient, here, to present a few examples of emphasis, for practical analysis, classified in such a manner as to suggest to the student and the teacher the modes of practice best adapted to produce a distinct, impressive, and discriminating emphasis.

It will give additional value to all exercises in emphasis, if the examples are thoroughly analyzed, so as to exhibit all the properties of elocution comprised in each. It becomes necessary, once more, to drop, here, a suggestion on the effect of practice, — that, in the first course of exercise, the full force of emphasis, in all its characteristics, is the object to be kept in view, so as to gain the power of throwing out the utmost expressive force, when impassioned utterance requires it; but that a subsequent course should be carefully added, so as to bring down and soften the emphasis of unimpassioned language into a quiet and moderate style of expression, marked by chaste and manly reserve. — Our current style of professional reading is justly complained of by foreigners, as being mechanical and studied in its emphasis; and our popular oratory, as characterized by violence rather than genuine force. Earnestness, it is true, is the soul of eloquence; but it rarely authorizes vehemence, and never vociferation, — a habit which, for the time, degrades man from his rational elevation of humanity to the level of animal life. Emotion, the true source of impassioned emphasis, may be, in the highest degree, vivid, without being turbulent.

EXAMPLES OF EMPHASIS.

I.—*Impassioned Emphasis.*

*Fierce Anger and Defiance.*

[CORIOLANUS, ENRAGED BY THE ACCUSATION OF THE TRIBUNES.]—*Shakspeare.*

("Aspirated guttural quality:" "Impassioned" and increasing "expulsive" force: "Compound and thorough stress:" "High" and progressively rising "pitch:" Downward "third," "fifth," and "octave" in the "slide:" "Emphatically slow movement.")

"Call me their *traitor!*—Thou *injurious* tribune!
Within thine eyes sat *twenty thousand deaths,*
In thine hands clutched as many MILLIONS, in
Thy lying tongue BOTH numbers, I would say,
Thou LIEST, unto thee, with a voice as free
As   do pray the gods."

### *Revenge.*

[OTHELLO, INSTIGATED BY IAGO, AGAINST CASSIO.]—*Shakspeare.*

("Aspirated pectoral quality:" Intensely "impassioned" "Expulsive" force: "Thorough stress:" "Low pitch:" Downward "slide," of the "fifth" and "third:" Emphatically deliberate and slow "movement.")

"Oh! that the slave had FORTY THOUSAND lives!
My great *revenge* had stomach for them ALL!"

### *Anger and Threatening.*

[CORIOLANUS, TO THE ROMAN SOLDIERS WHEN REPULSED.]—*Shakspeare*

("Aspirated guttural quality:" "Impassioned" force: "Vanishing," "radical," and "median stress:" "High pitch:" "Downward" "slide" of the fifth: "Movement" first "slow," then "quick."

"You souls of *geese*,
That bear the *shapes* of men, how have you run
From *slaves* that *apes* would beat!—PLUTO and HELL!
All hurt *behind;* *backs red*, and *faces pale*
With *flight* and *agued fear!*—MEND, and CHARGE HOME
Or by the *fires* of *heaven*, I'll leave the FOE,
And make my wars on YOU: *look to 't:* COME ON!"

### *Defiance.*

[EDMUND, IN REPLY TO ALBANY.]—*Shakspeare.*

("Orotund quality:" "Impassioned" force: "Thorough stress:" "Middle pitch:" Downward "fifths:" Deliberate "movement.")

"What in the world he is,
That names me *traitor*, villain-like he LIES:
Call by thy trumpet: he that dares approach,
On *him*, on *you*,—WHO NOT?—I will maintain
My *truth* and *honor firmly.*"

### II.—*Unimpassioned Emphasis.*

### *Emphasis of Designation.*

[DESCRIPTION OF A BOOKSELLER'S LITERARY DINNER.]—*Irving.*

"The host seemed to have adopted Addison's idea as to

EMPHASIS AND "EXPRESSION." 195

the literary precedence of his guests.—A *popular* [1] *pòet* had the post of *honor;* opposite to whom was a *hot-pressed traveller in quàrto,* with *plates.* A *grave-looking àntiquary,* who had produced several *sòlid* works, that were *much quòted* and *little rèad,* was treated with great respect, and seated next to a *neat, dressy gentleman* in *blàck,* who had written a *thin, genteel, hot-pressed octavo on political econòmy,* that was getting into fashion. Several *three-volume-duodècimo* men of fair currency, were placed about the *cèntre* of the table; while the *lówer* end was taken up with *small pòets, translàtors,* and authors who had not as yet risen with much *notoriety."*

*Emphasis of Comparison and Contrast in Equal and Single Parts.*

[EXTRACT FROM A SERMON.]

" The [2] *high* and the *lòw,* the *rich* and the *pòor,* approach, in point of real enjoyment, much nearer to each other, than is commonly imagined. Providence never intended that any state here should be either completely *hàppy,* or entirely *miserable.* If the feelings of *plèasure* are more numerous and more lively in the *higher* departments of life, such also are those of *pàin.* If greatness flatters our *vànity,* it multiplies our *dàngers.* If opulence increases our *gratificàtions,* it increases, in the same proportion, our *desires* and *demànds.* If the poor are confined to a *more nàrrow* circle, yet within that circle lie most of those *natural satisfàctions,* which, after all the refinements of art, are found to be the most *genuine* and *trùe.*

*Comparison and Contrast in Equal and Double Parts.*

[HOMER AND VIRGIL.]—*Blair.*

" In [3] *Hòmer,* we discern all the Greek *vivàcity;* in *Vìrgil,*

---

[1] Usually, a downward slide of the second accompanies the "emphasis of designation."
[2] In the parallel or antithesis of equal and single parts, the slides exhibit the intervals of the upward and downward " third."
[3] In contrasts of double parts, the primary members have the "slide" of the third;" yet the inferior ones that of the "second"

all the Roman *stàteliness*. *Hòmer's* imagination is by much the most rich and *cópious;* *Virgil's* the most *chaste* and *corrèct*. The strength of the *fòrmer* lies, in his power of *warming* the *fáncy;* that of the *làtter*, in his power of *touching* the *hèart*. *Hòmer's* style is more *simple* and *ánimated;* *Vírgil's* more *elegant* and *ùniform*. The *first* has, on many occasions, a *sublìmity* to which the *làtter* never *attáins;* but the *làtter*, in return, never *sinks belów* a certain degree of *epic dignity*, which cannot so clearly be pronounced of the *fòrmer*."

*Comparison and Contrast in Unequal Parts.*

" Better be
Where the extinguished Spartans still are free,
In their proud charnel of [1]THERMÒPYLÆ,
Than stagnate in our *mársh*."

*Phrases of Successive Emphatic Words.*

" The British army, traversing the Carnatic, after the desolation effected by Hyder Ali, beheld[2] *nót òne living thing, nòt óne màn, nòt óne wòman, nòt óne child, nòt óne fòur-footed béast, of àny description whatèver*."[3]

III.—"*Arbitrary Emphasis.*"

The form of utterance to which this designation may be applied is that "expression," or significance, whether of loudness, pitch "time," "melody," or other property of vocal effect, in consequence of which the sense, or the connexion and structure of the parts of a sentence, may be rendered apparent by modification of voice, applied extemporaneously, during the moment of reading, at the discretion and by the will of the reader, rather than in compliance with any general rule of feeling or of elocution. This "arbitrary emphasis" is greatly aided in its effect by a corresponding abatement or depression of voice, in clauses which precede or follow the word or phrase of "arbitrary emphasis," or which occur between two such words or

[1] The preponderant member has the downward,—the weaker, the upward "slide."
[2] In emphatic phrases, every word takes a distinct and opposite "slide."
[3] The subjects of "slide," ("inflection,") "rhetorical" pause, emphasis and the other grammatical and sentential parts of elocution, are discussed a greater length in the "Elocutionist." The present work is designed as manual of elementary practice in orthophony, and is limited, chiefly, to examples and exercises.

phrases This "discharging" of "expression," as it may be termed, — in reference to the analogous process of discharging ink or color from the surface of an object, will, of course, take place by a reduction, abatement or depression, of one or all the elements of vocal effect. The "arbitrary emphasis" may, at the pleasure of the reader, heighten the "expression" arising from "quality," force, pitch, "slide," "melodial phrase," "time," "quantity," "movement," &c.; so may the "*reduction*" of emphasis, diminish or subdue, or destroy any or all of these.

"Arbitrary emphasis," and "reduction" may be employed where but a single parenthetic word intervenes to break the current of language; as in the sentence, "The sprout was carefully protected by a *stratum*, or layer, of *leaves*." The words "stratum" and "leaves" are in this instance, pronounced with a slight additional force, an enlarged interval of "slide" and prolonged "quantity;" while the words "or layer" are reduced in force, shortened in "quantity," and levelled into "monotone," in the manner of parenthesis

The following example will exhibit the same effects more distinctly; as poetic language is naturally more expressive than prose

" On the other side,
Incensed with indignation, Satan stood
Unterrified, and like a *comet* (¹ burned,)
That fires the length of Ophiuchus huge,
In the arctic sky."

The arrangement of the words, in this sentence, throws the word "*burned*" into a parenthetic situation, in consequence of the grammatical connexion between the words "*comet*" and "*that.*" To atone to the ear for this verbal dislocation, the word "*comet*" takes on an additional force, a lower "slide," a longer "quantity" in its accented syllable, and a more descriptive swell of "stress," than it would otherwise have. The line, "*That fires,*" &c., is also read with a resuming force of expression, borrowed, as it were, from the style of voice in the word "*comet;*" while the word "*burned*," (which, as being a descriptive verb, must possess a degree of accent,) is rendered parenthetic in effect, by being thrown into "monotone," instead of a *downward* "slide," and by being somewhat reduced in force, and raised in pitch; while its descriptive power is retained by prolonged "quantity" and "median swell."

The following examples will illustrate the effect of "arbitrary emphasis" and "reduction," where a clause is to be partially parenthesized, so as to preserve the connexion of sense, on each side of it.

" Say first, for *Heaven*, (hides nothing from thy view,)
Nor the deep tract of hell."

¹ The crotchets of parenthesis are introduced here, not as belonging to the text but as an ocular aid, with a view to suggest the proper style of reading to the ear.

'Thus while he spake, *each passion* (dunmed his face
Thrice changed with pale,) *ire, envy,* and *despair:*"

"There was a Brutus once that would have *brooked*
(The eternal Devil to keep his state in Rome)
*As easily* | as a king."

The student may analyze for himself the effect of the "arbitrary emphasis" and "reduced expression," as indicated by the italics and the parenthesis.

The slight, level, and rapid "expression," which takes place on clauses such as that included within crotchets, Dr. Rush has termed the "flight" of the voice, and the emphatic connecting "expression," the "emphatic tie."

The effect of these modifications of voice will be rendered still more apparent by longer examples.

"He stood, and called
His legions, angel forms, who lay entranced
*Thick as autumnal leaves* (that strow the brooks
In Vallambrosa, where the Etrurian shades,
High over-arched, embower;) *or scattered sedge*
Afloat, when with fierce winds Orion armed
Hath vexed the Red-sea coast."

The same mode of reading applies to all actual parentheses, or similar qualifying phrases, and their context; as in the following instances, from Scripture.

"Therefore it is of faith, that it might be by grace; to the end the promise might be sure to all the seed: not to that only which is of the law, but to that also which is of the faith of Abraham, who is the father of us all, (as it is written, 'I have made thee a father of many nations,') before him whom he believed, even God, who quickeneth the dead, and calleth those things which be not, as though they were."

"For as many as have sinned without law, shall also perish without law; and as many as have sinned in the law, shall be judged by the law, (for not the hearers of the law are just before God, but the doers of the law shall be justified; for when the Gentiles, which have not the law, do by nature the things contained in the law, these, having not the law are a law unto themselves: which show the work of the law written in their hearts, their conscience also bearing witness, and their thoughts, the meanwhile, accusing, or else excusing one another;) in the day when God shall judge the secrets of men by Jesus Christ, according to my gospel."

[ZANGA, RELATING THE ORIGIN OF HIS HATRED OF ALONZO.]—*Young.*

" 'T is twice three years since that great man,
(Great let me call him, for he conquered me,)
Made me the captive of his arm in fight.

" One day, (may that returning day be night,
The stain, the curse, of each succeeding year!)
For something, or for nothing, in his pride
He struck me. (While I tell it do I live?)
He smote me on the cheek."

[CORPORAL TRIM'S ELOQUENCE.]—*Sterne*

——" My young master in London is dead," said Obadiah.—

" Here is sad news, Trim,"—[1] cried Susannah, wiping her eyes as Trim stepped into the kitchen,—" master Bobby is dead."

" I lament for him from my heart and my soul,"—[1] said Trim, fetching a sigh,—" Poor creature!—poor boy!—poor gentleman!"

" He was alive last Whitsuntide," said the coachman.—
'Whitsuntide! alas!"[2] cried Trim, extending his right arm, and falling instantly into the same attitude in which he read the sermon, " What is Whitsuntide, Jonathan," (for that was the coachman's name,) " or Shrovetide, or any tide or time past, to this? Are we not here now?" [2] continued the corporal, (striking the end of his stick perpendicularly upon the floor, so as to give an idea of health and stability,) " and are we not" (dropping his hat upon the ground) " gone! in a moment!"—It was infinitely striking! Susannah burst into

---

[1] Phrases occurring between two dashes, are sometimes equivalent to a parenthesis in effect.
[2] All intervening clauses and phrases of whatever length are read in the style of parenthesis.

a flood of tears.—We are not stocks and stones:—Jonathan Obadiah, the cookmaid, all melted.—The foolish fat scullior herself, who was scouring a fish-kettle upon her knees, was roused with it.—The whole kitchen crowded about the corporal.

"Are we not here now,—and gone in a moment?"—There was nothing in the sentence:—it was one of your self-evident truths we have the advantage of hearing every day; and if Trim had not trusted more to his hat than his head, he had made nothing at all of it.

"Are we not here now?" continued the corporal, "and are we not" (dropping his hat plump upon the ground,—and pausing before he pronounced the word) "gone! in a moment!"—The descent of the hat was as if a heavy lump of clay had been kneaded into the crown of it.—Nothing could have expressed the sentiment of mortality,—of which it was the type and forerunner,—like it: his hand seemed to vanish from under it; it fell dead; the corporal's eye fixed upon it, as upon a corpse;—and Susannah burst into a flood of tears."

## " EXPRESSION."

Emphasis, fully defined for the purposes of elocution, is prominent "expression," embodied in an accented syllable. It bears the same relation to "expression," in its full sense, that "syllabic accent" bears to "rhythmical accent." It may be restricted to a *single word:* "expression" applies, as in music, to the *sequence of sounds, in connected and consecutive utterance,* designed for the communication of *feeling.*

"Expression," however, while it contains the same elements with emphasis, comprises a few more. It includes the effects arising from "quality," in all its forms, " pure," " aspirated," &c., and from the " effusive," " expulsive," and " explosive" modes of utterance; from force in all its gradations from whispering to shouting; " stress," in its " radical,' " median," " vanishing," " compound," and " thorough ' forms; " tremor;" ' melody," " pitch," ' slide " and " wave " in a.l their forms; time," in all its influence over "movement," "rhythm," and metre. These modifications of voice have all been discussed and exemplified. But to all these, "expression" adds the effect of "drift," as it has been termed by Dr. Rush,—or, in other words, the impression produced on the ear by the frequent or successive recurrence of any mode or element of "expression."

"Drift," accordingly, is either an excellence or a fault, according to the circumstances in which it is adopted as a mode of effect. When a passage is so pervaded by one mood of feeling, and by one style of language and of structure, and even by one form of phrase, that a special unity of effect is obviously designed, as a result in audible expression,—a frequent trait of declamatory eloquence and even of poetic emotion, to which metre still farther contributes,—the "drift,"—or frequently recurring "quality," force, "stress," 'melody," pitch, "slide," "wave," "movement," or "rhythm,"—for a "drift" may be constituted by the frequent recurrence of one, or of several, or of all of these accidents of voice,—has the effect of deepening the impression arising from the sentiment as a whole. Hence we may observe that the "drift," of recurring "melody," or what, in popular language, is termed a "*tone*," is often a means of powerful and deep impression on the ear and on the external sympathies of an audience, when there is little of unity, force, or weight, in the sentiment which the speaker utters.

The ear of discerning judgment and of true taste, however, is always offended, rather than pleased, by any perceptible drift not authorized by a predominating emotion associated with the language of a speaker, or the composition in the hands of a reader. Still, a gentle and chaste "drift" is one of the natural secrets of effect, in elocution, and should be carefully observed and closely analyzed, by every student who is desirous of securing a master-key to the human heart.

It is unnecessary to dwell on this subject after the discussion and exemplification of emphasis. We will conclude with referring to two examples which will fully illustrate the effect of "drift." Let the student read aloud, with well-marked "expression," the first example of "impassioned emphasis," (the reply of Coriolanus to the tribunes,) and watch the impression produced on the ear by the recurrence of those vehement and infuriated downward "slides," which occur in the words marked by italics and capitals: and he will obtain a clear idea of the effect arising from the "drift" of that "slide." The student may then turn to the Appendix, and read aloud, for the sake of a wide contrast in "drift," the tender, pathetic, and "chromatic" lines illustrative of "feminine grief and sorrow," under the head of "SEMITONE," in which will be found the opposite "drift" of recurring "semitone," and other prevailing properties of kindred character.

# THIRD TABLE OF ORTHOPHONY.

EXERCISES ON THE ELEMENTS OF "EXPRESSION.

### WHISPERING.

" ALL's hushed as midnight, yet!
——— No noise! and enter."[1]

### HALF-WHISPER.

" Step softly, and speak low,
For the old year lies a dying!"

### " PURE TONE."

" Pale mourned the lily where the rose had died!"
" Oh! th t this lovely vale were mine!"
" Joy! joy forever! My task is done!'

### " OROTUND."

" Farewell! a long farewell to all my greatness."
" Hail! holy Light,—offspring of heaven, first-born!"
" Sound drums and trumpets, boldly and cheerfully!"

### FORCE.

*Very soft:*—" Oh! lightly, lightly tread!"
*Soft:*—" Take, holy Earth, all that my soul holds dear!"
*Moderate:*—" The breath of spring awakens the flowers."
*Loud:*—" Up! let us to the fields away!"
*Very loud:*—" Liberty! Freedom! Tyranny is dead!"

### STRESS.

*Impassioned Explosive Radical:*—" Up! comrades, up! In Rokeby's halls
Ne'er be it said our courage falls!"
*Unimpassioned Radical:*—" A clear, distinct articulation is an invaluable accomplishment."
*Median Stress:*—" Oh! I have lost you all, parents, and home and friends!"
" O Lord, my God, Thou art very great!"
" The shades of eve came slowly down."
*Vanishing Stress:*—" For Heaven's sake, Hubert, let me not be bound!"
" While a single foreign troop remained on my native shore, I would never lay down my arms. *Never* NEVER, NEVER!"

[1] Repeat, after every example, in its peculiar tone, the elements and a selection from the syllables and words in the first and second tables of Orthophony

ORTHOPHONY. 203

*Compound Stress:*—" What! to attribute the sacred sanctions of God and nature to the massacres of the Indian scalping-knife!"
*Thorough Stress:*—" Awake! arise! or be forever fallen!"

### PITCH.

*Lowest:*—" Silence how dead! and darkness how profound!"
*Low:*—" Dark flow thy tides o'er manhood's noble head."
*Middle:*—" Lovely art thou, O Peace, and lovely are thy children."
" He leadeth me by the still waters."
*High:*—" Now even now, my joys run high!"
*Highest:*—" Wheel the wild dance, till the morning break!"

### MOVEMENT.

*Slowest:*—" Creation sleeps:—'T is as the general pulse
Of life stood still, and Nature made a pause,—
An awful pause,—prophetic of her end!"
*Slow:*—" Now fades the glimmering landscape from the sight,
And all the air a solemn stillness holds."
*Moderate:*—" One great end to which all knowledge ought to be employed, is the welfare of humanity."
*Lively:*—" Crowned with her pail, the tripping milkmaid sings!"
*Brisk:*—" Haste thee, Nymph, and bring with thee
Mirth and youthful jollity!"
*Rapid:*—" And rushing and flushing and brushing and gushing,
And flapping and rapping and clapping and slapping,
And curling and whirling and purling and twirling,
Advancing and glancing and prancing and dancing,—
'T is this way the water comes down at Lodore."

# FOURTH TABLE OF ORTHOPHONY.

## COMBINATIONS OF EXPRESSION, IN TONES OF EMOTION.

### COURAGE.

*Orotund Quality, Loud Utterance, Thorough Stress, High Pitch, Brisk Movement.*

Come one, come all,—this rock shall fly
From its firm base as soon as I.[1]

### FEAR.

*Half Whisper, Suppressed Force, Explosive Radical Stress, Highest Pitch, Rapid Movement.*

" While thronged the citizens, with terror dumb,
Or whispering with white lips, ' The foe! they come, they come!' "

### JOY.

*Orotund Quality, Loudest Utterance, Thorough Stress, High Pitch, Lively Movement.*

" Joy, joy! shout, shout aloud for joy!"

### GRIEF.

*Orotund Quality, Subdued Force, Vanishing Stress and Tremor, Middle Pitch, Slow Movement.*

" Oh! pardon me, thou bleeding piece of earth!"

### AWE.

*Orotund, slightly aspirated, Suppressed Force, Median Stress, Lowest Pitch, Slowest Movement.*

" It thunders!—sons of dust in reverence bow!"

### ANGER.

*Aspirated Orotund, Loudest Utterance, Explosive Radical Stress, Middle Pitch, Rapid Movement.*

" Back to thy punishment, false fugitive!' "

### ADMIRATION.

*Pure Tone, Earnest Utterance, Median Stress, High Pitch Lively Movement.*

" Oh! speak again, bright angel!"

### HURRY.

*Aspirated Orotund, Loudest Utterance, Explosive Radical Stress, Middle Pitch, Rapid Movement.*

' Send out more horses! skirr the country round!' "

### TRANQUILLITY.

*Orotund Quality, Gentle Utterance, Median Stress, Middle Pitch, Slow Movement.*

" O'er all the peaceful world the smile of heaven shall lie!"

[1] After practising each example, repeat the elements and the words containing them, in the peculiar style of the example.

# FIFTH TABLE OF ORTHOPHONY.

EXERCISES IN THE DIFFERENT FORMS OF VERSE.

IAMBIC METRE.

*Blank Verse:*—" And earthly pride[1] | is like the passing flower,
That springs | to fall, and blossoms | but to die. '
*Heroic Verse:*—" Like leaves on trees | the race of man | is found;
Now | green in youth, now | withering on the ground."
*Octosyllabic Verse:*—" The spacious firmament | on high,
With all the blue ethereal sky,
And spangled heavens, a shining frame,
Their great Original proclaim."
*Common Metre:*—" Thy love | the power of thought bestowed
To Thee | my thoughts would soar:
Thy mercy | o'er my life has flowed,
That mercy | I adore."

TROCHAIC METRE.

" Softly sweet, in Lydian measures,
Soon he soothed his soul to pleasures:
War, he sung, is toil and trouble,—
Honor | but an empty bubble."

ANAPÆSTIC METRE.

" How fleet | is a glance of the mind!
Compared with the speed of its flight,
The tempest itself | lags behind,
And the swift-winged arrows of light."

" The evening was glorious, and light, through the trees,
Played the sunshine | and raindrops, the birds | and the breeze
The landscape, outstretching in loveliness, lay. |
On the lap of the year, in the beauty of May."

---

[1] The careful observance of these shorter pauses, is the surest means of avoiding the tendency to a jingling style in reading verse.

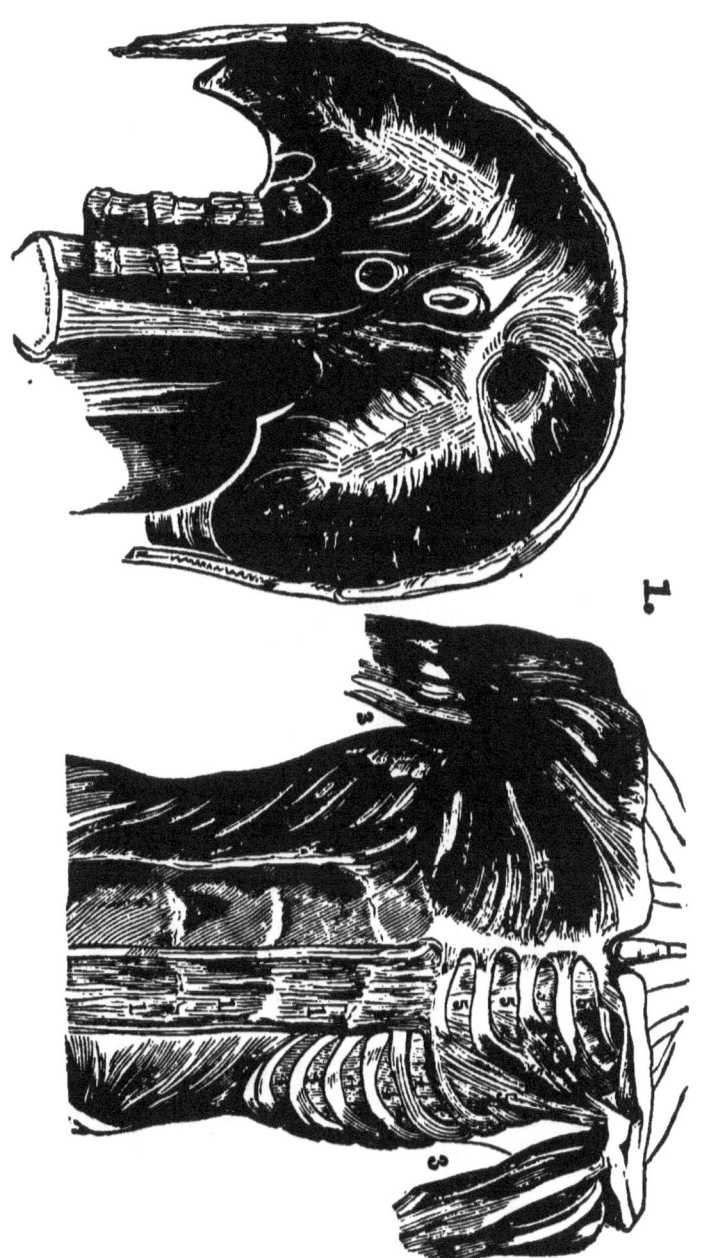

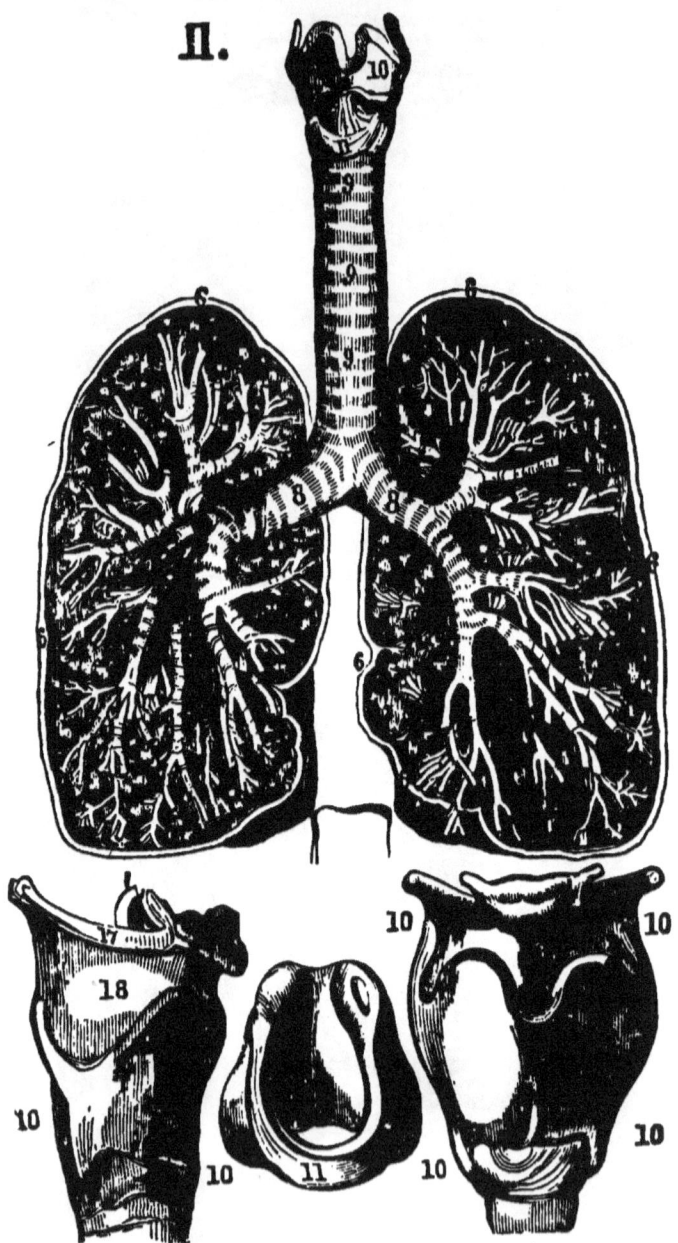

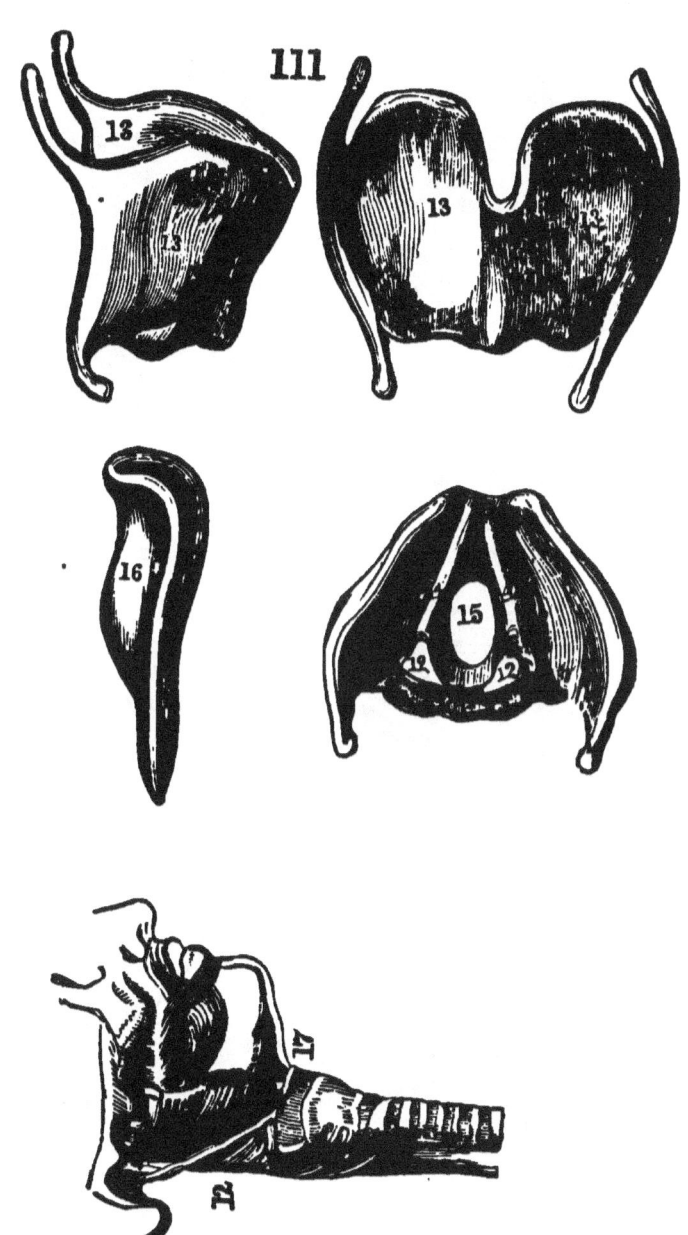

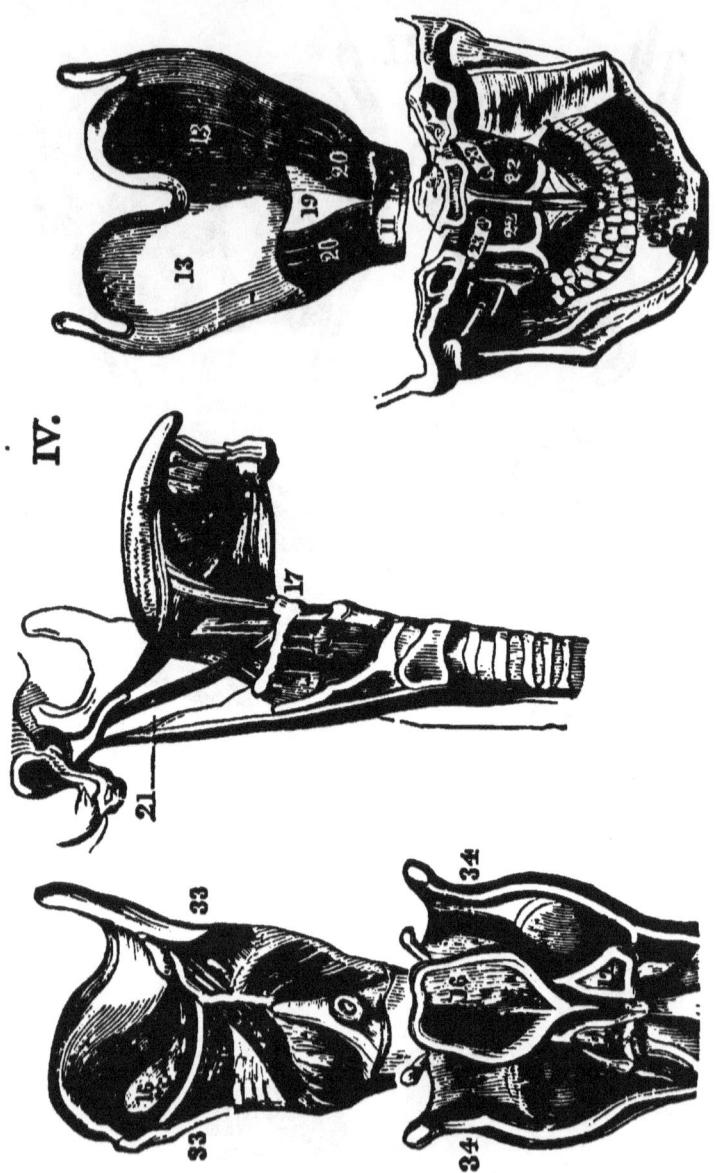

# APPENDIX.

## THE ORGANS OF VOICE.[1]

A LABORED and minute description of the organs of the human voice, would be incompatible with the design of a brief and practical work, such as this. Nor is an exact anatomical knowledge of these parts of the human frame, or a profound investigation of the physiology of their functions, essential to the purposes of culture. All that is aimed at, in the following observations, is, to impart such an idea of organic structure and action, as is indispensable to an intelligent, voluntary use of the vocal organs.

To examine the corporeal mechanism of speech, we commence with a survey of the trunk of the body, the great cavity, or main pipe, of vocal sound, and the seat of the principal apparatus whose motions give origin to voice. As the first step in our investigation, then, we wish to withdraw the student's attention entirely from the tongue, the mouth, and the throat, — the immediate, and, as it were conscious instruments of utterance, and to fasten the thoughts on the sources of voice, — the unconscious, and, in part, the involuntary, action of the muscles which enlarge and compress the cavity of the organic frame, and render it a resonant body.

The production of vocal sound, is, to a certain extent, identical with the function of breathing. A person in health, and free from pain, breathes without any perceptible sound, but that gentle whispering effect which is produced by inspiration and expiration, — drawing in and giving forth the breath. We observe this process exemplified in the tranquil breathing of one who is reading silently. But let the reader come to a passage of intense interest and exciting

---

[1] To facilitate the use of this manual in practical instruction, subjects which demand the attention of adult students pr.ncipally, are transferred to the appendix of this edition. Individuals who can command the requisite opportunities of acquiring actual information concerning the structure of the vocal organs, would do well to attend anatomical dissections, and particularly *post mortem* examinations of the parts ; as the tendency of the membranous lining of the organic apparatus to shrink, when cold, and to shrivel, when dry, does not easily admit of a true exhibition, — either in mannikin models, anatomical preparations, or engraved illustrations, — of the most important of all the instruments of phonation, — the surface of the vocal ligaments. M. Colombat de l'Isère, in his work on the hygiène and diseases of the voice, indicates the not uncommon errors, even of professional men, on this point.

emotion; and the breathing becomes, in consequence of the heightened organic action, caused by excessive feeling, hard and laborious: its force renders it plainly audible. A sigh, a sob, or a partial groan, perhaps, follows as the result of the over-excited action of the breathing apparatus. Breath thus becomes sound. We have here the history of involuntary voice.

A parallel illustration might be drawn from the hard breathing, the suppressed or loud groans, and the articulate exclamations, of a person suffering through the various stages of pain, from uneasiness to agony. But it is unnecessary to pursue examples of the fact that the function of breathing, when rendered intense, becomes vocal. To analyze the human voice, therefore, or to trace the organic mechanism of speech, we must examine the apparatus employed in the act of breathing.

We commence our investigation with the primary action of inspiration, or inhaling breath. A person in good health, draws in breath by an exertion, partly involuntary, partly voluntary, of those muscles which, by a combined act, expand, and, at the same time, raise the chest, and consequently enlarge the cavity called the thorax,— the region between the neck and the stomach. The degree of freedom and energy, in this muscular action, decides, of course, the extent to which the thoracic cavity is enlarged, and the volume of air which is inhaled: it decides also, as a natural consequence, the capacity of resonance in the chest, and the fulness of the supply of breath,— the material of sound.

These preliminary facts teach us the first practical lesson in the cultivation of the voice,— the necessity of maintaining an erect, free expansive, unembarrassed, posture of the chest, as an indispensable condition of full, clear, distinct, effective, and appropriate utterance

Continuing our investigation of voice, we return, for a moment, to the case of a person in the act of silent reading. Let the reader come to a passage, not of exciting effect or vivid emotion, but of profound and absorbing thought, which fixes the attention, with extreme earnestness, on an abstruse subject, rivets the mind on a single point, requiring the closest discrimination, or leads it away in a train of abstract thought: let there be, in one word, what we term a " breathless " attention; and we observe the person at once in the situation which we designate by the common phrase, " holding the breath." The reader, so situated, neither attempts to inhale a fresh breath, nor to let go that which he has inhaled; his chest becomes, as it were, fixed and immovable; in the intensity of his attention to a mental object, he forgets and neglects the organic demands of the vital processes; he unconsciously sympathizes with the stimulated condition of his brain; and his nervous energy takes that direction,— to the suspension, almost, of the functions of breathing, and even of circulation, and digestion,— hence the enfeebled state of the lungs, the paleness of the countenance, and the coldness of the extremities, which attend close mental application, when intense or long continued. Such is the condition of the human being, under the spell of the intellectual instincts, when nature is absorbing the powers of life, for the purposes of fixed thought, and is forbidding utterance, or expression, or any external manifestation of mind. Voice is, in such circumstances, silenced; and the organs are, for the time, irrevocably closed, by the stricture which is thrown over them.

But let us continue our observation of this silent reader; and we may perceive, perhaps, an immediate and entire change of phenomena. The spell of irresistible attraction in the page of the book, has ceased; the cloud of perplexity has passed away; the difficulty is solved; the discrimination is made; the doubt is cleared up; or the train of thought is come to an issue. As a consequence, the rigor of the brow relaxes; a radiant smile takes its place; the suspended breathing is resumed, with a deep and full expiration, which seems to let go the imprisoned function; the returning blood restores its hue to the cheek and the lip; animation once more sparkles in the eye; the heart resumes the throb of life; and a genial glow is diffused over the whole frame; an exclamation of joy, perhaps, succeeds; and a friend standing near, is invited, in cheerful accents, to partake the intellectual pleasure of the reader. The effect on the organs of speech, in such circumstances, is, then, that the breath is no longer held: the struggling prisoner escapes in a sigh of instinctive, reactive effort, or in an exclamation of delight.

The practical lesson here taught, is, that utterance demands a free expulsion, not less than a deep inhalation of breath; — that there must be a vigorous consentaneous action of the will, along with the silent involuntary process of nature

The full function of expiration, when carried to the extent of exclamation, as in the case supposed, implies an energetic use of the lower muscles of the trunk, — those which are termed the abdominal,[1] — to impart, by upward and inward impulse, a powerful percussion to the diaphragm, by which the breath contained in the air-cells of the lungs, is forced through the bronchial tubes and the trachea, towards the glottis and the larynx, where it is converted into sound, and thence into and through the mouth, and the cavity of the head, where it is modified into speech, by the action of the nasal passage, the tongue, the palate, the teeth, and the lips, in the various functions of articulate utterance.

The engraved figures will serve to impart a clearer idea than can be conveyed by words, of the place and form of the vocal organs, together with their action in the production of sound.

Figure 1 represents *the principal abdominal muscle*, by which the first expulsory movement terminating in sound, is produced. The action of this muscle, in energetic and abrupt forms of utterance, is nearly the same in kind, though not in degree, with that which takes place in the sudden shrinking from a blow, aimed at or below the

---

[1] In shouting and calling, and other violent exertions of voice, the *dorsal* muscles, — those of the lower part of the back, — partake in the expulsory effort.

stomach. In vigorous utterance of a steady and sustained character, or in the energetic singing of long notes, a powerful and continued upward and inward pressure of the abdominal muscles, takes place, as in the attitude observed in swift riding on horseback.

2. The *diaphragm*, which by an upward impulse, consentaneous with that of the abdominal muscles, and imparted to the pleura, or enveloping membrane of the lungs, forces the breath from the air cells into the bronchi, and thence into the trachea and the larynx.

3. The *thorax*, the great cavity of the chest. By the expansion and compression of this capacious organ, the process of breathing is conducted; and by its resonance, the voice receives depth and volume.

4. The *intercostal* muscles at the lower, and

5. The *thoracic* and *pectoral* muscles, at the upper part of the chest, serve to dilate and compress it, in the acts of breathing and of utterance.

6. The *pleura*, a membrane which envelopes the lungs, and propagates to their cells the impulse by which these are emptied of their successive supplies of air inhaled at the intervals of speaking or singing.

7. The *lungs*, a spongy body, in the form of lobes, into the cells, or little cavities, of which, the air inhaled in breathing, is drawn, and from which it is expelled by the impulse communicated, as mentioned before, by the pleura, and derived from the diaphragm and the abdominal muscles.

8. The *bronchi*, or two main branches of the trachea, or windpipe. These two tubes are themselves subdivided into many subordinate and minute *ramifications*, which serve to distribute to the air-cells of the lungs,—in which they terminate,—the breath inhaled through the trachea, and to convey that which is expelled from the lungs, by the impulsive action of the diaphragm, into the trachea, the larynx and the mouth. One important office of the bronchial ramifications, is to vibrate, and thereby aid in rendering vocal the column of air which is emitted from the cells of the lungs.

9. The *trachea*, or wind-pipe, a series of connected cartilaginous, or gristly, rings, forming the great air-tube, which receives and conducts the breath to and from the lungs, in the acts of inspiration and expiration, and in the function of utterance.

10. The *larynx*, a cartilaginous box, on the top of the trachea, the exterior projection of which is familiarly called the Adam's apple, in allusion to the fabled origin of this part, which was anciently said to have owed its existence to Adam's fatal offence in swallowing the forbidden fruit. The whole larynx is the immediate seat and general instrument of vocal sound. The portions of this organ, which are immediately concerned in the production of sound, are,

11. The *cricoïd* cartilage, situated immediately over the uppermost ring of the trachea, resembling, in form, a seal-ring, from which it takes its name, but having the broad part at the back, and the narrow in front. The form and position of this portion of the larynx, admit of the elevation and depression of its parts,—one step in the process by which tone is rendered grave or acute.

ORGANS OF VOICE. 215

12. The *arytænoid* cartilages, so called, from their fancied resemblance in shape, to a ladle, funnel, or pitcher. These fill up the space at the back of the thyroïd and cricoïd cartilages, and are connected with both; while they serve also as points of support and of tension, for the vocal ligaments.

13. The *thyroïd* cartilage, which has its name from its partial resemblance to the form of a buckler, or shield, but much bent. Its two main plates form the walls, or sides, of the larynx; and their size usually determines the capacity of the voice, as we observe, in their comparative smallness in females and children, and their great expansion and projection in men.

The comparative solidity of texture, in all these component portions of the larynx, and in the gristly rings of which the trachea is itself composed, give them the power of rendering the voice compact and sonorous.

14. The *vocal* ligaments extend across the upper part of the larynx, and form the lips of the glottis, and by their vibration, together with the action of the current of air expelled through the trachea and larynx, produce the phenomena of vocal sound or voice and, by their tension or remission, the effect of high or low pitch.

15. The *glottis*, so denominated from the partial resemblance of its shape to that of the tongue, is a small chink, or opening, which forms the mouth of the larynx. The opening and the contraction of this portion of the vocal apparatus, decide, in part, the gravity or the shrillness of tone.

All the parts of the larynx are interconnected by ligaments, and by muscles which move in concerted action, so as to expand or contract, raise or lower the whole larynx, and thus enlarge or diminish its capacity, and elevate or depress the pitch of the voice, and increase or diminish its force. The whole interior of the larynx is lined with a continuation of the mucous membrane of the mouth, which imparts to it a vivid sensibility and a unity of action. Hoarseness is the result of the embarrassment or obstruction of this membrane, by the mucous accumulations arising from colds or catarrh, or the injudicious habit of using cold water too freely, during the exercise of speaking.

16. The *epiglottis*, the valve, or lid, which, when the larynx is elevated, as in the act of swallowing, covers the glottis, or orifice of the windpipe, and prevents strangulation. Its usual erect position allows free ingress and egress to the breath. But, in some instances of intensely impassioned utterance, its pressure, against the glottis, becomes an additional preparative for the ultimate explosive eruption of voice.

17. At the root of the tongue, lies a small crescent-shaped or horseshoe-formed bone, called, from its resemblance to the Greek *υ*, the *hyoïd*, or *u-like* bone. This member serves, by its firm texture, as a gateway from the trachea and larynx to the mouth, or from the latter to the former. It forms a point of tension for the muscles which connect the larynx with the mouth. Its hard texture enables it to perform this office effectually, and thus to aid in giving, ⁊' ch to vocal sounds.

18. The *thyro-hyoïdean membrane* connects the thyroid cartilage with the instrument just described, and facilitates the functions of both, in elevating or depressing the pitch of the voice.

19. The *crico-thyroid ligament*, attaches, as its name implies, the cricoid to the thyroïd cartilage; and (20.) *the crico-thyroid muscle* facilitates their consentaneous movement, in the production of vocal sound, acute or grave.

21. The *pharynx*, or swallow, situated immediately behind and above the *larynx*, although not directly concerned in the production of sound, has, — by resonant space, — a great effect on its character. Persons in whom this organ is large, have usually a deep-toned voice; those in whom it is small, have comparatively a high pitch. When it is allowed to interfere with the sound of the voice, through negligence of habit, or bad taste, it causes a false and disagreeable guttural swell in the quality of the voice.[1]

22. The *nasal passages*. Through these channels the breath is inhaled in the usual tranquil function of breathing. The innermost part of the nostrils is united into one resonant channel, and opens into the back part of the mouth, behind the "veil," or pendent and movable part, of the palate, which serves as a curtain to part the nasal arch from the anterior portion of the mouth.

23. The *internal tubes of the ears*. Above the valve of the orifice of the windpipe, on each side of the root of the tongue, is a small opening, leading to a tube which communicates with the ear, and whose orifice is always opened, in the act of opening the mouth. These tubes have a great effect in rendering vocal tone clear and free; as is perceived in the case of obstructions arising from disease, from accident, or from cold, which impart a dull and muffled sound to the voice. "The ear," says an eminent writer on this subject "being formed of very hard bone, and containing the sonorous membrane of the drum, the sound of the voice entering it, through the air-tubes, must necessarily be increased by its passage along what may be termed the whispering galleries of the ear."

The effect of these passages, as conductors of vocal sound, may be traced in the fact, that the middle and innermost parts of the nostrils, open into several hollows, or cells, in the adjacent bones of the face and forehead. By this arrangement, the whole cavity of the head is rendered subservient to the resonance of the voice. That degree of clear, ringing, bell-like sound, which is so obvious a beauty of the human voice, seems to be dependent on this circumstance. Hence, too, the stifled tone caused by obstruction arising from cold, from accident, from the deleterious effect of snuff-taking, or from malformation of organic parts.

The fault of utterance which is termed nasal tone, arises from lowering too far the veil of the palate, — the membrane which separates the mouth from the nasal passages, and raising too high the root of the tongue, in producing a vocal sound. The consequence of these

---

[1] For a full and highly instructive statement of the effect of the pharynx on utterance, see a "Treatise on the Diseases and Hygiène of the Organs of the Voice, by Colombat de l'Isère." Translated by Dr. J. F. W. Lane, and published by Otis, Broaders, & Co., Boston.

errors, is that an undue proportion of breath is forced against the nasal passages, and that these organs are at once overcharged, and obstructed. Hence, the twanging and false resonance which constitutes " nasal " tone.

24. The *cavity*, and, more particularly (25) the *roof*, or ridgy arch, of the *mouth*, — in the anterior part of it, — together with (26) the *palate*, and (27) the *veil*, or pendent and movable part of *the palate*, and (28) the *uvula*, or the terminating tag of the veil of the palate in the back part of the mouth, as well as (29) the upper gum and (30) the teeth, in the fore part of it, all serve important purposes in modifying the sound of the voice, and aiding the function of speech.

The most satisfactory mode of forming a correct idea of these organs, is, to inspect the interior of the mouth, by the use of a looking-glass. In this way, the position and action of all these parts, in the function of speech, may be distinctly observed.

The mouth, by its arched structure, exerts a great influence in moulding the sound of the voice. It serves at once to give it scope, and partial reverberation. It gives sweetness and smoothness to tone; as we perceive in contrasting the voice duly modified by it, with that which loses its softening effect, in undue nasal ring, or guttural suffocation.

To give the voice the full effect of round, smooth, and agreeable tone, the free use of the cavity of the mouth, is indispensable: the whole mouth must be thrown open, by the unimpeded action and movement of the lower jaw. A smothered, imperfect, and lifeless utterance, is the necessary consequence of restraint in the play of this most effective implement of speech. A liberal opening of the mouth, is the only condition on which a free and effective utterance can be produced.

30. The *teeth*. These instruments, by their hard and sonorous texture, serve to compact and define the volume of the voice, while they aid one of the important purposes of distinct articulation, in the function of speech. Used with exact adaptation to their office, they give a clear and distinct character to enunciation; but remissly exerted, they cause a coarse hissing, resembling the sibilation of the inferior animals.

31. The *tongue*. The various positions and movements of this organ, are the chief means of rendering vocal sound articulate, and thus converting it into speech. They exert, at the same time, a powerful influence on the quality of the voice, by contracting or enlarging the cavity of the mouth, and giving direction to vocal sound: it is the position and action of the root of the tongue, which render the voice guttural, nasal, or oral, in its effect on the ear.

32. The *lips*. These important aids to articulation, not only give distinctness to utterance, but fulness of effect to the sounds of the voice. Imperfectly used, they produce an obscure mumbling, instead of definite enunciation; and, too slightly parted, they confine the voice within the mouth and throat, instead of giving it free egress and emissive force. In vigorous speech, rightly executed, the lips are slightly rounded, and even partially, though not boldly, projected

They thus become mos'. effective aids to the definite projection and conveyance of vocal sound: they emit the voice well moulded, and as it were, exactly aimed at the ear.

Figures 33 and 34 are intended to exhibit the effect of the epiglottis on the character of vocal sound. — When the voice is thrown out with abruptness, or even with a clear, decided force and character of sound, there is first a momentary occlusion of the glottis, attended, in impassioned utterance, by the downward pressure of the epiglottis, (the ii of the glottis,) as in the act of swallowing: see figure 33. To this preparatory rallying of the muscular apparatus, and its accompanying effect of resistance, — the natural preliminary to a powerful and sudden effort, — succeeds an abrupt and instantaneous explosion of breath and sound, produced by the sudden upward impulse of the abdominal muscles and the diaphragm, acting on the pleura, and the air-cells of the lungs, and forcing the breath upward, through the bronchi and the trachea, to the larynx. The breath, thus impelled, bursts forth, parting, in the act, the glottis from the epiglottis, (34,) and issues from the mouth, in the form of vocal sound.

Such is the history of the function of vocal explosion, — the inseparable characteristic of all impassioned utterance, and, in greater or less degree, accompanying all vivid expression, and all distinct articulation.

## ADDITIONAL BREATHING EXERCISES.

### Sighing.

The following exercises may be practised in addition to those which are prescribed at the beginning of this volume.

Sighing, as a natural effort, designed to relieve the lungs and accelerate the circulation, when depressing emotions or organic impediments cause a feeling as if the breath were pent up, consists in a sudden and large inspiration and a full, strong, effusive expiration. In vocal training, it becomes a most efficacious means of free, unembarrassed respiration, and, consequently of organic energy and of full voice. It should be repeated as the other exercises, and practised both through the nostrils and the mouth; the former being its gentler, — the latter, its more forcible form. It should be practised, also, in the tremulous style of inspiration, in which the sigh resembles a series of prolonged and subdued sobs.

### Sobbing.

Sobbing, as an instinctive act, consists in a slightly convulsive, subdued and whispering gasp, by which an instantaneous supply of breath is obtained, when the stricture caused by the suffocating effect of grief, would otherwise obstruct or suspend too long the function of inspiration. The practice of the sob facilitates the habit of easy and rapid inspiration, and the expression of pathetic emotion.

### Gasping.

Gasping is an organic act corresponding somewhat to sobbing, but much more violent, as belonging to the expression of fierce emotions

Its effects as an exercise, in disciplining the organs, are very powerful, and its use in vehement expression in dramatic passages, highly effective, and, indeed, indispensable to natural effect.

## Panting.

Panting, as a natural act, in a highly excited state of circulation, whether caused by extreme muscular exertion, or by intense emotion, consists in sudden and violent inspiration and expiration, the latter process predominating in force and sound. It is the only form of respiration practicable in high organic excitement. The practice of panting as an exercise, imparts energy to the function of respiration, and vigor to the organs. Its effect is inseparable from the expression of ardor and intense earnestness in emotion.

## ANALYSIS OF "SLIDES."

Before proceeding to the study of the other forms of the "slide," it will be an important aid to definite ideas and appropriate applications of those which have been exemplified, to pause here, and review the practice of the forms of "concrete" and "radical pitch," on elementary sounds, on syllables, and words, and to add a thorough and extensive course of practice on all gradations of the "slide," but especially its three chief forms, — the "third," "fifth," and "octave," both upward and downward.

The following diagram may be used as an ocular suggestion, to prompt and regulate the ear; each character being intended to represent the sound of an element, syllable, or word. The exercise commences with a slide of the "second," the usual interval, in "concrete pitch," between the "radical" and the "vanish" of an element, — as uttered in the common progression of the unemphatic and inexpressive "melody" of speech or reading, — and extends through all other intervals to that of the "octave." The forms which are of most frequent occurrence in reading, are repeated separately.

The bulb of each character in the diagram, represents the "radical," — the stem, the "vanish."

But it will be of great use, as a matter of practice, with a view to facility in the command of the voice, to add to the sound of the "slide," the effects of "effusion," "expulsion," and "explosion;" "radical," "median," "vanishing," "compound," "thorough stress," and "tremor;" together with those of "pure tone," "orotund," and "aspiration;" and all stages of force from the softest "subdued," to that of "shouting."

The "slide" being, in speech and reading, the only means of marking to the ear the peculiar character of many emotions, and the distinctions of thought and language, as well as the relative port'ons of sentences; the frequent practice of this element of vocal expression, becomes exceedingly important. Equally so is a discriminating and appropriate *use* of the "slide." Speech or reading, divested of its aid, becomes merely mechanical, unmeaning articulation; as we observe the fact in the syllabic reading of little children.

220                          APPENDIX.

I. *Scale of Progressive "Upward and Downward Slides;" from the "Second" to the "Octave."* [1]

II. *"Upward Slide" of the "Second."*

III. *"Upward Slide" of the "Third."*

IV. *"Upward Slide" of the "Fifth."*

V. *"Upward Slide" of the "Octave."*

VI. *Alternate "Slides" of the "Third."*

VII. *Alternate "Slides" of the "Fifth."*

VIII. *Alternate "Slides" of the "Octave."*

[1] The lowest "radical" on these diagrams, is set, for convenience' sake on E on the "first line" of the tenor clef. But, to avoid the disagreeable

The unmeaning style so often and justly complained of in school reading, and, sometimes, in professional performances, is, to a great extent, owing to want of perception in regard to the nature and effect of the "slide."

Persons who know what an expenditure of time and labor is requisite, to train the organs to clear and just execution, and even to correct intonation, in vocal music, will not be surprised at the extent of practice suggested in this department of elocution. Nor is there any branch of the subject in which close application and persevering practice are more sure of an ample reward. The ability to read aright the plainest passage of narrative, descriptive, or didactic writing, is wholly dependent on the just and discriminating use of the "slide."

### THE "WAVE," OR "CIRCUMFLEX."

One of the natural modes of "expression," in the "melody of speech," is, in the language of peculiar emotion, or marked distinction, the use of a double "slide," the upward and the downward on the same sound. This mode of voice, called the "wave," is the characteristic utterance of *sarcasm, mockery, raillery*, and other intense and keen emotions: it marks, likewise, the expression of *humor, irony,* and *wit,* and *pungent antithesis*, whether serious or humorous. In its lowest perceptible form, it aids the "swell" or "median stress" of *solemn* and *sublime* feeling. The "wave," like the single "slide," exists in all varieties of effect, from the slightest undulation of *solemnity*, in the interval of the "second," (or the "concrete" downward transition from one note of the scale to the next below,) to the "third," "fifth," and "octave." The "wave" is termed "direct," when it slides first upward and then downward "inverted," when the "downward slide" precedes, and the "upward" follows. It is termed "equal," when the "slides" are of equal height and depth; the upward and the downward being each a "third," "fifth," or "octave:" "unequal," when the one "slide" traverses a wider interval of the scale than the other; the upward, for example, being a "third," and the downward, an "octave." — Grave and sedate feeling, or the affectation of such feeling, inclines to the use of the "equal wave;" keen and sarcastic expression prefers the "unequal wave," from its greater pungency to the ear.

This element of expression, is one of the most impressive in the whole range of vocal effect. It gives, in its subdued form, a sustained dignity and grandeur to utterance, without which the long-drawn sounds of *solemnity*, would sink into monotony and feebleness. *Sarcastic* and *ironical* expression cannot be given without it. *Close distinctions of sense and meaning*, lose their point and discrimination,

---

falsette of *E* in the "fourth space," in some male voices, it may be advisable to pitch the lowest radical, in execution, on *C* on the 'first leger line below.' This change will cause no hinderance in practice; as the intervals are not affected by it, and the slides, consequently, remain the same relatively

when deprived of it. *Wit* and *humor* cease to exist to the ear, if th ambiguous and equivocal, or graphic effect of the "wave," is dropped.

An intelligent and discriminating use of this element, is indispensable, however, to its right effect. Adopted too frequently, and expressed too pointedly, it offends the ear; as it implies a want of skill on the part of the reader or speaker, and a want of perception on that of the hearer. It forms, when given in excess, the striking feature in overdone emphasis, or that which seems, by its obtrusiveness, to forestall the judgment of the person who is addressed, and compel his perceptions. It is the usual resort of the author of a pun so poor, that, without his syllabic and waving enunciation, you could not have surmised its existence.

The "wave" exists sometimes, as a mere local accident of usage, in what is termed national accent. The dialects of Scotland and of New England, furnish striking examples of the unmeaning prevalence of the "wave." The popular "Yankee story," and, not unfrequently, the emphasis of well-educated people, abound in instances of this local intonation.

The use of the "wave" should be carefully practised, in the spirit of the closest analysis, on the following examples, and, in its principal forms, applied to "tonic" elements, long syllables, and expressive words and phrases.

### EXAMPLES.

1. — *The "Equal Wave."*

*Solemnity and Sublimity.*

("Effusive orotund:" "Subdued" force: Full and prolonged "median swell:" "Low pitch:" "Equal wave of the second." The "wave" so slight as barely to be discernible.)

1. — FROM THE MORNING HYMN. — *Milton.*

" His [1] *praise*, ye *winds* that from *four quarters* **blow**
Breathe *soft* or *loud*; and *wave* your *tops*, ye *pines*,
With every *plant*, in sign of *worship wave*! "

2. — FROM AN EVENING HYMN. — *H. M. Williams.*

" While *Thee* I *seek*, protecting *Power*!
Be my *vain* wishes *stilled*;
And may this *consecrated hour*
With *better hopes* be *filled*! "

[1] The " wave " occurs on the letters denoted by italic type.

THE "WAVE." 223

*Pointed Antithesis. Serious Expression.*

1.

("Pure tone:" "Animated" force: "Radical and median stress:' "Middle Pitch:" "Equal wave of the third.")

MORAL TO A FABLE.—*Jane Taylor.*

"Let any man resolve to do right ¹ nŏw leaving ¹ thĕn to do as it can; and if he were to live to the age of Methuşelah, he would never do wrong.—But the common error is to resolve to act right after brĕakfast, or ăfter dinner, or to-mŏrrow mŏrning, or nĕxt tĭme. But nŏw, just nŏw, this ŏnce, we must go on the same as ever."

2.

("Pure tone:" "Moderate" force, "grave" style: "Median stress" "Middle pitch:" "Equal wave of the third.")

CHANCE.—*Shakspeare.*

"Alas! the while!
If Hercules, and Lichias, play at dĭce
Which is the better man, the grĕater thrŏw
May turn by fortune from the wĕaker hând."

*Pointed Antithesis. Half-humorous Style.*

3.

("Pure tone:" "Animated" force: "Median stress:" "Middle pitch ' "Equal wave of the third.")

ROMAN CITIZEN, MURMURING AGAINST THE PATRICIANS.—*Shakspeare.*

"Wê are accounted pŏor citizens; the patrĭcians gôod What authôrity sŭrfeits on, would relĭeve ûs. If they would yield us but the superfluity, while it were whŏlesome, we might guess they relieved us humânely; but they think we are too dêar: the lĕanness that afflicts ŭs, the object of our misery, is an invĕntory to particularize thĕir abŭndance: ôur sŭfferance is a găin to thêm.—Let us revenge this with our pĭkes, ere we become răkes: for the gods know I spɛak this in hûnger for brĕad, not in thĭrst for revĕnge.

---

¹ The "direct wave" is marked by the usual circumflex accent, the " inverted wave," by an inverted circumflex.

### Wit.

("Pure tone," laughing voice: "Radical and median stress" "High pitch:" "Equal wave of the third.")

BEATRICE, SPEAKING OF BENEDICK. — *Shakspeare.*

"In our last conflict, fóur of his fíve wits went halting off, and now is the whole man governed with ône: so that if he have wit enough to keep himself wărm, let him bear it for a difference between himself and his horse; for it is all the wit that he hath lêft, to be known a rĕasonable crêature."

### *Raillery.*

("Pure tone:" "Animated" force: "Median stress:" "High pitch: "Equal wave of the third.")

MENENIUS, TO THE TRIBUNES BRUTUS AND SICINIUS. — *Shakspeare.*

"You blame Marcius for being prôud?

*Brutus.* We do it not alône, sir.

*Men.* I know you can do very little alône; for your hĕlps are mâny; or else your âctions would grow wŏndrous single: your abilities are too înfant-like for doing much alône. You talk of príde: Oh! that you could turn your eyes towards the napes of your nĕcks, and make but an interior survey of your gŏod sêlves!"

### II. — *The Unequal Wave.*

### *Irony and Derision.*

("Pure tone:" "Animated" force: "Stress" varying from "radical" to "median:" "High pitch:" Unequal wave of the "third" and "fifth.")

THE CRITIC. — *Sterne.*

"How did Garrick speak the soliloquy, last night?" — "Oh! against all rule, my lord, most ungrammatically! Betwixt the substantive and the adjective, which should agree together in number case, and gender, he made a breach thus — stopping, as if the point wanted settling; and betwixt the nominative case, which, your lordship knows, should govern the verb, he suspended his voice in the epilogue, a dozen times, three seconds and three fifths by a stop-watch, my lord, each time." "Âdmi·.ble grammarian! — But, is

THE "WAVE." 225

suspending his voice, — was the sense suspended? — Did no expression of attitude or countenance fill up the chasm! — Was the eye silent? Did you narrowly look?"—"I looked only at the stopwatch, my lord!"—"Excellent observer!"

*Contempt and Derision.*

( Aspirated quality:" "Impassioned" force: "Median stress "High pitch:" "Unequal waves.")

NORVAL, IN THE QUARREL WITH GLENALVON.—*Home.*

"And who is Norval in Glenalvon's eyes?
*Glenalvon.* A pĕasant's sôn, [3. & 5.]¹ a wândering bĕggar bôy! [3. & 8.]
[3. & 5.] At bêst no more,—even if he speaks the trŭth. [3. & 5.]
[5. & 3.] "Hĕar him, my lord: he's wŏndrous condescênd ing! [5. & 3.]
Mark the *humility* of *shĕpherd Nôrval!*" [3. & 8.]

*Scorn and Derision.*

(" Aspirated pectoral and guttural quality:" "Impassioned" force: "Vanishing stress:" "High pitch:" "Unequal wave.")

CORIOLANUS, TO THE SENATORS, WHEN HIS ELECTION TO THE CONSULATE IS CONTRAVENED BY THE TRIBUNES BRUTUS AND SICINIUS; THE LATTER HAVING USED THE WORD "SHALL" IN HIS VETO.—*Shakspeare.*

"*Shăll!* [" semitone and octave."]
They chose their magistrate;
And such a one as he, who puts his *shăll*, [as before.]
His pŏpular *shăll*, against a graver bench, [as before.]
Than ever frowned in Greece!"

THE "MONOTONE."

This designation, like many others used in the technical language of elocution, is not strictly applicable to the fact of voice which it is

¹ The figures indicate the "unequal wave of the "*third*" and "*fifth*," &c In these exemplifications it is not intended that either a weaker or a stronger "expression," an infer:or or a greater "wave," may not be approrriately used If it be not out of proportion to the context. In the stronger expressions there might even be a prolonged and repeated, or "double" "wave," in highly animated reading.

used to denote. The word "monotone" should import a *strict musical sameness* of sound; but, in actual usage, it applies, rather, to successive repetitions of the same "radical" and "concrete pitch," in the common form of the latter, as in the "radical" and "vanish" of unimpassioned or inexpressive utterance.

Two causes have contributed to the license of language, in the vague use of this term: first, the fact that what is termed *monotone*, as differing from mere monotony, (the one being an intentional and impressive effect; the other, an accidental fault of the ear and habit,) is, usually, the utterance of a long, and even protracted, vowel sound, with a peculiarly full "median stress," which absorbs the attention, and occupies the ear, to the exclusion of the differential sounds of the "radical" and the "vanish." The style in "monotone" approaches comparatively near to that of music, as contradistinguished from speech by more or less of the "swell." Hence the middle point of each sound will be most impressive to the ear, and obliterate the effect of the extremes. An *apparent* absolute monotone, is thus produced. — Another cause of error in the designation of "monotone," is the effect of the close and frequent recurrence of apparently the same note, in the repetition of the same "radical" and "concrete pitch," on successive words; as what is termed "monotone" is usually a partial sameness of voice on several, or on many words, in succession.

The term "monotone," then, when used in the language of elocution, must be understood as conventional, and employed merely to avoid circumlocution. It implies the successive repetition of the same "radical" and "concrete" pitch, with the addition of a full and prolonged "median stress," so executed as to occupy the ear to the exclusion, nearly, of the "radical" and "vanish" of the sounds to which it is applied. The partial sameness of voice, thus produced, has been, not inaptly compared, as mentioned before, to the repeated sounds of a deep-toned bell; as the "monotone" is usually the expression of low-pitched, solemn utterance, analogous in effect, to the bell's perpetually recurring low note. The "monotone" is, in the true, natural, and unstudied use of the voice, — the invariable standard of elocution, — the style of *awe, reverence, solemnity, sublimity, grandeur, majesty, power, splendor,* and all other modes of feeling which imply *vastness* and *force*, particularly when associated with the idea of *supernatural* influence or agency. It expresses, also, the feelings of *amazement, terror,* and *horror,* or whatever emotion arises from the contemplation of *preternatural* effects.

The reason why this peculiar form of utterance is associated with the extremes of emotion, seems to be the same that we observe when we hear a person who has been an eye-witness of an awful event, relating what he has seen: the excess of feeling denies him the power of varied utterance; and his perpetually low, husky note, which seems to come from the depths of his inmost frame, thrills the hearer with a feeling from which a varied intonation would be an instantaneous relief. The same principle divested of the associations of horror, applies, in degree, to scenes and objects of overpowering majesty and splendor. The impression is, in such instances, too powerful to allow the varied and free play of ordinary utterance.

The "monotone," therefore, as the indication of vastness and power, pervades the style of all the noblest and most impressive forms of human language in poetry, and, not unfrequently, in prose of a high-wrought style. It abounds, particularly, in the reading of the sacred Scriptures; and it is indispensable in the devotional language of hymns. It is used likewise in verse, and in poetic prose, for melody of effect, instead of the "downward slide of complete sense."

The "monotone" does not, it is true, occur so frequently as most other modifications of voice. But, from its special office, it acquires peculiar importance. Without it, the tones of a devotional exercise, or the reading of many parts of the Scriptures, are unavoidably associated with irreverence, or utter absence of appropriate feeling. The language of Milton or of Young, becomes parody to the ear, when divested of the due effect of this impressive element of voice.

A great error, however, to be carefully avoided in actual reading and speaking, is the prevalent use of this mode of voice, without distinction of circumstances. The wearisome sameness of school reading, and of the style of many professional speakers, arises from the habitual unintentional use of this element. The monotony thus produced can be tolerated only in a law paper, a state document, a bill of lading, or an invoice, in the reading of which, the mere distinct enunciation of the words, is deemed sufficient. In other circumstances it kills, with inevitable certainty, everything like feeling or expression.

The student of elocution will derive great benefit, in his practice on "monotone," from a repetition of the elements and of words, on the recurring identical successive "radical and concrete," with full prolongation and ample "median stress."

The following examples will serve to suggest others of similar character.

EXAMPLES OF "MONOTONE."

*Devotional Awe and Reverence.*

["Effusive orotund quality:" "Subdued" force: "Median stress:"
"Very low pitch."]

[EXTRACTS FROM THE SCRIPTURES.]

¹ " Hōly! hŏly! hōly! Lōrd Gōd of Sabaoth! "

The "monotone" is usually distinguished by this horizontal mark.

"Bless the Lord, O my soul; and all that is within me, bless his holy name!"

"Unto Thee I lift up mine eyes, O Thou that dwellest in the heavens!'

*Awe, Sublimity, Majesty, Power, Horror.*

("Quality," force, "stress," and pitch, as before.)

"And I beheld when he had opened the sixth seal, and lo! there was a great earthquake. And the sun became black as sackcloth of hair, and the moon became as blood; and the stars of heaven fell unto the earth, even as a fig-tree casteth her untimely figs, when she is shaken of a mighty wind. [¹And the heaven departed as a scroll when it is rolled together; and every mountain and island were moved out of their places.] ¹And the kings of the earth, and the great men, and the rich men, and the chief captains, and the mighty men, and every bond-man, and every free-man, hid themselves in the dens and in the rocks of the mountains; and said to the mountains and rocks, ¹ 'Fall on us, and hide us from the face of Him that sitteth on the throne, and from the wrath of the Lamb: ¹ for the great day of his wrath is come; and who shall be able to stand?'"

*Amazement and Terror.*

("Aspirated pectoral quality:" "Suppressed force:" "Median stress:" "Very low pitch.")

"In thoughts from the visions of the night, when deep sleep falleth on men, ¹ fear came upon me and trembling, which made all my bones to shake. ¹ Then a spirit passed before my face; ¹ the hair of my flesh stood up. — It stood still; but I could not discern the form thereof. An image was before mine eyes; ¹ there was silence; and I heard a voice saying, ¹ 'Shall mortal man be more just than God? Shall a man be more pure than his Maker?'"

*Majesty and Grandeur*

("Orotund quality:" "Moderate" force: "Median stress:" "Low pitch.")

[DESCRIPTION OF SATAN.]—*Milton.*

"His form had not yet lost
All her original brightness, nor appeared

---

¹ A deeper note commences at each of the places thus marked. The whole passage is a succession of "monotones."

"Less than archangel ruined, and the excess
Of glory obscured ; as whēn the sūn nēw risen
Looks thrōugh the horizōntal mīsty āir,
Shorn of his beams, or from behīnd the mōon
In dim eclīpse, disāstrous twīlight shēds
On half the nations, and with fear of change
Perplexes monarchs."

*Sublimity and Splendor.*

(" Orotund quality :" "Moderate" force: "Median stress:" "Low pitch.")

[SUMMER.] —*Thomson.*

" But yonder comes the powerful King of Day,
Rejoicing in the east. The lessening cloud,
The kindling azure, and the mountain's brow,
Illumed with fluid gold, his near approach
Betoken glad. Lō! nōw, appārent āll,
Aslānt the dēw-brīght ēarth, and cōlored āir,
He lōoks in boundless mājesty abrōad,
And shēds the shīning dāy, that būrnished plays
On rōcks, and hīlls, and tōwers, and wāndering streams,
High gleaming from afār."

*Vastness, Sublimity, and Solemnity.*

( ' Orotund quality :" "Impassioned" force: "Median stress:" Low pitch.")

[THE OCEAN.] —*Byron.*

" Thou glorious mirror! where the Almighty's form
  Glasses itself in tempests ; in all time,
Calm or convulsed, — in breeze, or gale, or storm, —
  Icing the pōle, or in the tōrrid clīme
Dark heaving ; — boundless, endless, and sublime, -
  The image of Eternity, — the throne
Of the Invisible ; even from out thy slime
The monsters of the deep are made ; each zone
Obeys thee, — thou go'st forth, dread, fathomless, alone ! "

*"Poetic Monotone."*

[The " poetic monotone " is properly, the distinctive " second ' which gives to the language of *verse* or of *poetic prose*, when no marked by emphatic or impassioned force, its peculiar melody, as contrasted with the "partial cadence" of "complete sense in clauses." The two faults commonly exemplified in passages such as the following, are, 1st, that of terminating a clause which forms complete sense, with a "partial cadence,"—2d, that of terminating it with the upward "slide" of the "third." Both these errors turn verse into prose, or render poetic language in prose, dry and inexpressive; as both these modes of voice are the appropriate language of *fact*, and not of *feeling* or *melody*.]

("Pure tone:" "Subdued force: "Median stress:" "High pitch.")

1. — [Music.] —*Moore.*

" For mine is the lay that lightly floats,
And mine are the murmuring dying notes,
That fall as soft as snow on the sea,
And melt in the heart as instantly."

("Pure tone:" "Subdued" force: " Median stress:' ' Low pitch ")

2. — [Autumn Scene.] —*Mellen.*

" The winds of autumn came over the woods,
As the sun stole out from their solitudes;
The moss was white on the maple's trunk;
And dead from its arms the pale vine shrunk;
And ripened the mellow fruit hung; and red
Were the tree's withered leaves round it shed."

( 'Pure tone:" "Moderate" force: "Median stress:" "Low pitch ")

3. — [The Ocean Depths.] —*Percival.*

" Deep in the wave is a coral grove,
Where the purple mullet and gold-fish rove,
Where the sea-flower spreads its leaves of blue,
That never are wet with falling dew,
But in bright and changeful beauty shine
Far down in the green and glassy brine."

(" Quality," force, " stress," and pitch, as before )

4. — [Nature.] —*Bryant.*

" Still shall sweet summer, smiling, linger here,
And wasteful winter lightly o'er thee pass;
Bright dews of morning jewel thee, and all
The silent stars watch over thee at night;

"The mountains clasp thee lovingly within
Their giant arms, and ever round thee bow
The everlasting forests."

"*Poetic Monotone,*" in *Descriptive Prose.*

("Quality," &c., as before.)

1. — [Spring.] —*Anonymous.*

" In the calm spring evenings, what delightful hours the cottager spends in his little garden! — He is not without a feeling — unuttered though it be — of the sweetness of spring, and the delights of the passing hour; for, as the shades of night fall darkly on the scene, he leans upon his spade, and lingers to breathe the odorous air, to hear the faint murmur of his wearied bees, now settling peaceably in their hive for the night, and the glad notes of birds, dying melodiously away in the inner woods."

("Quality," &c., as before.)

2. — [The Chosen Grave.] —*Anonymous.*

" The thought is sweet to lay our bones within the bosom of our native soil. The verdure and the flowers I love, will brighten around my grave; — the same trees whose pleasant murmurs cheered my living ears, will hang their cool shadows over my dust; — and the eyes that met mine in the light of affection, will shed tears over the sod that covers me, keeping my memory green within their spirits "

" SEMITONIC OR CHROMATIC MELODY."

The uses of the musical scale, which occur, either in the natural and accustomed forms of speech, or the exercise of reading, have been, thus far in our analysis, of the character termed " diatonic." That is to say, the intervals, or the transitions, of voice, hitherto discussed in this volume, have all been such as extend to at least the interval of a full tone, or occupy the entire space necessarily traversed, in passing from one note to another, at the relative distance of a *whole tone.* The term " diatonic " may therefore be applied to all the melodial functions of voice to which we have been attending ; and the " diatonic melody " of a sentence may be briefly thus reviewed. — In the simple statement of fact or of thought, in unimpassioned narration, and in plain definition or description, the " current melody " of a sentence will consist of, 1st, the usual upward " concrete " produced by the " radical " and " vanish " of the elements of speech, traversing a tone, or occupying the interval of a " second ;" 2d, an occasional downward " concrete " of the " second ;" 3d, the differential " radical pitch," in the forms of upward and downward

## APPENDIX.

ditone," "tritone," and "alternate phrase;" 4th, the termination of the "sentential melody" by the "triad of the cadence." In impassioned narration, description, or statement, "expression" may demand, instead of the sedate and reserved effect of such "melody," the vivid style of the upward and downward "slides" of the "third," the "fifth," the "octave;" and, in extreme emotion, even a wider interval. In a still higher stage of excitement, the "wave," or double slide, of the same intervals, may be requisite; and, in extremely deep and solemn feeling, the prolonged "second," called "monotone."

This enumeration would exhaust the chief forms of "diatonic melody;" as the intervals of the "fourth," "sixth," and "seventh," are rarely found in the regulated functions of speech or in reading. *Conscious guilt, shame,* and *cowardice,* will be found, in consequence of their agitated, suppressed, and unhinged utterance, to substitute, sometimes, the imperfect effect of the downward "second" for the downward "third," a struggling and choking upward "second" for an upward "third," — the "fourth," in the same style, when the voice seems aiming at a "fifth," — and a "seventh" for an "octave." The ungovernable voice of *inebriety* sometimes shoots over the "third" into the "fourth," and so of the other intervals, or falls a tone short of its aim, through untuned ear, and organic paralysis, so as to give the peculiarly dissonant and inharmonious effect of its characteristic utterance. Boyhood, in its wild freaks of ungoverned feeling, sometimes delights to execute these anomalies of voice, for sportive effect.

But the next practically important stage of voice, connected with the study of melody as a branch of elocution, is that which is exhibited in the use of the "semitone," or half tone. To persons to whom the technical nomenclature of music is familiar, it would be sufficient to say that we have now to do with the "chromatic" scale, or that which ascends and descends by half instead of whole tones. Students of elocution who have not paid attention to musical terms, may be directed to the interval under consideration by the general statement that it is that which gives to any sound, vocal, or instrumental, or accidental, (as in the occasional tones of the wind, or of the Æolian harp,) the effect which is universally termed "plaintive."

An exact idea of the "semitone," would be formed by thinking of it as occupying precisely half the interval of the usual " concrete " of the "radical" and "vanish" of the "second" upward or downward. The student may be able to give it correct exemplification by attempting to utter a common "concrete," with a whining or plaintive tone. He will find that, in this case, his voice glides upward or downward in a style barely perceptible, and falling obviously short of that of the "diatonic concrete."

The voice of the mother condoling with her grieving child, is a vivid natural exemplification of the effect of "semitone;" as is, also, the tone of sorrow or regret, in the utterance of childhood. Even the manly expression of grief, takes this mode of utterance, especially in the language of dramatic poetry, in passages in which grief is not violent, but subdued, in its tone. The excess and caricature of this mode of voice, occurs in the whine of the dispirited child, of the exhausted invalid, of the languishing hypochondriac, or of the pathetic sentimentalist. It is thrown out still more perceptibly on the ear, in the child's whimpering approach to crying, when he is overcome by pain or apprehension. The extensive range of circumstances which require or produce the " semitone," may be distinctly apprehended, if we pass, at once, to the example afforded in the deep and peculiar tones of penitence or contrition, and of supplication,— feelings in the true and just utterance of which, it always predominates, and which cannot be expressed to the ear without it

The " semitone," or " chromatic " interval, is the appropriate expressive note of all *pathetic* and *tender* emotion. It gives utterance to *affectionate sympathy, commiseration, compassion, pity,* and *tenderness.* It is, also, the characteristic of *grief* and *sorrow* in their subdued forms, of *regret, penitence, contrition, complaint, condolence supplication,* and *entreaty.*

" Chromatic " is a term borrowed from the art of painting, and transferred to that of music, by one of those customary licenses of speech, by which the terms of one art, addressed to one sense, are transferred to another art, addressed to a different sense. This proceeding in language is owing, in most instances, to comparative paucity of appropriate terms, in the art which borrows the use of words. But it sometimes, though not always, produces a happy effect, in the form of figurative illustration, and facilitates a vivid apprehension of the idea to which a borrowed term is applied. Thus, the word " chromatic " was originally applied to the painter's scale of gradation in colors, when these are arranged not for contrast but gradual approximation to each other. Suppose, for example, a colored scale of degrees, in which one degree should be yellow ; the next, red ; the next, black. The colors would, in this case, stand forth perfectly distinct from each other ; as the tones of the " diatonic " scale exist to the ear. Suppose, again, a scale of colors divided into successive half degrees, thus ; passing gradually from the bright to the dark tint, through intervening hues, — yellow, *orange,* red, *brown,* black. We should now have a softened or mitigated transition of approximated, or half-blended, tints ; the effect corresponding, as regards the eye, to that of " chromatic " or " semitonic " progression of notes to the ear.

The effect of the " semitone " extends over all the intervals, " concrete " and " discrete," from the mere " radical " and " vanish " up to the " octave," and so downward, as designated in the " diatonic " scale. But the " octave " is comparatively seldom used in the semitonic form. The principal applications of the " semitone " are found in the " monotone," the " semitone " proper, the " third," and the " fifth." The " chromatic melody," takes effect, likewise, in all the " phrases of sentential melody," both in the " current " and the closing strains, with this peculiar exception, that the change by radical pitch " in the " chromatic current," although it is by

20*

"semitone," when *upward*, is through the interval of a "tone," when it *descends*.

The importance of "chromatic melody," as an element of elocution, will be at once perceived, when we advert to the fact of its great power over sympathy, and its value, as an instrument of effect, in the hands of the orator, the reciter, and the reader. The speaker who relies wholly on his power to overawe, to arouse, or to impel, will always be found unfit for the treatment of all subjects which appeal to human sympathy and tenderness. The orator is deficient in power, who cannot touch and soften, and melt and subdue; ne is incapable of exerting the easiest and surest sway over the heart. Genuine pathos is "the gentle hand, that leads the elephant by a hair."

The application of the semitone, as an implement of vocal effect, needs peculiar skill; as the least approach to excess in its use, or to artificial aiming at its object, renders a reader or speaker ridiculous. Some readers, however, (and the number is large among young ladies,) through habitual languor or feebleness, allow themselves to fall into "semitone," as a habit of the voice, and consequently read, on all occasions, with a gratuitous pathos of tone throughout, and in cadences, more particularly, with what the poet terms "a dying, dying fall."

A thorough command of pathetic utterance, needs a close and discriminating application to the different effects of "tone" and "semitone;" and every student of elocution, who is not master of these distinctions, should practise carefully with a musician, till he can execute, with perfect and instantaneous precision, all the applications of the "semitone" as it affects the intervals of the "semitone proper," and of the "third," and "fifth," — the forms in which it most frequently occurs in "expression."

The practice of the following examples, should be accompanied by frequent and extensive exercises on the elements, and on words and phrases, as well as lines and sentences of appropriate character. Additional examples may be found by referring to passages quoted under other heads, in various parts of this manual, for the purpose of exemplifying pathetic and tender emotions, in the various particulars of "quality," "force," "stress," "pitch," &c.

EXAMPLES OF "SEMITONE."

*Affectionate Sympathy.*

("Pure tone:" "Impassioned" force: "Vanishing stress," and "Tremor:" "High pitch:" "Semitone," throughout, — interval of the "fifth.")

ADAM, [TO ORLANDO.] — *Shakspeare.*

"What! my young master! — O my gentle master!
O my sweet master! O you memory
Of old Sir Rowland! — why, what make you here?
Why are you virtuous? Why do people love you?

And wherefore are you gentle, strong, and valiant ?
Your praise is come too swiftly home before you.
Oh! what a world is this, when what is comely
Envenoms him that bears it!"

( Pure tone:" "Moderate" force: "Median stress:" "Middle pitch:"
"Semitone," throughout, — interval of the "third.")

ORLANDO, [TO ADAM.] — *Shakspeare.*

" O good old man! how well in thee appears
The constant service of the antique world,
When service sweat for duty, not for meed! —
" But poor old man! thou prun'st a rotten tree,
That cannot so much as a blossom yield,
In lieu of all thy pains and husbandry!"

*Commiseration.*

(" Pure tone:" "Impassioned" force: "Vanishing stress," and "tremor:" Weeping utterance: "Semitone proper," throughout; and occasional "chromatic thirds" and "fifths.")

CORDELIA, [WATCHING OVER HER FATHER, AFTER HIS EXPOSURE TO THE TEMPEST.] — *Shakspeare.*

" O my dear father! — Restoration, hang
Thy medicine on my lips; and let this kiss
Repair those violent harms, that my two sisters
Have in thy reverence made!
" Had you not been their father, these white flakes
Had challenged pity of them. Was this a face
To be exposed against the warring winds?
To stand against the deep, dread-bolted thunder?
In the most terrible and nimble stroke
Of quick, cross lightning? — to watch, (poor perdu,)
With this thin helm! Mine enemy's dog,
Though he had bit me, should have stood that night
Against my fire; And wast thou fain, poor father,
To hovel thee with swine, and rogues forlorn,
In short and musty straw? Alack, alack!
'T is wonder that thy life and wits, at once,
Had not concluded all!"

## Compassion.

("Pure 'one:" "Subdued" force: "Median stress: "Middle pitch 'Semitone proper," and "chromatic third," prevalent.

BRUTUS [ON THE NIGHT BEFORE THE BATTLE OF PHILIPPI, TO THE BOY LUCIUS, HIS ATTENDANT.] —*Shakspeare.*

"Bear with me, good boy, I am much forgetful.
Canst thou hold up thy heavy eyes awhile,
And touch thy instrument a strain or two?
I trouble thee too much; but thou art willing.
I should not urge thy duty past thy might,
I know young bloods lack for a time of rest.
I will not hold thee long: if I do live,
I will be good to thee. [*Lucius plays and sings.*]
"This is a sleepy tune: — O murderous Slumber!
Lay'st thou thy leaden mace upon my boy,
That plays thee music? — Gentle knave, good night!
I will not do thee so much wrong to wake thee.
If thou dost nod, thou break'st thy instrument:
I'll take it from thee; and, good boy, good night!"

## Pity and Tenderness.

("Pure tone:" "Subdued" force: "Median" and "Vanishing stress: "High pitch:" "Semitone proper," and "chromatic fifth," throughout.)

MIRANDA, [TO FERDINAND, WHEN HE IS UNDERGOING THE TASK OF CARRYING AND PILING LOGS, AT THE COMMAND OF HER FATHER.] —*Shakspeare.*

"Alas! now, pray you,
Work not so hard: I would the lightning had
Burned up those logs, that you are enjoined to pile!
Pray, set it down and rest you: when this burns,
'T will weep for having wearied you. My father
Is hard at study, — pray now, rest yourself:
He's safe for these three hours.

"If you'll sit down,
I'll bear your logs the while: pray, give me that, —
I'll carry it to the pile!'"

## THE "SEMITONE." 237

*Feminine Grief and Sorrow.*

(" Pure tone:" "Subdued" force: "Median stress:" "High pitch. "Semitone," throughout, and occasional "chromatic third"

[DEATH OF A CHILD AT SEA.] —*Anonymous.*

My boy refused his food, forgot to play,
And sickened on the water, day by day;
He smiled more seldom on his mother's smile;
He prattled less, in accents void of guile,
Of that wild land, beyond the golden wave,
Where I, not he, was doomed to be a slave;
Cold o'er his limbs the listless languor grew;
Paleness came o'er his eye of placid blue, —
Pale mourned the lily where the rose had died;
And timid, trembling, came he to my side. —
He was my all on earth. Oh! who can speak
The anxious mother's too prophetic woe,
Who sees death feeding on her dear child's cheek,
And strives, in vain, to think it is not so?
Ah! many a sad and sleepless night I passed,
O'er his couch, listening in the pausing blast,
While on his brow, more sad from hour to hour,
Drooped wan dejection like a fading flower!"

*Manly Grief and Sadness.*

("Effusive orotund:" "Subdued" force: "Median stress:' "Low pitch:" "Semitone" prevalent, with occasional "chromatic third.")

[THE EXILE OF THE "FOREST SANCTUARY," RECALLING HIS WIFE'S VESPER HYMN AT SEA.] —*Mrs. Hemans.*

"Thy sad, sweet hymn, at eve, the seas along, —
  Oh! the deep soul it breathed! — the love, the woe,
The fervor, poured in that full gush of song,
  As it went floating through the fiery glow
Of the rich sunset! — bringing thoughts of Spain,
With all her vesper voices, o'er the main,
  Which seemed responsive in its murmuring flow —
'*Ave sanctissima!*' — how oft that lay
Hath melted from my heart the martyr strength away!

'*Ora pro nobis, mater!*' — What a spell
  Was in those notes, with day's last glory dying

On the flushed waters . — seemed they not to swell
From the far dust wherein my sires were lying,
With crucifix and sword ? — Oh ! yet how clear
Comes their reproachful sweetness to mine ear ! —
'Ora !' — with all the purple waves replying, —
All my youth's visions rising in the strain ; —
And I had thought it much to bear the rack and chain ! "

*Regret, Penitence, Contrition.*

("Pure tone :" "Subdued" force : "Vanishing" stress : "Low pitch :
"Semitone," throughout, with occasional "chromatic third.")

[REFLECTIONS AND RESOLVE OF THE PRODIGAL SON.]

' How many hired servants of my father's have bread enough and to spare, and I perish with hunger ! I will arise and go to my father, and will say unto him, Father, I have sinned against heaven and before thee, and am no more worthy to be called thy son : make me as one of thy hired servants ! "

*Complaint.*

(" Aspirated pectoral quality :" "Impassioned" force : "Vanishing stress :" "Low pitch :" "Semitone" throughout, with occasiona. "chromatic third" and "fifth.")

[LAMENTATION OF JOB.]

" And now my soul is poured out upon me ; the days of affliction have taken hold upon me. My bones are pierced in me, in the night season : and my sinews take no rest. — He hath cast me into the mire; and I am become like dust and ashes. I cry unto thee, and thou dost not hear me : I stand up, and thou regardest me not. Thou art become cruel to me : with thy strong hand thou opposest thyself against me. Thou liftest me up to the wind ; thou causest me to ride upon it, and dissolvest my substance. For I know that thou wilt bring me to death, and to the house appointed for all living ! "

*Condolence.*

("Pure tone :" "Subdued" force : Gentle "vanishing stress :" "Middle pitch :" "Semitone," throughout, with occasional "chromatic third" and "fifth.")

[CROMWELL, TO WOLSEY ON HIS DOWNFALL.] — *Shaksptare.*

" O my lord,
Must I then leave you ! must I needs forego

So good, so noble, and so true a master!
Bear witness, all that have not hearts of iron,
With what a sorrow Cromwell leaves his lord. —
The king shall have my service; but my prayers
Forever and forever shall be yours!"

*Pathetic Supplication and Intercession.*

( Effusive orotund:" "Subdued" force: " Median stress :'' "Low pitch :'' "Semitone," throughout, with occasional "chromatic third.")
} — [KING HENRY VI. AT THE DEATH-BED OF CARDINAL BEAUFORT.] —
Shakspeare.

" O Thou eternal mover of the heavens,
Look with a gentle eye upon this wretch!
Oh! beat away the busy, meddling fiend,
That lays strong siege unto this wretch's soul;
And from his bosom purge this black despair!"

*Penitential Supplication and Entreaty.*

(' Pure tone, pectoral quality:". "Subdued" force: Soft, but earnest "vanishing stress :'' "Very low pitch:" "Semitone," throughout, with occasional "chromatic third" and "fifth.")

[THE PSALMIST'S SELF-HUMILIATION AND CONTRITION.]

" Have mercy upon me, O God, according to thy loving kindness: according unto the multitude of thy tender mercies, blot out my transgressions! Wash me thoroughly from mine iniquity and cleanse me from my sin. For I acknowledge my transgressions; and my sin is ever before me. Against thee, thee only, have I sinned, and done this evil in thy sight. Hide thy face from my sins, and blot out all mine iniquities! Deliver me from blood-guiltiness, O God thou God of my salvation!"

---

## CULTIVATION OF PURE TONE.

[Our desire to render this manual conducive, as far as possible, to perfect development of the voice, induced us to solicit the aid arising from the perfect discipline to which the organs are subjected, in the elementary practice of the art of music. Professor G. J. Webb, of the Boston Academy of Music, has, in compliance with our request, furnished the following directions for 'he cultivation of perfect purity of tone, the want of which, in elocution, is a prevalent fault, both in public speaking and private reading.]

It is important that the pupil, at the very outset of vocal study, should have the ability of appreciating purity of tone. Unless he has some distinct perception of it; in other words, unless a model of pure tone has been formed in his own mind, all merely physical effort to acquire it will be likely to fail.

The practice of the scale in swelling tones, is chiefly relied upon by teachers of vocal music, for developing the voice, and for acquiring purity, mellowness, flexibility, and an adequate breadth of tone.

Immediately before singing each sound, breath should be taken so as completely to inflate the lungs; and after pausing an instant with the chest well expanded, the sound should commence with firmness, but with great softness, then gradually augmented to the loudest degree, succeeded by being as gradually diminished to the degree of force with which it began. Each tone should be prolonged from eighteen to twenty seconds.

This exercise, as a general rule, should be continued for about two months; singing the scale daily about four times.

In the delivery of the tones of the "chest register," the air ought to escape without touching the surfaces of the mouth; the tones of the "medium register," are best acquired by directing the air a little above the upper front teeth: — in those of the "head register," the air is directed vertically

## CULTIVATION OF PURE TONE. 241

To adapt the above exercise to the Contralto and Bass voice, it must be transposed a third or fourth lower.

This mark $pp \mathrel{<} \!\! f \!\! \mathrel{>} pp$ is designed to indicate the swelling tone; the double comma before each note, the place for breathing

# EXTRACTS FOR PRACTICE.

### EXERCISES IN "PURE TONE."

("Subdued" force, or softened utterance.)

I. — *Pathos.*

1 — [THE GRAVE OF A FAMILY.] — *Gray.*

"I wandered on, scarce knowing where I went,
Till I was seated on an infant's grave.
Alas! I knew the little tenant well:
She was one of a lovely family,
That oft had clung around me like a wreath
Of flowers, the fairest of the maiden spring: —
It was a new-made grave, and the green sod
Lay loosely on it; yet affection there
Had reared the stone, her monument of fame.
I read the name I loved to hear her lisp: —
'T was not alone; but every name was there,
That lately echoed through that happy dome.

"I had been three weeks absent: — in that time
The merciless destroyer was at work,
And spared not one of all the infant group.
The last of all I read the grandsire's name,
On whose white locks I oft had seen her cheek,
Like a bright sunbeam on a fleecy cloud,
Rekindling in his eye the fading lustre,
Breathing into his heart the glow of youth, —
He died, at eighty, of a broken heart,
Bereft of all for whom he wished to live."

2. — [HEROISM OF THE PILGRIMS.] — *Choate.*

["I acknowledge the splendor of the scene of Thermopylæ in all its aspects. I admit its morality, too, and its useful influence on every Grecian heart, in that greatest crisis of Greece.]

"And yet, do you not think, that whoso could, by adequate description, bring before you that winter of the Pilgrims, its brief sunshine, the nights of storm slow waning; the damp and icy breath, felt to the pillow of the dying; its destitutions, its contrasts with all their former experience in life; its insulation and loneliness; its death-beds and burials; its memories; its apprehensions; its hopes; the consultations of the prudent; the prayers of the pious, the occasional cheerful hymn, in which the strong heart threw off its burthen, and, asserting its unvanquished nature, went up like a bird of dawn, to the skies;—do ye not think that whoso could describe them calmly waiting in that defile, lonelier and darker than Thermopylæ, for a morning that might never dawn, or might show them, when it did, a mightier arm than the Persian, 'raised as in act to strike,' would sketch a scene of more difficult and rarer heroism?"

II.— *Solemnity.*

("Subdued" force,— soft and deep tone.)

1.— [STANZA OF A RUSSIAN HYMN.]—*Bowring.*

"Thou breathest;— and the obedient storm is still,
Thou speakest;— silent the submissive wave:
Man's shattered ship the rushing waters fill;
And the hushed billows roll across his grave.
Sourceless and endless God! compared with Thee,
Life is a shadowy, momentary dream;
And time, when viewed through Thy eternity,
Less than the mote of morning's golden beam."

2.— [MIDNIGHT MUSINGS.]—*Irving.*

"I am now alone in my chamber. The family have long since retired. I have heard their steps die away, and the doors clap to after them. The murmur of voices, and the peal of remote laughter, no longer reach the ear. The clock from the church in which so many of the former inhabitants of this house lie buried, has chimed the awful hour of midnight.

"I have sat by the window, and mused upon the dusky landscape, watching the lights disappearing, one by one, from the distant village; and the moon rising in her silent majesty, and leading up all the silver pomp of heaven. As I have gazed upon these quiet groves and shadowing lawns, silvered over and imperfectly lighted by streaks of dewy moonshine, my mind has been crowded by 'thick-coming fancies' concerning those spiritual beings which

'Walk the earth,
Unseen, both when we wake and when we sleep.'"

3.— [FROM THE THANATOPSIS.]— *Bryant.*

"Go forth under the open sky, and list
To Nature's teachings, while from all around, —

Earth and her waters, and the depths of air, —
Comes a still voice. — ' Yet a few days, and thee
The all-beholding sun shall see no more
In all his course; nor yet in the cold ground,
Where thy pale form was laid, with many tears,
Nor in the embrace of ocean shall exist
Thy image. Earth, that nourished thee shall claim
Thy growth, to be resolved to earth again;
And, lost each human trace, surrendering up
Thine individual being, shalt thou go
To mix forever with the elements,
To be a brother to the insensible rock,
And to the sluggish clod, which the rude swain
Turns with his share, and treads upon.
    ' Thou shalt lie down
With patriarchs of the infant world, — with kings,
The powerful of the earth, — the wise, the good,
Fair forms and hoary seers of ages past,
All in one mighty sepulchre. — The hills,
Rock-ribbed and ancient as the sun, — the vales,
Stretching in pensive quietness between ;
The venerable woods, — rivers that move
In majesty, and the complaining brooks
That make the meadows green ; and poured round all,
Old ocean's gray and melancholy waste, —
Are but the solemn decorations all
Of the great tomb of man.' "

### III. — *Tranquillity.*

("Subdued" force, — gentle and level utterance.)

1. — [CONSTANTINOPLE, ON THE EVE OF THE LAST ASSAULT.] — *Mrs. Hemans.*

" The streets grow still and lonely; and the star,
 The last bright lingerer in the path of morn,
Gleams faint; and in the very lap of war,
 As if young Hope with Twilight's ray were born,
 Awhile the city sleeps : — her throngs, o'erworn
With fears and watchings, to their homes retire ;
 Nor is the balmy air of day-spring torn
With battle sounds ; the winds in sighs expire ;
And Quiet broods in mists, that veil the sunbeam's fire."

2. — [CONTEMPLATION.] — *Moir.*

"The sea is waveless as a lake ingulfed
'Mid sheltering hills, — without a ripple spreads
Its bosom, silent, and immense, — the hues
Of flickering day have from its surface died,
Leaving it garbed in sunless majesty.
With bosoming branches round, yon village hangs
Its rows of lofty elm trees; silently
Towering in spiral wreaths to the soft sky,
The smoke from many a cheerful hearth ascends
Melting in ether.

"As I gaze, behold
The evening star illumines the blue south
Twinkling in loveliness. O holy star,
Thou bright dispenser of the twilight dews,
Thou herald of Night's glowing galaxy,
And harbinger of social bliss! how oft,
Amid the twilights of departed years,
Resting beside the river's mirror clear,
On trunk of mossy oak, with eyes upturned
To thee in admiration, have I sat
Dreaming sweet dreams, till earth-born turbulence
Was all forgot, and thinking that in thee,
Far from the rudeness of this jarring world,
There might be realms of quiet happiness!"

3. — [PEACE.] — *Anonymous.*

"Lovely art thou, O Peace! and lovely are thy children; and ovely are the prints of thy footsteps in the green valleys.

"Blue wreaths of smoke ascend through the trees, and betray the half-hidden cottage: the eye contemplates well-thatched ricks and barns bursting with plenty: the peasant laughs at the approach of winter.

"White houses peep through the trees; cattle stand cooling in the pool; the casement of the farm-house is covered with jessamine and honeysuckle; the stately green-house exhales the perfume of summer climates.

"Children climb the green mound of the rampart: and ivy holds together the half-demolished buttress

"The lame, the blind, and the aged, repose in hospitals.
"Justice is dispensed to all: law sits steady on her throne."

4.—[SABBATH MORNING.]—*Grahame.*

'How still the morning of the hallowed day!
Mute is the voice of rural labor, hushed
The ploughboy's whistle, and the milkmaid's song.
The scythe lies glittering in the dewy wreath
Of tedded grass, mingled with faded flowers,
That yestermorn bloomed waving in the breeze.
Sounds the most faint attract the ear,—the hum
Of early bee, the trickling of the dew,
The distant bleating midway up the hill.
Calmness sits throned on yon unmoving cloud.
To him who wonders o'er the upland leas,
The blackbird's note comes mellower from the dale
And sweeter from the sky the gladsome lark
Warbles his heaven-tuned song; the lulling brook
Murmurs more gently down the deep-worn glen;
While from yon cottage-roof whose curling smoke
O'ermounts the mist, is heard, at intervals,
The voice of psalms,—the simple song of praise."

" MODERATE FORCE."

I.—" *Grave*" *Style.*

(Tone smooth, but inclining to deep.)

1.—[ADMONITION.]—*Anonymous.*

" 'T is not in man
To look unmoved upon that heaving waste,
Which, from horizon to horizon spread,
Meets the o'erarching heavens on every side,
Blending their hues in distant faintness there.

" 'T is wonderful!—and yet, my boy, just such
Is life. Life is a sea as fathomless,
As wide, as terrible, and yet sometimes
As calm and beautiful. The light of heaven
Smiles on it; and 't is decked with every hue
Of glory and of joy. Anon dark clouds
Arise; contending winds of fate go forth;—
And Hope sits weeping o'er a general wreck.

" And thou must sail upon this sea, a long

Eventful voyage. The wise *may* suffer wreck,—
The foolish *must*. Oh! then be early wise!
Learn from the mariner his skilful art
To ride upon the waves, and catch the breeze,
And dare the threatening storm, and trace a path
'Mid countless dangers, to the destined port
Unerringly secure. Oh! learn from him
To station quick-eyed Prudence at the helm,
To guard thy sail from Passion's sudden blast,
And make Religion thy magnetic guide,
Which, though it trembles as it lowly lies,
Points to the light that changes not,—in heaven."

2.—[Cosrou's Address to Mirza.]—*Hawksworth.*

"Be not offended: I boast of no knowledge that I have not received. As the sands of the desert drink up the drops of the rain, or the dew of the morning, so do I also, who am but dust, imbibe the instructions of the Prophet. Believe, then, it is he who tells thee, all knowledge is profane which terminates in thyself; and by a life wasted in speculation, little even of this can be gained. When the gates of paradise are thrown open before thee, thy mind shall be irradiated in a moment: here, thou canst do little more than pile error upon error,—there thou shalt build truth upon truth. Wait, therefore, for the glorious vision.

"Much is in thy power; and therefore much is expected of thee. Though the Almighty only can give virtue, yet, as a prince, thou mayest stimulate those to beneficence, who act from no higher motive than immediate interest: thou canst not produce the principle, but mayst enforce the practice. Let thy virtue be thus diffused; and if thou believest with reverence, thou shalt be accepted above.

"Farewell! May the smile of Him who resides in the heaven of heavens, be upon thee; and against thy name, in the volume of His will, may happiness be written!"

II.—"*Serious*" *Style.*

(Tone, smooth and level, but spirited.)

1.—[Uses of Knowledge.]—*Alison.*

"One great end to which all knowledge ought to be employed, is the welfare of humanity. Every science is the foundation of some art beneficial to men; and while the study of it leads us to see the beneficence of the laws of nature, it calls upon us also to follow the great end of the Father of nature, in their employment and application.

"I need not say what a field is thus opened to the benevolence of knowledge; I need not tell you, that, in every department of learning, there is good to be done to mankind. I need not remind you, that the age in which we live has given us the noblest examples in this kind, and that science now finds its highest glory in improving the condition, or in allaying the miseries of humanity."

2.— [EARLY RISING.]—*Hurd.*

"Rise with the lark, and with the lark to bed.
The breath of night's destructive to the hue
Of every flower that blows. Go to the field,
And ask the humble daisy why it sleeps
Soon as the sun departs: Why close the eyes
Of blossoms infinite, ere the still moon
Her oriental veil puts off? Think why,
Nor let the sweetest blossom be exposed
That nature boasts, to night's unkindly damp.
Well may it droop, and all its freshness lose,
Compelled to taste the rank and poisonous steam
Of midnight theatre, and morning ball.
Give to repose the solemn hour she claims;
And, from the forehead of the morning, steal
The sweet occasion. Oh! there is a charm
That morning has, that gives the brow of age
A smack of youth, and makes the lip of youth
Breathe perfumes exquisite. Expect it not,
Ye who till noon upon a down bed lie,
Indulging feverish sleep, or, wakeful, dream
Of happiness no mortal heart has felt,
But in the regions of romance."

3 — [COUNSELS OF POLONIUS TO LAERTES.]—*Shakspeare.*

"These few precepts in thy memory
Look thou character. Give thy thoughts no tongue
Nor any unproportioned thought his act.
Be thou familiar, but by no means vulgar.
The friends thou hast, and their adoption tried,
Grapple them to thy soul with hooks of steel;

But do not dull thy palm with entertainment
Of each new-hatched unfledged comrade. Beware
Of entrance to a quarrel; but, being in,
Bear it that the opposer may beware of thee.
Give every man thine ear, but few thy voice :
Take each man's censure but reserve thy judgment.
Costly thy habit as thy purse can buy,
But not expressed in fancy; rich, not gaudy;
For the apparel oft proclaims the man:
Neither a borrower nor a lender be;
For loan oft loses both itself and friend;
And borrowing dulls the edge of husbandry.
This above all, — To thine own self be true;
And it must follow, as the night the day,
Thou canst not then be false to any man."

III. — *"Animated,"* or *Lively Style.*

(Tone smooth, but inclining to high.)

1. — [MORNING.] — *Beattie.*

" The cottage curs at early pilgrim bark :
Crowned with her pail the tripping milkmaid sings;
  The whistling ploughman stalks afield; and hark!
Down the rough slope the ponderous wagon rings;
Through rustling corn the hare astonished springs;
  Slow tolls the village clock the drowsy hour;
The partridge bursts away on whirring wings;
  Deep mourns the turtle in sequestered bower,
And shrill lark carols clear from her aërial tower "

2. — [MORNING.] — *Thomson.*

· " With quickened step,
Brown Night retires : young Day pours in apace,
And opens all the lawny prospect wide.
The dripping rock, the mountain's misty top,
Swell on the sight, and brighten with the dawn.
Blue, through the dusk, the smoking currents shine;
And from the bladed field the fearful hare
Limps awkward; while along the forest glade
The wild deer trip, and often, turning, gaze
At early passenger. Music awakes
The native voice of undissembled joy;

And thick around the woodland hymns arise.
Roused by the cock, the soon clad shepherd leaves
His mossy cottage where with Peace he dwells;
And from the crowded fold, in order drives
His flock, to taste the verdure of the morn."

3.— [ANIMAL HAPPINESS.]—*Paley.*

"The atmosphere is not the only scene of animal enjoyment Plants are covered with insects, greedily sucking their juices, and constantly, as it should seem, in the act of sucking. It cannot be doubted that this is a state of gratification. What else should fix them so closely to the operation and so long? Other species are running about, with an alacrity in their motions, which carries with it every mark of pleasure. Large patches of ground are sometimes half covered with these brisk and sprightly natures.

"If we look to what the waters produce, shoals of the fry of fish frequent the margins of rivers, of lakes, and of the sea itself. These are so happy, that they know not what to do with themselves Their attitudes, their vivacity, their leaps out of the water, their frolics in it, all conduce to show their excess of spirits, and are simply the effects of that excess."

IV.—"*Gay,*" *or Brisk, Style.*

(Tone, smooth and high.)

1.— [RUSTIC SUPERSTITIONS.]—*Milton*

" Then to the spicy nut brown ale,
With stories told of many a feat,
How fairy Mab the junkets eat:
She was pinched and pulled, she said;
And he by friar's lantern led,
Tells how the drudging goblin sweat,
To earn his cream bowl duly set,
When in one night, ere glimpse of morn.
His shadowy flail hath threshed the corn,
That ten day-laborers could not end;
Then lies him down, the lubber fiend,
And, stretched out all the chimney's length
Basks at the fire his hairy strength;
And crop-full, out of doors he flings,
Ere the first cock his matin rings."

## "PURE TONE:"—"GAY" STYLE.

(Tone smooth, high, and loud.)

2.—[FROM THE ODE ON THE PASSIONS.]—*Collins*

" But oh! how altered was its sprightlier tone,
When Cheerfulness, a nymph of healthiest hue,—
Her bow against her shoulder flung,
Her buskins gemmed with morning dew,—
Blow an inspiring air, that dale and thicket rung,
The hunter's call, to Faun and Dryad known.
The oak-crowned Sisters, and their chaste-eyed Queen
   Satyrs and Sylvan boys, were seen
   Peeping from forth their alleys green:
Brown Exercise rejoiced to hear,
And Sport leaped up, and seized his beechen spear

" Last came Joy's ecstatic trial:—
He, with viny crown advancing,
First to the lively pipe his hand addressed;—
But soon he saw the brisk awakening viol,
Whose sweet entrancing voice he loved the best.
They would have thought, who heard the strain,
They saw in Tempe's vale her native maids,
Amidst the festal sounding shades
To some unwearied minstrel dancing;
While, as his flying fingers kissed the strings,
   Love framed with Mirth a gay fantastic round,—
   Loose were her tresses seen, her zone unbound;
   And he, amid his frolic play,
   As if he would the charming air repay,
Shook thousand odors from his dewy wings."

3.—[THE FALL OF LODORE.]—*Southey.*

" How does the water come down at Lodore?
   Receding and speeding,
   And shocking and rocking
   And darting and parting,
   And dripping and skipping,
   And whitening and brightening,
   And quivering and shivering,
   And hitting and splitting,
   And rattling and battling,
   And running and stunning,

And hurrying and skurrying,
And glittering and frittering,
And gathering and feathering;
And clattering and battering and shattering,
And rushing and flushing and brushing and gushing,
And flapping and rapping and clapping and slapping
Advancing and prancing and glancing and dancing,
And so never ending but always descending,
Sounds and motions forever and ever are blending."

V. — *"Humorous," or Playful, Style.*

*Exercise.*

[In the reading of the following scene, the tone of humor is exemplified in the laughing and bantering utterance in which the audience make their remarks on the absurd attempts at sublimity, solemnity, and pathos, which are made by the clownish amateur actors. These worthies have, it may be recollected, volunteered a play on the story of Pyramus and Thisbe, for the entertainment of the court of Theseus, " duke " of Athens, during a season of festivity.]

(Tone smooth, but in laughing utterance, in the italic passages.)

[SCENE FROM THE MIDSUMMER NIGHT'S DREAM.] — *Shakspeare.*

"*Enter Lion and Moonshine.*

"*Lion*   You ladies, you whose gentle hearts do fear
The smallest monstrous mouse that creeps on floor,
May now, perchance, both quake and tremble here,
When lion rough in wildest rage doth roar.
Then know, that I, one Snug, the joiner, am, —
No lion fell, nor else no lion's dam;
For if I should as lion come in strife
Into this place, 't were pity of my life.
*Theseus. A very gentle beast, and of good conscience.*
*Demetrius. The very best at a beast, my lord, that e'e- I saw*
*Lysander. This lion is a very fox for his valor.*
*Thes. True; and a goose for his discretion.*
*Dem. Not so, my lord: for his valor cannot carry his discretion and the fox carries the goose.*

---

[1] The remarks which exemplify the mode of utterance mentioned above are distinguished by italics.

*Thes. His discretion, I am sure, cannot carry his valor; for the goose carries not the fox. It is well': leave it to his discretion; and let us listen to the moon.*
Moon. 'This lantern doth the horned moon present:
'Myself the man i' the moon do seem to be.'
*Thes. This is the greatest error of all the rest: the man should be put into the lantern. How is it else the man i' the moon?*
*Dem. He does not come there for the candle; for, you see, it is already in snuff.*
*Hippolyta. I am aweary of this moon: would he would change!*
*Thes. It appears, by his small light of discretion, that he is in the wane: but yet, in courtesy, in all reason, we must stay the time.*
*Lys. Proceed, moon*
Moon. 'All that I have to say, is, to tell you that the lantern is the moon; I, the man in the moon; this thorn-bush my thorn-bush; and this dog, my dog.'
*Dem. Why, all these should be in the lantern: for they are in the moon. — But silence! — here comes Thisbe."*

## EXERCISES IN "OROTUND" UTTERANCE.

To young persons whose organs are yet pliant, and susceptible of the full effects of cultivation, and to students who are desirous of acquiring a perfect command over the vocal organs, for the purposes of effective public speaking, as well as to persons who wish to attain facility in the strong impassioned expression of vocal music, as exemplified in occasional passages of the oratorio and the opera, the power of orotund utterance, in all its extent, is indispensable as an accomplishment. Capacious and vigorous organs, a high state of health, an energetic will, a deep and quick susceptibility of the inspiration of poetic passion, enable some individuals to become powerful vocalists and speakers, with comparatively little training or express practice. But the vast majority of human beings cannot attain the effective expression of intense emotion, without the aid of systematic culture and persevering application; and, to all classes of students, such assistance is of immense advantage: the more regular and extensive the discipline, the greater is always the result in power of voice.

For these reasons, it will be of the utmost service, as an efficacious mode of training, to repeat, with due frequency, previous to commencing the following exercises, the organic functions of *breathing* in its different forms, as before suggested, and the *yawning* :*gh ing*, *crying*, and *laughing* modes of utterance, on the "ton*e* elements," and on words selected from the "exercises in enunciation"

I. — "EFFUSIVE OROTUND."

1. -- *Pathos and Gloom, or Melancholy, united with Grandeur*

1. — [OSSIAN'S APOSTROPHE TO THE SUN.] — *Macpherson.*

"O thou that rollest above, round as the shield of my fathers! whence are thy beams, O sun! thy everlasting light? Thou comest forth in thy awful beauty: the stars hide themselves in the sky; the moon, cold and pale, sinks in the western wave. But thou thyself movest alone: who can be a companion of thy course! The oaks of the mountains fall; the mountains themselves decay with years; the ocean shrinks and grows again; the moon herself is lost in the heavens; but thou art forever the same, rejoicing in the brightness of thy course. When the world is dark with tempests, when thunders roll and lightnings fly, thou lookest in thy beauty from the clouds, and laughest at the storm. — But to Ossian thou lookest in vain; for he beholds thy beams no more; whether thy yellow hair floats on the eastern clouds, or thou tremblest at the gates of the west. But thou art, perhaps, like me, — for a season: thy years will have an end. Thou wilt sleep in thy clouds, careless of the voice of the morning."

2. — [MILTON'S ALLUSION TO HIS LOSS OF SIGHT.]

"Seasons return! But not to me returns
Day, or the sweet approach of even or morn;
Or sight of vernal bloom, or summer's rose,
Or flocks or herds or human face divine;
But cloud, instead, and ever-during dark
Surround me, from the cheerful ways of men
Cut off, and, for the book of knowledge fair,
Presented with a universal blank
Of nature's works, to me expunged and razed,
And wisdom at one entrance quite shut out!"

3. — [FROM THE ODE ON THE PASSIONS.] — *Collins.*

"With eyes upraised as one inspired,
Pale Melancholy sat retired,
And from her wild, sequestered seat,
In notes by distance made more sweet,
Poured through the mellow horn her pensive soul;
And, dashing soft from rocks around,
Bubbling runnels joined the sound;
Through glades and glooms the mingled measure stole;

Or, o'er some haunted stream, with fond delay
Round a holy calm diffusing,
Love of peace and lonely musing,
In hollow murmurs died away."

II   *Solemnity and Sublimity, combined with Tranquillity.*

[FROM THE THANATOPSIS.] — *Bryant.*

" Yet not to thy eternal resting place
Shalt thou retire alone, nor couldst thou wish
Couch more magnificent. Thou shalt lie down
With patriarchs of the infant world, — with kings,
The powerful of the earth, — the wise, the good,
Fair forms and hoary seers of ages past,
All in one mighty sepulchre. The hills,
Rock-ribbed, and ancient as the sun; the vales,
Stretching in pensive quietness between;
The venerable woods, rivers that move
In majesty, and the complaining brooks
That make the meadows green; and, poured round all,
Old ocean's gray and melancholy waste, —
Are but the solemn decorations all
Of the great tomb of man! The golden sun,
The planets, all the infinite host of heaven,
Are shining on the sad abodes of death,
Through the still lapse of ages. All that tread
The globe are but a handful to the tribes
That slumber in its bosom. Take the wings
Of morning, and the Barcan desert pierce,
Or lose thyself in the continuous woods,
Where rolls the Oregon, and hears no sound,
Save his own dashings, — yet the dead are there ;
And millions in those solitudes, since first
The flight of years began, have laid them down
In their last sleep; — the dead reign there alone!"

III. — *Reverence, and Adoration.*[1]

1. — [FROM THE MORNING HYMN IN PARADISE.] — *Milton.*

" These are Thy glorious works, Parent of Good,

The appropriate tone of *devotion* is uniformly characterized by "effusive orotund" utterance.

Almighty! Thine this universal frame
Thus wondrous fair,—Thyself how wondrous thee
Unspeakable! who sitt'st above these heavens
To us invisible, or dimly seen
'Midst these thy lowest works.
Yet these declare Thy goodness beyond thought
And power divine!"

2.—[ADORATION OFFERED BY THE ANGELS.]—*Milton*

"Thee, Father, first they sung, omnipotent,—
Immutable, immortal, infinite,—
Eternal King! Thee Author of all being,
Fountain of light, thyself invisible
Amidst the glorious brightness where Thou sitt'st
Throned inaccessible, but when Thou shad'st
The full blaze of thy beams, and, through a cloud
Drawn round about Thee, like a radiant shrine,
Dark with excessive bright, thy skirts appear,
Yet dazzle Heaven that brightest seraphim
Approach not, but with both wings veil their eyes."

II.—" EXPULSIVE OROTUND."

I.—*"Declamatory" Style.*

1.—*Oratorical Invective.*

[AGAINST WARREN HASTINGS.]—*Burke.*

'By the order of the House of Commons of Great Britain, I impeach Warren Hastings of high crimes and misdemeanors.

'I impeach him in the name of the Commons of Great Britain in Parliament assembled, whose parliamentary trust he has abused.

"I impeach him in the name of the Commons of Great Britain, whose national character he has dishonored.

"I impeach him in the name of the people of India, whose laws, rights, and liberties he has subverted.

"I impeach him in the name of the people of India, whose property he has destroyed, whose country he has laid waste and desolate.

"I impeach him in the name of human nature itself, which he has cruelly outraged, injured, and oppressed, in both sexes. And I impeach him in the name and by the virtue of those eternal laws of justice, which ought equally to pervade every age, condition, rank and situation, in the world."

## 2.—*Oratorical Apostrophe and Interrogation*

[FROM CICERO'S ACCUSATION OF VERRES.]

" O Liberty!—O sound once delightful to every Roman ear!— O sacred privilege of Roman citizenship!—Once sacred, now trampled upon. But what then? Is it come to this? Shall an inferior magistrate, a governor, who holds his whole power of the Roman people, in a Roman province, within sight of Italy, bind, scourge, torture with fire and red hot plates of iron, and at last put to the infamous death of the cross, a Roman citizen? Shall neither the cries of innocence expiring in agony, nor the tears of pitying spectators, nor the majesty of the Roman commonwealth, nor the fear of the justice of his country, restrain the licentious and wanton cruelty of a monster, who, in confidence of his riches, strikes at the root of liberty, and sets mankind at defiance!"

## 3.—*Vehement Oratorical Address.*

[FROM PATRICK HENRY'S WAR SPEECH.]

"They tell us, sir, that we are weak, unable to cope with so formidable an adversary. Sir, we are not weak, if we make a proper use of those means which the God of nature hath placed in our power. Three millions of people, armed in the holy cause of liberty, and in such a country as that which we possess, are invincible by any force which our enemy can send against us.

"But, sir, we shall not fight our battles alone. There is a just God, who presides over the destinies of nations, and who will raise up friends to fight our battles for us. The battle, sir, is not to the strong alone: it is to the vigilant, the active, the brave.

"Besides, sir, we have no election. If we were base enough to desire it, it is now too late to retire from the contest. There is no retreat but in submission and slavery. Our chains are forged. Their clanking may be heard on the plains of Boston. The war is inevitable; and let it come! I repeat it, sir, let it come!

"It is in vain, sir, to extenuate the matter. Gentlemen may cry ' Peace, peace!'—but there is no peace: the war is actually begun. — The next gale that sweeps from the north, will bring to our ears the clash of resounding arms! Our brethren are already in the field! Why stand we here idle? What is it that gentlemen wish? What would they have?—Is life so dear, or peace so sweet, as to be purchased at the price of chains and slavery?—Forbid it, Almighty God! I know not what course others may take; but as for me, give me liberty or give me death!"

# APPENDIX.

## II. — "*Impassioned Expression.*"

### 1. — *Poetic Invective: Epic Style.*

-[Moloch's Address.] — *Milton.*

" My sentence is for open war: of wiles,
More unexpert, I boast not: them let those
Contrive who need, or when they need, — not now
For, while they sit contriving, shall the rest,
Millions that stand in arms, and, longing, wait
The signal to ascend, sit lingering here,
Heaven's fugitives, and for their dwelling-place
Accept this dark opprobrious den of shame,
The prison of his tyranny who reigns
By our delay? No! let us rather choose,
Armed with hell flames and fury, all at once
O'er heaven's high towers to force resistless way,
Turning our tortures into horrid arms
Against the Torturer; when, to meet the noise
Of his almighty engine, he shall hear
Infernal thunder, and, for lightning, see
Black fire and horror shot, with equal rage,
Among his angels, and his throne itself
Mixed with Tartarean sulphur and strange fire, —
His own invented torments."

### 2. — *Poetic Apostrophe.*

[From Coleridge's Hymn to Mont Blanc.]

" Ye ice-falls! ye that from the mountain's brow
Adown enormous ravines slope amain, —
Torrents, methinks, that heard a mighty voice,
And stopped at once amid their maddest plunge!
Motionless torrents! silent cataracts!
Who made you glorious as the gates of heaven
Beneath the keen full moon? Who bade the sun
Clothe you with rainbows? Who with living flowers
Of loveliest blue, spread garlands at your feet? —
God! let the torrents, like a shout of nations,
Answer! and let the ice-plains echo, God! —
And they, too, have a voice, — yon piles of snow
And in their perilous fall shall thunder, God!

"Ye living flowers that skirt the eternal frost!
Ye wild goats sporting round the eagle's nest.
Ye eagles, playmates of the mountain storm!
Ye lightnings, the dread arrows of the clouds!
Ye signs and wonders of the elements!
Utter forth God, and fill the hills with praise!"

### 3. — *Poetic Invective: Lyric Style.*

[LOCHIEL'S REPLY TO THE SEER.] — *Campbell.*

"False wizard, avaunt! I have marshalled my clan:
Their swords are a thousand, — their bosoms are one!
They are true to the last of their blood and their breath,
And like reapers descend to the harvest of death.
Then welcome be Cumberland's steed to the shock!
Let him dash his proud foam like a wave on the rock.
But woe to his kindred, and woe to his cause,
When Albyn her claymore indignantly draws;
When her bonneted chieftains to victory crowd,
Clan Ranald, the dauntless, and Moray the proud;
All plaided and plumed in their tartan array!"

### 4. — *Ecstatic Poetic Apostrophe.*

[THE RESURRECTION OF CHRIST.] — *Young.*

"Hear, O ye nations! hear it, O ye dead!
He rose, He rose, — he burst the bars of death.
The theme, the joy, how then shall men sustain?
Oh! the burst gates! crushed sting! demolished throne!
Last gasp of vanquished Death! Shout, earth and heaven,
That sum of good to man! whose nature then
Took wing, and mounted with him from the tomb.
—————— "Man, all immortal, hail!
Hail, Heaven, all lavish of strange gifts to man!
Thine all the glory! man's the boundless bliss!"

### *Shouting.*

CITIZENS, [AFTER ANTONY'S ORATION OVER THE BODY OF CÆSAR.] —
*Shakspeare.*

"Come, brands, ho! fire-brands! — To Brutus'! to Cassius'! —
burn all! Some to Decius' house, and some to Casca's; some to
Ligarius: — away! o!"

**WILLIAM TELL,** [TO THE MOUNTAINS, ON REGAINING HIS LIBERTY]— *J. S. Knowles.*

"Ye crags and peaks, I'm with you once again!
I hold to you the hands you first beheld,
To show they still are free.

"Ye guards of liberty,
I'm with you, once again! I call to you
With all my voice!—I hold my hands to you
To show they still are free!"

III.—" EXPLOSIVE OROTUND."

1.—*Anger, excited to Rage.*

[FROM THE LORD OF THE ISLES.]— *Scott.*

**Lorn,** [*about to assault Bruce.*] "Talk not to me
Of odds or match!—When Comyn died,
Three daggers clashed within his side!
Talk not to me of sheltering hall!—
The Church of God saw Comyn fall!
On God's own altar streamed his blood;
While o'er my prostrate kinsman stood
The ruthless murderer, even as now,—
With armed hand and scornful brow.—
Up! all who love me!—blow on blow!
And lay the outlawed felons low!"

2.—*Wrath and Scorn.*

[FROM THE LADY OF THE LAKE.]—*Scott.*

**Roderick Dhu,** [*to Malcom Græme.*] "Back! beardless boy
Back! minion!—Holdst thou thus at naught
The lesson I so lately taught?—
This roof, the Douglas, and that maid,
Thank thou for punishment delayed!

*Anger and Defiance.*

**Malcom.** Perish my name, if aught afford
Its chieftain safety, save his sword!

*Indignant Rebuke*

**Douglas** Chieftains, forego!

I hold the first who strikes, my foe.—
Madmen! forbear your frantic jars!"

### 3. — *Scorn and Defiance.*[1]

[From Paradise Lost.] — *Milton.*

*Satan*, [*to Death.*] " Whence and what art thou, execrable shape!
That dar'st, though grim and terrible, advance
Thy miscreated front athwart my way
To yonder gates? Through them I mean to pass,—
That be assured,— without leave asked of thee:
Retire! or taste thy folly ; and learn by proof,
Hell-born! not to contend with spirits of heaven."

### *Wrath and Threatening.*[1]

*Death*, [*in reply.*] " Back to thy punishment,
False fugitive! and to thy speed add wings ;
Lest with a whip of scorpions I pursue
Thy lingering, or, with one stroke of this dart,
Strange horror seize thee, and pangs unfelt before!"

### 4. — *Infuriate Anger.*

The Doge of Venice, [on the eve of his execution, in the concluding words of his curse on the city.] — *Byron's Marino Faliero.*

" Thou den of drunkards with the blood of princes!
Gehenna of the waters! thou sea Sodom!
Thus I devote thee to the infernal gods!
Thee and thy serpent seed!
[*To the executioner.*] Slave, do thine office!
Strike as I struck the foe! Strike as I would
Have struck those tyrants! Strike deep as my curse,
Strike — and but once!"

### 5. — *Courage.*

[Bozzaris, to his band of Suliotes.] — *Halleck.*

" Strike till the last armed foe expires!
Strike for your altars and your fires!
Strike for the green graves of your sires,
God and your native land!"

---

[1] The fierceness of emotion, in some instances, adds "aspirated quality" to orotund.

## EXERCISES IN "ASPIRATED QUALITY."

### I. — "EFFUSIVE" UTTERANCE.

**1.** — *Awe, in its gentlest form, with moderate " Aspiration.'*

("Pectoral Quality.")

*Note.* The effect intended here is but the slightest approach to a whisper, — a barely perceptible breathing sound accompanying the utterance, — not unlike, in its effect, to a slight hoarseness.

[JACOB'S EXCLAMATION AFTER HIS DREAM.]

" How dreadful is this place! This is none other than the house of God, and the gate of heaven! "

*2. — The same emotion deepened.*

[FROM THE BOOK OF PSALMS.]

"Of old hast Thou laid the foundation of the earth; and the heavens are the work of Thy hands. They shall perish, but Thou shalt endure; yea, all of them shall wax old like a garment; as a vesture shalt Thou change them, and they shall be changed: but Thou art the same; and Thy years shall have no end.

" Before the mountains were brought forth, or ever Thou hadst formed the earth and the world, even from everlasting to everlasting, Thou art God.

" Thou turnest man to destruction; and sayest, ' Return, ye children of men.' For a thousand years, in Thy sight, are but as yesterday, when it is past, and as a watch in the night.

" Thou carriest them away as with a flood; they are as a sleep: in the morning, they are like grass which groweth up. In the morning it flourisheth and groweth up: in the evening, it is cut down, and withereth."

**3.** —*Awe, still deeper in " expression," and stronger in " aspiration*

[NATURE, SHRINKING FROM DEATH.] — *Campbell*

" Yet half I hear the parting spirit sigh,
' It is a dread and awful thing to die! ' —
Mysterious worlds, untravelled by the sun, —
Where Time's far-wandering tide has never run, —
From your unfathomed shades, and viewless spheres,
A warning comes, unheard by other ears.
'T is Heaven's commanding trumpet, long and loud,

Like Sinai's thunder pealing from the cloud!
While Nature hears, with terror-mingled trust,
The shock that hurls her fabric to the dust,
And, like the trembling Hebrew, when he trod
The roaring waves, and called upon his God,
With mortal terrors clouds immortal bliss,
And shrieks, and hovers, o'er the dark abyss!"

4. — *Awe, extending to Fear: with still stronger " aspiration*
[FROM A RUSSIAN HYMN.] — *Bowring.*

"It thunders! Sons of dust, in reverence bow!
Ancient of days! thou speakest from above:
Thy right hand wields the bolt of terror now;
That hand which scatters peace and joy and love.
Almighty! trembling like a timid child,
I hear Thy awful voice, — alarmed, afraid,
I see the flashes of Thy lightning wild,
And in the very grave would hide my head!"

5. — *Horror and Fear: the effect transcending that of Awe; the*
" *aspiration* " *nearly a whisper.*

MACBETH, [MEDITATING THE MURDER OF DUNCAN.] — *Shakspeare.*

"Now o'er the one half world
Nature seems dead; and wicked dreams abuse
The curtained sleep; now witchcraft celebrates
Pale Hecate's offerings; and withered murder,
Alarumed by his sentinel, the wolf,
Whose howl 's his watch, thus with his stealthy pace,
Towards his design
Moves like a ghost. — Thou sure and firm-set earth!
Hear not my steps, which way they walk; for fear
The very stones prate of my whereabout,
And take the present horror from the time,
Which now suits with it."

II. — " EXPULSIVE " UTTERANCE.

1 — *Horror and Amazement:* " *aspiration*" *increased by* " *expulsion.*"
(" Pectoral Quality.")

HAMLET, [TO THE GHOST OF HIS FATHER.] — *Shakspeare.*

"What may this mean,
That thou, dead corse, again, in complete steel,

Revisit'st thus the glimpses of the moon,
Making night hideous; and we fools of nature
So horridly to shake our disposition
With thoughts beyond the reaches of our souls!"

2. — *Horror and Terror: effect still farther increased*

CLARENCE, [RELATING HIS DREAM.] — *Shakspeare*

"Oh! I have passed a miserable night,
So full of fearful dreams, of ugly sights,
That, as I am a Christian faithful man,
I would not spend another such a night,
Though 't were to buy a world of happy days
So full of dismal terror was the time!
———— " My dream was lengthened after life: —
Oh! then began the tempest to my soul! ——
" With that, methought, a legion of foul fends
Environed me, and howled in mine ears
Such hideous cries, that, with the very noise
I trembling waked, and, for a season after,
Could not believe but that I was in hell;
Such terrible impression made my dream!"

3. — *Fear.*

(Whispering Voice: "Guttural Quality.")

CALIBAN, [CONDUCTING STEPHANO AND TRINCULO TO THE CELL OF PROSPERO.] — *Shakspeare.*

" Pray you tread softly, — that the blind mole may not
Hear a foot fall: we are now near his cell
            Speak softly!
All 's hushed as midnight yet.
            See'st thou here!
This is the mouth o' the cell: no noise! and enter

4. — *Fear and Alarm.*

(Forcible Half-Whisper: "Pectoral Quality.")

ALONZO, [WHO, WITH GONZALO, IS SUDDENLY AWAKENED BY THE INTERVENTION OF ARIEL, AND FINDS THE CONSPIRATORS, SEBASTIAN AND ANTONIO, WITH THEIR SWORDS DRAWN.] — *Shakspeare.*

" Why, how now, ho! — awake! — Why are you drawn!

Wherefore this ghastly looking?
*Gonzalo.* What's the matter?
*Sebastian.* Whiles we stood here, securing your repose,
Even now, we heard a hollow burst of bellowing
Like bulls or rather lions: did it not wake you?
It struck mine ear most terribly.
*Antonio.* Oh! 't was a din to fright a monster's ear:
To make an earthquake! — sure, it was the roar
Of a whole herd of lions!"

III. — " EXPLOSIVE " UTTERANCE.

("Guttural and Pectoral Quality.")

1. — *Hatred.*

SHYLOCK, [REGARDING ANTONIO.]

" How like a fawning publican he looks!
I hate him for he is a Christian;
But more, for that, in low simplicity,
He lends out money gratis, and brings down
The rate of usuance with us here in Venice.
If I can catch him once upon the hip,
I will feed fat the ancient grudge I bear him!
He hates our sacred nation; and he rails,
Even there where merchants most do congregate,
On me, my bargains, and my well-won thrift,
Which he calls interest. — Cursed be my tribe,
If I forgive him!"

2. — *Scorn and Abhorrence.*

("Guttural and Pectoral Quality.")

MASANIELLO, [IN REPLY TO THE BASE SUGGESTIONS OF GENUINO.]

"I would that now
I could forget the monk who stands before me;
For he is like the accursed and crafty snake!
Hence! from my sight! — Thou Satan, get behind me
Go from my sight! — I hate and I despise thee!
*These* were thy pious hopes; and I, forsooth,
Was in thy hands a pipe to play upon;
And at thy music my poor soul to death
Should dance before thee! ———

Thou standst at length before me undisguised,—
Of all earth's grovelling crew the most accursed.
Thou worm! thou viper!—to thy native earth
Return!—Away!—Thou art too base for man
To tread upon.—Thou scum! thou reptile!"

3.—*Revenge.*

("Guttural and Pectoral Quality.")

Shylock, [REFERRING TO THE POUND OF FLESH, THE PENALTY ATTACHED TO ANTONIO'S BOND.]—*Shakspeare.*

"If it will feed nothing else it will feed my revenge. He hath disgraced me, and hindered me of half a million; laughed at my losses, mocked at my gains, scorned my nation, thwarted my bargains, cooled my friends, heated my enemies. And what's his reason? I am a Jew! Hath not a Jew eyes? Hath not a Jew hands, organs, dimensions, senses, affections, passions? Is he not fed with the same food, hurt with the same weapons, subject to the same diseases, healed by the same means, warmed and cooled by the same summer and winter, as a Christian is? If you stab us, do we not bleed? If you tickle us, do we not laugh? If you poison us, do we not die? And if you wrong us, shall we not revenge? If we are like you in the rest, we will resemble you in that. If a Jew wrong a Christian, what is his humility? Revenge. If a Christian wrong a Jew, what should his sufferance be by Christian example? Why, revenge. The villany you teach me, I will execute; and it shall go hard, but I will better the instruction."

4 —*Hatred, Rage, Horror.*

("Guttural and Pectoral Quality:" fierce "aspiration.")

SATAN, [IN SOLILOQUY.]—*Milton.*

"Be then his love accursed! since love or hate,
To me alike, it deals eternal woe.
Nay, cursed be thou! since against his thy will
Chose freely what it now so justly rues.
Me miserable! which way shall I fly
Infinite wrath and infinite despair?
Which way I fly is Hell,—myself am Hell:
And in the lowest deep, a lower deep,
Still threatening to devour me, opens wide,
To which the Hell I suffer seems a Heaven!

5. — *Horror, Terror, and Alarm.*

("Pectoral Quality.")

MACBETH, [TO THE GHOST OF BANQUO.] — *Shakspeare.*

"Avaunt! and quit my sight! Let the earth hide thee!
Thy bones are marrowless, thy blood is cold:
Thou hast no speculation in those eyes
Which thou dost glare with!
"Hence, horrible shadow!
Unreal mockery, hence!"

## EXERCISES IN FORCE.

I. — [1] "SUPPRESSED" FORCE.

1. — *Whispering.*

("Effusive" Utterance.)

*Pathos.*

[DYING REQUEST.] — *Mrs. Hemans.*

"Leave me! — thy footstep with its lightest sound,
The very shadow of thy waving hair,
Wakes in my soul a feeling too profound,
Too strong for aught that lives and dies, to bear: —
Oh! bid the conflict cease!"

("Expulsive" utterance.)

*Rapture.*

[FROM THE DYING CHRISTIAN.] — *Pope.*

"Hark! they whisper, — angels say,
'Sister spirit! come away!'"

("Explosive" utterance.)

*Terror.*

[FROM BYRON'S LINES ON THE EVE OF WATERLOO.]

——— "The foe! they come, they come!"

---

"*Suppressed* force is not limited exclusively to the forms of the *whisper* or the *half-whisper*. Still, it is usually found in one or other of these; and, on this account, although sometimes intensely earnest and energetic in the expression of feeling, it is a gradation of utterance which, in point of "vocality," ranks below even the "moderate" and "subdued" forms of "pure tone." We regard, at present, its value in *vocal force,* — not in "expression."

## APPENDIX.

*Half-whisper.*

("Effusive" utterance.)

*Awe.*

[FROM THE FATE OF MACGREGOR.] — *Hogg.*

"They oared the broad Lomond, so still and serene;
And deep in her bosom now awful the scene!
Over mountains inverted the blue water curled,
And rocked them o'er skies of a far nether world!"

(' Expulsive" utterance.)

*Fear.*

" Few minutes had passed, ere they spied on the stream,
A skiff sailing light, where a lady did seem :
Her sail was a web of the gossamer's loom, —
The glow-worm her wake-light, the rainbow her boom,
A dim rayless beam was her prow, and her mast
Like wold-fire at midnight, that glares o'er the waste!"

("Explosive" utterance.)

*Terror.*

"The fox fled in terror; the eagle awoke,
As slumbering he dozed in the shelve of the rock;—
Astonished, to hide in the moonbeam he flew,
And screwed the night-heaven, till lost in the blue!"

II. —[1] " SUBDUED " FORCE

("Pure tone:" "Effusive" utterance.)

1. — *Pathos.*

[FROM THE DEATH OF KÖRNER.] — *Mrs. Hemans.*

'It was thy spirit, brother! which had made
The bright world glorious to her youthful eye,
Since first, in childhood, 'midst the vines ye played
And sent glad singing through the free blue sky.

The degree of force implied in the epithet "*subdued*," is equivalent, in general, to that which, in music, would be indicated by the term "*piano*," and which suggests an obvious *softening* of the voice from even its moderate or ordinary energy. *Pathos, solemnity,* and *tranquillity*, when so arranged in succession, imply a slight increase of energy at every stage. But all three are still inferior to "*moderate*" or ordinary force.

Ye were but two,—and when that spirit passed,
  Woe to the one, the last!

" Woe, yet not long;—she lingered but to trace
  Thine image from the image in her breast,
Once, once again to see that buried face
  But smile upon her, ere she went to rest.
Too sad a smile! its living light was o'er,—
  It answered hers no more.

" The earth grew silent when thy voice departed,
  The home too lonely whence thy step had fled;—
What then was left for her, the faithful-hearted!—
  Death, death,—to still the yearning for the dead.
Softly she perished:—be the Flower deplored
  Here with the Lyre and Sword!"

### 2. — *Solemnity.*

[DEATH.] — *Bryant.*

" Leaves have their time to fall,
And flowers to wither at the north wind's breath,
  And stars to set;—but all,
Thou hast all seasons for thine own, O Death!

" We know when moons shall wane,
When summer birds from far shall cross the sea,
  When autumn's hue shall tinge the golden grain:—
But who shall teach us when to look for thee?"

### 3. — *Tranquillity.*

[EVENING.] — *Moir.*

" 'T is twilight now:
How deep is the tranquillity!—The trees
Are slumbering through their multitude of boughs,
Even to the leaflet on the frailest twig!
A twilight gloom pervades the distant hills,
An azure softness mingl'ng with the sky "

### 4. — *Profound Repose.*

[ASPECT OF DEATH: FROM BYRON'S DESCRIPTION OF GREECE.]

" He who hath bent him o'er the dead,
Ere the first day of death is fled,—

The first dark day of nothingness,
The last of danger and distress, —
(Before Decay's effacing fingers
Have swept the lines where Beauty lingers,)
And marked the mild angelic air, —
The rapture of repose that 's there, —
The fixed yet tender traits that streak
The languor of the placid cheek,
And, — but for that sad, shrouded eye,
    That fires not, — wins not, — weeps not, — now, —
And but for that chill, changeless brow
Whose touch thrills with mortality,
And curdles to the gazer's heart,
As if to him it could impart
The doom he dreads, yet dwells upon, —
Yes, — but for these and these alone,
Some moments, — ay, — oné treacherous hour,
He still might doubt the tyrant's power:
So fair, — so calm, so softly sealed,
The first — last look — by death revealed!"

    ($^1$ "Orotund quality:" "Effusive" utterance.)

       1. — *Pathos and Sublimity.*

    WOLSEY, [ON HIS DOWNFALL.] — *Shakspeare.*

" Farewell, a long farewell, to all my greatness!
This is the state of man: To-day he puts forth
The tender leaves of hope, to-morrow blossoms,
And bears his blushing honors thick upon him:
The third day comes a frost, a killing frost;
And, — when he thinks, good easy man, full surely
His greatness is a ripening, — nips his root,
And then he falls as I do. I have ventured, —
Like little wanton boys that swim on bladders, —
This many summers, in a sea of glory,
But far beyond my depth: my high-blown pride
At length broke under me, and now has left me,

---

$^1$ The effect of " orotund quality," as transcending " pure tone," is that of a deeper, fuller, rounder, and more resonant utterance, — implying, therefore, an increase of *force*, although still a " subdued," or softened force, when compared with even an ordinary degree. In music, the distinction would still be that of "*piano.*"

Weary and old with service, to the mercy
Of a rude stream that must forever hide me!"

2. — *Solemnity and Sublimity.*

[IMMORTALITY.] — *Dana.*

"Oh! listen, man!
A voice within us speaks that startling word,
'Man, thou shalt never die!' Celestial voices
Hymn it unto our souls; according harps,
By angel fingers touched, when the mild stars
Of morning sang together, sound forth still
The song of our great immortality:
Thick-clustering orbs, and this our fair domain,
The tall, dark mountains, and the deep-toned seas,
Join in this solemn, universal song.
Oh! listen ye, our spirits; drink it in
From all the air. 'T is in the gentle moonlight;
'T is floating midst Day's setting glories; Night,
Wrapped in her sable robe, with silent step
Comes to our bed, and breathes it in our ears:
Night, and the dawn, bright day, and thoughtful eve,
All time, all bounds, the limitless expanse,
As one vast mystic instrument, are touched
By an unseen, living Hand; and conscious chords
Quiver with joy in this great jubilee.
The dying hear it; and, as sounds of earth
Grow dull and distant, wake their passing souls
To mingle in this heavenly harmony."

3. — *Tranquillity and Sublimity.*

[NIGHT.] — *Byron's Marino Faliero.*

"Around me are the stars and waters,—
Worlds mirrored in the ocean;—
And the great element, which is to space
What ocean is to earth, spreads its blue depths
Softened with the first breathings of the spring
The high moon sails upon her beauteous way,
Serenely smoothing o'er the lofty walls
Of those tall piles and sea-girt palaces,
Whose porphyry pillars and whose costly fronts,

Fraught with the orient spoils of many marbles,
Like altars ranged along the broad canal,
Seem each a trophy of some mighty deed ·
Reared up from out the waters, scarce less strangely
Than those more massy and mysterious giants
Of architecture, those Titanian fabrics,
Which point in Egypt's plains to times that have
No other record."

### 4. — *Reverence.*

[FROM THE HYMN OF THE SEASONS.] —*Thomson*

" These, as they change, Almighty Father! these
Are but the varied God. The rolling year
Is full of Thee. ——
And oft Thy voice in dreadful thunder speaks;
And oft at dawn, deep noon, or falling eve,
By brooks and groves, in hollow-whispering gales. —
In Winter, awful Thou! with clouds and storms
Around Thee thrown, tempest o'er tempest rolled, —
Majestic darkness! On the whirlwind's wing,
Riding sublime, Thou bidd'st the world adore,
And humblest Nature, with Thy northern blast."

### III. — [1] " MODERATE " FORCE.

(" Pure tone :" " Expulsive " utterance.)

"*Grave*" *Style.*

[UNDUE INDULGENCE.] —*Alison.*

" The inordinate love of pleasure is equally fatal to happiness as to virtue. To the wise and virtuous, to those who use the pleasures of life only as a temporary relaxation, as a resting-place to animate them on the great journey on which they are travelling, the hours of amusement bring real pleasure: to them the well of joy is ever full; while to those who linger by its side, its waters are soon dried and exhausted.

" I speak not now of those bitter waters which must mingle themselves with the well of unhallowed pleasure, — of the secret re-

---

[1] The term "*moderate*" is generally equivalent to "*mezzo*," in music. It has many gradations, however; of which "*grave*" is the softest. The successive steps are intimated in the arrangement of the exercises.

preaches of accusing conscience,—of the sad sense of shame and dishonor,—and of that degraded spirit, which must bend itself beneath the scorn of the world: I speak only of the simple and natural effect of unwise indulgence;—that it renders the mind callous to enjoyment; and that even though the 'fountain were full of water,' the feverish lip is incapable of satiating its thirst. Alas! here, too, we may see the examples of human folly: we may see around us, everywhere, the fatal effects of unrestrained pleasure;—the young, sickening in the midst of every pure and genuine enjoyment; the mature hastening, with hopeless step, to fill up the hours of a vitiated being; and, what is still more wretched, the hoary head wandering in the way of folly, and, with an unhallowed dotage, returning again to the trifles and the amusements of childhood."

"*Serious*" *Style*

[INFLUENCE OF LEARNING.] — *Moodie.*

"If learned men are to be esteemed for the assistance they give to active minds in their schemes, they are not less to be valued for their endeavors to give them a right direction, and moderate their too great ardor. The study of history will teach the legislator by what means states have become powerful; and in the private citizen it will inculcate the love of liberty and order. The writings of sages point out a private path of virtue, and show that the best empire is self-government, and that subduing our passions is the noblest of conquests."

"*Animated*," *or Lively, Style.*

[CHEERFULNESS.] —*Addison.*

"The cheerful man is not only easy in his thoughts, but a perfect master of all the powers and faculties of the soul: his imagination is always clear, and his judgment undisturbed; his temper is even and unruffled, whether in action or solitude. He comes with a relish to all those goods which Nature has provided for him, tastes all the pleasures of the creation which are poured about him, and does not feel the full weight of those accidental evils which may befall him.

"A cheerful mind is not only disposed to be affable and obliging, but raises the same good humor in those who come within its influence. A man finds himself pleased, he knows not why, with the cheerfulness of his companion: it is like a sudden sunshine, that awakens a secret delight in the mind, without her attending to it. The heart rejoices of its own accord, and naturally flows out into friendship and benevolence towards the person who has so kindly an effect upon it."

## "*Gay*," or *Brisk, Style*

[HABITS OF EXPRESSION.] — *Spectator.*

" Next to those whose elocution is absorbed in action, and who converse chiefly with their arms and legs, we may consider the professed *speakers*, — and, first, the emphatical, — who squeeze and press and ram down every syllable with excessive vehemence and energy. These orators are remarkable for their distinct elocution and force of expression: they dwell on the important particles *of* and *the*, and the significant conjunction *and*, — which they seem to hawk up, with much difficulty, out of their own throats, and to cram, — with no ess pain, — into the ears of their auditors. — These should be suffered only to syringe, (as it were,) the ears of a deaf man, through a hearing trumpet; though I must confess that I am equally offended with the *whisperers* or low speakers, who seem to fancy all their acquaintance deaf, and come up so close to you, that they may be said to measure noses with you. — I would have these oracular gentry obliged to talk at a distance, through a speaking trumpet, or apply their lips to the walls of a whispering gallery. — The *wits*, who will not condescend to utter anything but a *bon mot*, and the *whistlers*, or tune-hummers, who never talk at all, may be joined very agreeably together in a concert; and to these 'tinkling cymbals' I would also add the 'sounding brass,' the *bawler*, who inquires after your health with the bellowing of a town-crier."

## "*Humorous*" *Style.*

[THE CRITIC.] — *Sterne.*

" And what of this new book the whole world makes such a noise about?" — " Oh! 't is out of all plumb, my lord, — quite an irregular thing! — not one of the angles at the four corners was a right angle. I had my rule and compasses, my lord, in my pocket!" — " Excellent critic!"

" And for the epic poem your lordship bid me look at — upon taking the length, breadth, height, and depth of it, and trying them at home upon an exact scale of Bossu's — 't is out, my lord, in every one of its dimensions." — "Admirable connoisseur! — And did you step in to take a look at the great picture. on your way back?" —
"'T is a melancholy daub, my lord! — not one principle of the

'pyramid,' in any one group! — and what a price! — for there is nothing of the coloring of Titian, — the expression of Rubens, — the grace of Raphael, — the purity of Domenichino, — the *corregiescity* of Corregio, — the learning of Poussin, — the airs of Guido, — the taste of Caracci, — or the grand contour of Angelo!"

IV. — " DECLAMATORY " FORCE.

[THE AMERICAN UNION.] — *Webster.*

' While tne Union lasts, we have high, exciting, gratifying prospects spread out before us, for us and for our children. Beyond that I seek not to penetrate the veil. God grant that, in my day, at least, that curtain may not rise! God grant that on my vision never may be opened what lies behind — When my eyes shall be turned to oehold, for the last time, the sun in the heaven, may I not see him shining on the broken and dishonored fragments of a once glorious Union; on States dissevered, discordant, belligerent; — on a land rent with civil feuds, or drenched, it may be, in fraternal blood! Let their last feeble and lingering glance rather behold the gorgeous ensign of the republic, now known and honored throughout the earth, and still ' full high advanced,' — its arms and trophies streaming in their original lustre, — not a stripe erased or polluted, nor a single star obscured; — bearing, for its motto, no such miserable interrogatory as, ' What is all this worth?' nor those other words of delusion and folly, ' Liberty first, and Union afterwards,' — but everywhere spread all over, in characters of living light, blazing on all its ample folds, as they float over the sea and over the land, and in every wind under the whole heavens, that other sentiment, dear to every true American heart, — ' Liberty *and* Union, now and forever, one and inseparable!' "

*Scorn, Abhorrence, and Detestation.*

[HELEN MACGREGOR, TO THE SPY, MORRIS.] — *Scott.*

" I could have bid you live, had life been to you the same weary and wasting burden that it is to me, — that it is to every noble and generous mind. — But you, wretch! you could creep through the world unaffected by its various disgraces, its ineffable miseries, its constantly accumulating masses of crime and sorrow; — you could live and enjoy yourself, while the noble-minded are betrayed, — while nameless and birthless villains tread on the neck of the brave and long-descended: — you could enjoy yourself, like a butcher's dog in the shambles, battening on garbage, while the slaughter of the brave went on around you! This enjoyment you shall not live to partake of: you shall die, base dog!—and that before yon cloud has passed over the sun!"

V.—" IMPASSIONED" FORCE.

("Aspirated pectoral quality:" "Explosive orotund,

*Anger and Threatening.*

CATILINE, [ADDRESSING THE SENATE.]—*Croly.*

Here I devote your senate! I've had wrongs,
To stir a fever in the blood of age,
Or make the infant's sinews strong as steel.
This day's the birth of sorrows!—This hour's work
Will breed proscriptions.—Look to your hearths, my lord,
For there henceforth shall sit, for household gods,
Shapes hot from Tartarus!—all shames and crimes.—
Wan Treachery, with his thirsty dagger drawn;
Suspicion, poisoning his brother's cup;
Naked Rebellion, with the torch and axe,
Making his wild sport of your blazing thrones;
Till Anarchy come down on you like Night,
And Massacre seal Rome's eternal grave!"

*Indignant and Enthusiastic Address.*

("Expulsive orotund.")

RIENZI, [TO THE PEOPLE.]—*Miss Mitford.*

" Rouse, ye Romans!—Rouse, ye slaves!
Have ye brave sons? Look in the next fierce brawl
To see them die. Have ye fair daughters? Look
To see them live, torn from your arms, distained,
Dishonored; and, if ye dare call for justice,
Be answered by the lash. Yet, this is Rome,
That sat on her seven hills, and from her throne
Of beauty ruled the world! Yet, we are Romans.
Why in that elder day, to be a Roman
Was greater than a king!—And once again,—
Hear me, ye walls that echoed to the tread
Of either Brutus!—Once again, I swear,

The eternal city shall be free! her sons
Shall walk with princes!"

VI. — *Shouting.*

("Expulsive orotund:" intense force )

RIENZI, [TO THE CONSPIRATORS.] — *Ibid.*

"Hark! — the bell, the bell!
The knell of tyranny, — the mighty voice
That to the city and the plain, to earth
And listening heaven, proclaims the glorious tale
Of Rome re-born, and freedom!"

VII. — *Shouting and Calling.*

("Expulsive orotund," "pure tone," intense "sustained" force

[MACDUFF'S OUTCRY ON THE MURDER OF DUNCAN.] — *Shakspeare*

"Awake! awake!
Ring the alarm-bell: — Murder! and treason! —
Banquo, and Donalbain! Malcolm! awake!"

---

## MISCELLANEOUS PIECES.

### EXTRACTS FOR GENERAL PRACTICE.

EXERCISE I. — A SEA-VOYAGE. — *Irving.*

[This extract exemplifies, in its diction, the forms of *narrative, descriptive,* and *didactic* style. The emotions arising from the subject and the language, are those of *tranquillity, wonder, admiration, pathos,* and *awe.*

The first of these emotions prevails through the first two paragraphs, and produces, in the vocal "expression," "pure tone," decreasing gradually from gentle "expulsion" to "effusion:" the "force" is "moderate:" the stress, at first, "unimpassioned radical," gradually changing to a soft "median:" the "pitch" is on 'middle notes," — the "melody," "diatonic," in prevalent "intervals of the second," varying from the "simple concrete" to the "wave:" the "movement." is "slow," — the pauses moderately long, — the "rhythm" requires an attentive but delicate marking.

*Wonder* is the predominating *emotion* expressed in the third paragraph. It produces a slight deviation from perfect "purity of tone" towards "aspiration:" the "force" increases gently, after the first sentence: a slight tinge of "vanishing stress" pervades the first sentence; an simple "median" prevails in the first two clauses of the second, and a vivid "radical" in the third clause; and, in the third sentence, a stronger "vanishing stress" than before, becomes distinctly audible, in proportion to the increasing emphasis: the "pitch" of this paragraph is moderately "low," at first, and gradually descends, throughout, as far as to the last semicolon of the paragraph; — the "slides" are principally downward "seconds and thirds:" the "movement" is "slow," excepting in the last clause of the second sentence, in which it is "lively;" the pauses are long; and the "rhythm" still requires perceptible marking.

*Admiration* is the prompting *emotion* in the "expression" of the fourth paragraph. — After the first sentence, which is neutral in effect, the voice passes from "pure tone" to "orotund," as the "quality" required in the union of *beauty* and *grandeur:* the force passes from "moderate" to "declamatory:" the "stress" becomes bold "median expulsion:" the "middle pitch," inclining to "low," for dignity of effect; and downward "thirds" in emphasis: the "movement" is "moderate;" the pauses correspondent; and the "rhythm" somewhat strongly marked.

The fifth and sixth paragraphs are characterized, in "expression," by *pathos* and *awe*. The first two sentences of the fifth paragraph, are in the neutral or unimpassioned utterance of common narrative and remark; the next three sentences introduce an increasing effect of the "pure tone" of *pathos;* the last three of the paragraph are characterized by the expression of *awe* carried to its deepest effect; and the preceding pure tone, therefore, gives way to "aspiration," progressively, to the end of the paragraph. The "force," in the first part of the paragraph, is "subdued;" — in the latter, it is "suppressed:" the "stress" is "median," throughout, — *gently* marked in the *pathetic* part, and *fully*, in that expressive of *awe*. The "pitch" is on "middle" notes, inclining high in the *pathetic* expression, and "low," descending to "lowest," in the utterance of *awe;* the "melody" contains a few slight effects of "semitone," on the emphatic words in the *pathetic* strain, and full downward "slides" of "third" and "fifth," in the language of *awe*. The "movement" is "slow" in the *pathetic* part, and "very slow" in the utterance of *awe;* the pauses correspond; and the "rhythm" is to be exactly kept in the pauses of the latter, as they are the chief source of effect.

The first two sentences of the sixth paragraph, are characterized by the expression of *deep pathos*, differing from that of the first part of the preceding paragraph, by greater force, lower notes, fuller "stress," slower "movement," and longer pauses. The "expression" of the third sentence, passes through the successive stages of *apprehension*, or *fear*, *awe* and *horror*, — marked by increasing "aspiration" and force, deepening notes, slower "movement," and longer pause, so as, at last, to reach the extreme of these elements of effect. The fourth sentence expresses still deeper *pathos* than before, and by the increased effect of the same modes of utterance In the last sentence, in which *awe* combines with *pathos*, the "expression" becomes yet deeper and slower but without increase of "force."

A similar analysis should be performed on all the following pieces previcus to the exercise of reading them. The analogy of emotion exemplified in the numerous examples contained in the body of the book, will be found a sufficiently definite guide for this purpose.]

To an American visiting Europe, the long voyage he has to make is an excellent preparative. From the moment you lose sight of the land you have left, all is vacancy, until you step on the opposite shore, and are launched at once into the bustle and novelties of another world.

I have said that at sea all is vacancy. I should correct the expression. To one given up to day-dreaming, and fond of losing himself in reveries, a sea-voyage is full of subjects for meditation; but then they are the wonders of the deep, and of the air, and rather tend to abstract the mind from worldly themes. I delighted to loll over the quarter-railing, or climb to the main-top on a calm day, and muse for hours together on the tranquil bosom of a summer's sea; or to gaze upon the piles of golden clouds just peering above the horizon, fancy them some fairy realms, and people them with a creation of my own; or to watch the gentle undulating billows rolling their silver volumes, as if to die away on those happy shores.

There was a delicious sensation of mingled security and awe, with which I looked down from my giddy height on the monsters of the deep at their uncouth gambols: shoals of porpoises tumbling about the bow of the ship; the grampus slowly heaving his huge form above the surface; or the ravenous shark, darting like a spectre through the blue waters. My imagination would conjure up all that I had heard or read of the watery world beneath me; of the finny herds that roam its fathomless valleys; of shapeless monsters that lurk among the very foundations of the earth: and those wild phantasms that swell the tales of fishermen and sailors.

Sometimes a distant sail gliding along the edge of the ocean would be another theme of idle speculation. How interesting this fragment of a world hastening to rejoin the great mass of existence! What a glorious monument of human invention, that has thus triumphed over wind and wave; has brought the ends of the earth in communion; has established an interchange of blessings, pouring into the sterile regions of the north all the luxuries of the south; diffused the light of knowledge and the charities of cultivated life; and has thus bound together those scattered portions of the human race, between which nature seemed to have thrown an insurmountable barrier!

We one day descried some shapeless object drifting at a distance. At sea, everything that breaks the monotony of the surrounding expanse attracts attention. It proved to be the mast of a ship th a must have been completely wrecked; for there were the remains of handkerchiefs, by which some of the crew had fastened themselves to this spar, to prevent their being washed off by the waves. There was no trace by which the name of the ship could be ascertained. The wreck had evidently drifted about for many months; clusters of shell-fish had fastened about it, and long sea-weeds flaunted at its sides. But where, thought I, is the crew? Their struggle has long been over;—they have gone down amidst the roar of the tempest;—their bones lie whitening in the caverns of the deep. Silence—oblivion,—like the waves, have closed over them; and no one can tell the story of their end.

What sighs have been wafted after that ship! what prayers offered up at the deserted fire-side of home! How often has the mistress, the wife, and the mother, pored over the daily news, to catch some casual intelligence of this rover of the deep! How has expectation darkened into anxiety—anxiety into dread—and dread into despair! Alas! not one memento shall ever return for love to cherish. All that shall ever be known is, that she sailed from her port, " and was never heard of more."

II.—DEATH OF MORRIS.—*Scott.*

(Vivid Narrative, exemplifying, after the introductory sentence, Sympathetic Horror, then successively, Terror, Scorn, Revenge, Horror, and Awe.)

It was under the burning influence of revenge that the wife of Macgregor commanded that the hostage, exchanged for her husband's safety, should be brought into her presence. I believe her sons had kept this unfortunate wretch out of her sight, for fear of the consequences; but if it was so, their humane precaution only postponed his fate. They dragged forward, at her summons, a wretch, already half dead with terror, in whose agonized features, I recognized, to my horror and astonishment, my old acquaintance Morris.

He fell prostrate before the female chief with an effort to clasp her knees, from which she drew back, as if his touch had been pollution, so that all he could do in token of the extremity of his humiliation, was to kiss the hem of her plaid. I never heard entreaties for life poured forth with such agony of spirit. The ecstasy of fear was such, that, instead of paralyzing his tongue, as on ordinary occasions it even rendered him eloquent; and, with cheeks as pale as ashes hands compressed in agony, eyes that seemed to be taking their last out of all mortal objects, he protested, with the deepest oaths, his total ignorance of any design on the life of Rob Roy, whom he swore he loved and honored as his own soul. — In the inconsistency of his terror, he said, he was but the agent of others, and he muttered the name of Rashleigh. — He prayed but for life — for life he would give all he had in the world; — it was but life he asked — life, if it were to be prolonged under tortures and privations; — he asked only breath though it should be drawn in the damps of the lowest caverns of their hills.

It is impossible to describe the scorn, the loathing, and contempt, with which the wife of Macgregor regarded this wretched petitioner for the poor boon of existence.

'I could have bid you live," she said, " had life been to you the same weary and wasting burden that it is to me — that it is to every noble and generous mind. — But you — wretch! you could creep through the world unaffected by its various disgraces, its ineffable miseries, its constantly accumulating masses of crime and sorrow, — you could live and enjoy yourself, while the noble-minded are betrayed, — while nameless and birthless villains tread on the neck of the brave and long-descended, — you could enjoy yourself, like a butcher's dog in the shambles, battening on garbage, while the slaughter of the brave went on around you! This enjoyment you shall not live to partake of; you shall die, base dog, and that before yon cloud has passed over the sun."

She gave a brief command, in Gaelic, to her attendants two of whom seized upon the prostrate suppliant, and hurried him to the brink of a cliff which overhung the flood. He set up the most piercing and dreadful cries that fear ever uttered — I may well term them dreadful; for they haunted my sleep for years afterwards. As the murderers, or executioners, call them as you will, dragged him along, he recognized me even in that moment of horror, and exclaimed, in the last articulate words I ever heard him utter, " O, Mr. Osbaldistone, save me! — save me!"

I was so much moved by this horrid spectacle, that, although in momentary expectation of sharing his fate, I did attempt to speak in his behalf, but, as might have been expected, my interference was sternly disregarded. The victim was held fast by some, while others, binding a large heavy stone in a plaid, tied it round his neck and others again eagerly stripped him of some part of his dress Half naked, and thus manacled, they hurried him into the lake, there about two or three feet deep, drowning his last death-shriek with a loud halloo of vindictive triumph, over which, however, the yell of mortal agony was distinctly heard. The heavy burden splashed in the darkblue waters of the lake; and the Highlanders, with their pole-axes and swords, watched an instant, to guard, lest, extricating himself from the load to which he was attached, he might have struggled to regain the shore. But the knot had been securely bound; the victim sunk without effort; the waters, which his fall had disturbed, settled calmly over him; and the unit of that life for which he had pleaded so strongly, was forever withdrawn from the sum of human existence.

III. — THE PLANETARY SYSTEMS. — *Hervey.*

(Serious, Descriptive, and Didactic Style.)

To us, who dwell on its surface, the earth is by far the most extensive orb that our eyes can anywhere behold: it is also clothed with verdure, distinguished by trees, and adorned with a variety of beautiful decorations; whereas, to a spectator placed on one of the planets, it wears a uniform aspect, looks all luminous, and no larger than a spot. To beings who dwell at still greater distances, it entirely disappears. That which we call alternately the morning and the evening star, — as in one part of her orbit she rides foremost in the procession of night, in the other ushers in and anticipates the dawn, — is a planetary world, which, and the four others, that so wonderfully vary their mystic dance, are in themselves dark bodies, and shine only by reflection; have fields, and seas, and skies of their own, are furnished with all accommodations for animal subsistence, and are supposed to be the abodes of intellectual life; all which, together with our earthly habitation, are dependent on that great and dispenser of divine munificence, the sun; receive their light from the distribution of his rays, and derive their comfort from his benign agency.

This sun, however, with all its attendant planets, is but a very little part of the grand machine of the universe: every star, though in appearance no bigger than the diamond that glitters upon a lady's ring, is really a vast globe, like the sun in size and in glory; no less spacious, no less luminous, than the radiant source of the day: so that every star is not barely a world, but the centre of a magnificent system; has a retinue of worlds, irradiated by its beams, and revolving round its attractive influence, all which are lost to our sight in immeasurable wilds of ether.

It is observed by a very judicious writer, that if the sun himself which enlightens this part of the creation, were extinguished, and all the host of planetary worlds, which move about him, were annihilated, they would not be missed by an eye that can take in the whole compass of nature, any more than a grain of sand upon the sea-shore. The bulk of which they consist, and the space which they occupy, are so exceeding little in comparison of the whole, that their loss would scarce leave a blank in the immensity of God's works.

### IV.—CHATHAM'S REBUKE OF LORD SUFFOLK.

(Declamatory Interrogation, Detestation, and Abhorrence.)

Who is the man, that, in addition to the disgraces and mischiefs of the war, has dared to authorize and associate to our arms the tomahawk and scalping-knife of the savage? — to call into civilized alliance, the wild and inhuman inhabitant of the woods? — to delegate to the merciless Indian, the defence of disputed rights, and to wage the horrors of his barbarous war against our brethren? My lords, these enormities cry aloud for redress and punishment. But, my lords, this barbarous measure has been defended, not only on the principles of policy and necessity, but also on those of morality; "for it is perfectly allowable," says Lord Suffolk, "to use all the means, which God and nature have put into our hands." I am astonished, I am shocked, to hear such principles confessed; to hear them avowed in this house, or in this country!

My lords, I did not intend to encroach so much on your attention; but I cannot repress my indignation — I feel myself impelled to speak. My lords, we are called upon as members of this house, as men, as Christians, to protest against such horrible barbarity! — "That God and nature have put into our hands!" What ideas of God and nature, that noble lord may entertain, I know not; but I know, that such detestable principles are equally abhorrent to religion and humanity. What! to attribute the sacred sanction of God and nature, to the massacres of the Indian scalping-knife! to the canniba. savage, torturing, murdering, devouring, drinking the blood of his mangled victims! Such notions shock every precept of morality every feeling of humanity, every sentiment of honor. These abominable principles, and this more abominable avowal of them, demand the most decisive indignation.

I call upon that right reverend, and this most learned bench, to vindicate the religion of their God, to support the justice of their country. I call upon the bishops, to interpose the unsullied sanctity of their lawn; — upon the judges, to interpose the purity of their

ermine, to save us from this pollution. I call upon the honor of you.
lordships to reverence the dignity of your ancestors, and to maintain
your own. I call upon the spirit and humanity of my country, to
vindicate the national character. I solemnly call upon your lord
ships, and upon every order of men in the state, to stamp upon
this infamous procedure, the indelible stigma of the public abhorrence. More particularly, I call upon the holy prelates of our
religion, to do away this iniquity; let them perform a lustration, to
purify the country from this deep and deadly sin.

V.—EXTRACT FROM PATRICK HENRY'S SPEECH IN FAVOR OF THE WAR
OF INDEPENDENCE.

(Declamatory Expostulation, Courage, Confidence, Resolute Defiance,
Rousing Appeal, Deep Determination.)

They tell us, sir, that we are weak — unable to cope with so formidable an adversary. But when shall we be stronger? Will it be
the next week, or the next year? Will it be when we are totally
disarmed; and when a British guard shall be stationed in every
house? Shall we gather strength by irresolution and inaction?
Shall we acquire the means of effectual resistance, by lying supinely
on our backs, and hugging the delusive phantom of hope, until our
enemies shall have bound us hand and foot?

Sir, we are not weak, if we make a proper use of those means,
which the God of nature hath placed in our power. Three millions
of people, armed in the holy cause of liberty, and in such a country
as that which we possess, are invincible by any force which our
enemy can send against us. Besides, sir, we shall not fight alone.
There is a just God, who presides over the destinies of nations, and
who will raise up friends to fight our battles for us.

The battle, sir, is not to the strong alone: it is to the vigilant, the
active, the brave. — Besides, sir, we have no election. If we were
base enough to desire it, it is now too late to retire from the contest.
There is no retreat, but in submission and slavery! Our chains are
forged. Their clanking may be heard on the plains of Boston!
The war is inevitable — and let it come! I repeat it, sir, let it
come!

It is in vain, sir, to extenuate the matter. Gentlemen may cry
peace, peace, — but there is no peace. The war is actually begun.
The next gale, that sweeps from the north, will bring to our ears
the clash of resounding arms! Our brethren are already in the field.
Why stand we here idle? What is it that gentlemen wish? What

would they have!—Is life so dear, or peace so sweet, as to be purchased at the price of chains and slavery? Forbid it, Almighty God!—I know not what course others may take; but as for me —give me liberty, or give me death!

VI.—THE OCEAN.—*Byron.*

Roll on, thou deep and dark blue ocean—roll!
Ten thousand fleets sweep over thee in vain;
Man marks the earth with ruin—his control
   Stops with the shore;—upon the watery plain
   The wrecks are all thy deed; nor doth remain
A shadow of man's ravage, save his own,
   When, for a moment, like a drop of rain,
He sinks into thy depths with bubbling groan,
Without a grave, unknelled, uncoffined, and unknown!

The armaments, which thunderstrike the walls
   Of rock-built cities, bidding nations quake,
And monarchs tremble in their capitals—
   The oak leviathans, whose huge ribs make
   Their clay Creator the vain title take
Of lord of thee, and arbiter of war—
   These are thy toys; and, as the snowy flake
They melt into thy yeast of waves, which mar
Alike the Armada's pride, or spoils of Trafalgar.

Thy shores are empires, changed in all save thee—
   Assyria, Greece, Rome, Carthage, what are they?
   Thy waters wasted them while they were free,
And many a tyrant since; their shores obey
   The stranger, slave, or savage; their decay
Has dried up realms to deserts—not so thou,
   Unchangeable save to thy wild waves' play—
Time writes no wrinkle on thy azure brow—
Such as Creation's dawn beheld, thou rollest now!

Thou glorious mirror, where the Almighty's form
   Glasses itself in tempests!—in all time—
Calm or convulsed, in breeze or gale or storm,
   Icing the pole, or in the torrid clime
Dark heaving—boundless, endless, and sublime!

# APPENDIX.

The image of Eternity! — the throne
Of the Invisible. — Even from out thy slime
The monsters of the deep are made! Each zone
Obeys Thee! Thou go'st forth; dread! fathomless! alone

## VII. — BATTLE OF WATERLOO. — *Byron.*

There was a sound of revelry by night;
And Belgium's capital had gathered then
Her Beauty and her Chivalry, and bright
The lamps shone o'er fair women and brave men:
A thousand hearts beat happily; and when
Music arose with its voluptuous swell,
Soft eyes looked love to eyes which spake again,
And all went merry as a marriage bell; —
But hush! hark! a deep sound strikes like a rising knell.

Did ye not hear it? — No; 't was but the wind,
Or the car rattling o'er the stony street:
On with the dance! let joy be unconfined;
No sleep till morn, when Youth and Pleasure meet
To chase the glowing Hours with flying feet —
But, hark! — that heavy sound breaks in once more,
As if the clouds its echo would repeat;
And nearer, clearer, deadlier than before!
Arm! Arm! it is! — it is! — the cannon's opening roar.

Ah! then and there was hurrying to and fro,
And gathering tears, and tremblings of distress,
And cheeks all pale, which but an hour ago —
Blushed at the praise of their own loveliness;
And there were sudden partings, such as press
The life from out young hearts, and choking sighs
Which ne'er might be repeated: who could guess
If ever more should meet those mutual eyes,
Since upon night so sweet such awful morn could rise!

And there was mounting in hot haste; the steed,
The mustering squadron, and the clattering car,
Went pouring forward with impetuous speed,
And swiftly forming in the ranks of war;
And the deep thunder, peal on peal, afar,

And near, the beat of the alarming drum,
  Roused up the soldier ere the morning star;—
While thronged the citizens with terror dumb,
Or whispering, with white lips—" The foe! they come! they
    come!"

And wild and high the " Cameron's gathering" rose!
  The war-note of Lochiel, which Albyn's hills
Have heard;—and heard, too, have her Saxon foes:—
  How in the noon of night that pibroch thrills,
  Savage and shrill! But with the breath which fills
Their mountain-pipe, so fill the mountaineers
  With the fierce native daring, which instils
The stirring memory of a thousand years;
And Evan's, Donald's fame rings in each clansman's ears!

And Ardennes waves above them her green leaves,
  Dewy with nature's tear-drops, as they pass,
Grieving,—if aught inanimate e'er grieves,—
  Over the unreturning brave,—alas!
Ere evening to be trodden like the grass
  Which now beneath them, but above shall grow
In its next verdure, when this fiery mass
  Of living valor, rolling on the foe,
And burning with high hope, shall moulder cold and low!

Last noon beheld them full of lusty life,
  Last eve in Beauty's circle proudly gay,
The midnight brought the signal-sound of strife,
  The morn, the marshalling in arms,—the day
Battle's magnificently-stern array!
  The thunder-clouds close o'er it, which when rent
The earth is covered thick with other clay,
  Which her own clay shall cover,—heaped and pent,
Rider and horse,—friend, foe,—in one red burial blent!

VIII.—Satan rallying the Fallen Angels.—*Milton.*

He scarce had ceased when the superior fiend
Was moving toward the shore; his ponderous shield
Ethereal temper, massy, large, and round,
Behind him cast, the broad circumference
Hung on his shoulders, like the moon, whose orb,

# APPENDIX.

Thro' optic glass, the Tuscan artist views,
At evening, from the top of Fiesole,
Or in Valdarno, to descry new lands,
Rivers, or mountains, on her spotty globe.
His spear, to equal which the tallest pine
Hewn on Norwegian hills to be the mast
Of some great admiral, were but a wand,
He walked with to support uneasy steps
Over the burning marl : (not like those steps
On Heaven's azure !) and the torrid clime
Smote on him sore besides, vaulted with fire.
Nathless he so endured till on the beach
Of that inflamed sea he stood, and called
His legions, angel forms, who lay, entranced,
Thick as autumnal leaves that strew the brooks
In Vallombrosa, where the Etrurian shades,
High over-arched embower; or scattered sedge
Afloat, when with fierce winds, Orion armed,
Hath vexed the Red Sea coast, whose waves o'erthrew
Busiris and his Memphian chivalry,
While with perfidious hatred they pursued
The sojourners of Goshen, who beheld
From the safe shore, their floating carcases
And broken chariot wheels : so thick bestrown,
Abject and lost, lay these, covering the flood,
Under amazement of their hideous change.
He called so loud, that all the hollow deep
Of hell resounded.
    "Princes ! Potentates !
Warriors ! the flower of heaven, once yours, now lost,
If such astonishment as this can seize
Eternal spirits : or have ye chosen this place,
To rest your wearied virtue, for the ease ye find
To slumber here, as in the vales of heaven ?
Or in this abject posture have you sworn
To adore the Conqueror, who now beholds
Cherub and seraph rolling in the flood,
With scattered arms and ensigns; till, anon,
His swift pursuers, from heaven gates discern
The advantage, and descending, tread us down
Thus drooping; or with linked thunderbolts

Transfix us to the bottom of this gulf!
Awake! arise! or be forever fallen!"


IX.—HYMN TO MONT BLANC.—*Coleridge.*

Hast thou a charm to stay the morning star
In his steep course! so long he seems to pause
On thy bald awful head, O sovran Blanc!
The Arvé and Arveiron at thy base
Rave ceaselessly, while *thou*, dread mountain form,
Risest from forth thy silent sea of pines
How silently! Around thee and above
Deep is the sky and black: transpicuous deep
An ebon mass! methinks thou piercest it
As with a wedge! But when I look again
It seems thine own calm home, thy crystal shrine,
Thy habitation from eternity.
O dread and silent form! I gazed on thee
Till thou, still present to my bodily eye,
Didst vanish from my thought.— Entranced in prayer
I worshipped the Invisible alone,
Yet thou, methinks, wast working on my soul,
E'en like some deep enchanting melody,
So sweet we know not we are listening to it.
But I awake, and with a busier mind
And active will, self-conscious, offer now,
Not, as before, involuntary prayer
And passive adoration.
    Hand and voice
Awake, awake! and thou, my heart, awake!
Green fields and icy cliffs! all join my hymn!
And thou, O silent mountain, sole and bare,
O blacker than the darkness, all the night,
And visited all night by troops of stars,—
Or when they climb the sky, or when they sink,—
Companion of the morning star, at dawn,
Thyself earth's rosy star, and of the dawn
Co-herald! wake, oh! wake, and utter praise!
 Who sank thy sunless pillars in the earth?
Who filled thy countenance with rosy light?
Who made thee father of perpetual streams?
And you, ye five wild torrents, fiercely glad,

# APPENDIX.

Who called you forth from night and utter death?
From darkness let you loose, and icy dens,
Down those precipitous, black, jagged rocks,
Forever shattered, and the same forever?
Who gave you your invulnerable life,
Your strength, your speed, your fury, and your joy,
Unceasing thunder and eternal foam? —
 And who commanded — and the silence came,
"Here shall the billows stiffen and have rest?"
Ye ice-falls! ye that from your dizzy heights
Adown enormous ravines steeply slope, —
Torrents, methinks, that heard a mighty noise,
And stopped at once amidst their maddest plunge, —
Motionless torrents! silent cataracts!
Who made you glorious as the gates of heaven,
Beneath the keen full moon? Who bade the Sun
Clothe you with rainbows? Who with lovely flowers
Of living blue spread garlands at your feet? —
God! God! the torrents like a shout of nations
Utter: the ice-plain bursts, and answers, God! —
God! sing the meadow streams with gladsome voice,
And pine-groves with their soft and soul-like sound.
 The silent snow-mass, loosening, thunders, God!
Ye dreadless flowers, that fringe the eternal frost!
Ye wild goats bounding by the eagle's nest!
Ye eagles, playmates of the mountain blast!
Ye lightnings, the dread arrows of the clouds!
Ye signs and wonders of the elements,
Utter forth God! and fill the hills with praise!
And thou, O silent form, alone and bare, —
Whom as I lift again my head, bowed low
In silent adoration, I again behold,
And to thy summit upward from thy base
Sweep slowly, with dim eyes suffused with tears, —
Awake thou mountain form! Rise like a cloud,
Rise, like a cloud of incense, from the earth!
Thou kingly spirit throned among the hills,
Thou dread Ambassador from earth to heaven,
Great Hierarch, tell thou the silent sky,
And tell the stars, and tell the rising sun,
Earth with her thousand voices calls on GOD.

## MISCELLANEOUS PIECES.

### X.—ODE ON THE PASSIONS.—*Collins.*

When Music, heavenly maid, was young,
While yet in early Greece she sung,
The Passions oft, to hear her shell,
Thronged around her magic cell,
Exulting, trembling, raging, fainting,—
Possessed beyond the Muse's painting.
By turns they felt the glowing mind
Disturbed, delighted, raised, refined:
Till once, 't is said, when all were fired,
Filled with fury, rapt, inspired,
From the supporting myrtles round
They snatched her instruments of sound;
And, as they oft had heard apart
Sweet lessons of her forceful art,
Each, (for madness ruled the hour,)
Would prove his own expressive power

First, Fear, his hand, its skill to try,
   Amid the chords bewildered laid ;—
And back recoiled, he knew not why,
   Even at the sound himself had made.

Next, Anger rushed: his eyes on fire,
   In lightnings owned his secret stings.—
With one rude clash he struck the lyre,
   And swept with hurried hands the strings.

With woful measures, wan Despair—
   Low sullen sounds his grief beguiled;
A solemn, strange, and mingled air:
   'T was sad, by fits;—by starts, 't was wild.

But thou, O Hope! with eyes so fair,
   What was thy delighted measure?
   Still it whispered promised pleasure,
And bade the lovely scenes at distance hail.
   Still would her touch the strain prolong;
And from the rocks, the woods, the vale,
   She called on Echo still through all her song:
     And, where her sweetest theme she chose,
      A soft responsive voice was heard at every close,
And Hope, enchanted, smiled, and waved her golden hair!

# APPENDIX.

And longer had she sung — but, with a frown,
    Revenge impatient rose.
He threw his blood-stained sword in thunder down
    And, with a withering look,
    The war-denouncing trumpet took,
And blew a blast, so loud and dread,
Were ne'er prophetic sounds so full of woe:
    And ever and anon, he beat
    The doubling drum with furious heat.
    And though sometimes, each dreary pause between,
      Dejected Pity at his side,
      Her soul-subduing voice applied,
    Yet still he kept his wild unaltered mien;
While each strained ball of sight seemed bursting from his head

Thy numbers, Jealousy, to nought were fixed;
Sad proof of thy distressful state!
Of differing themes the veering song was mixed:
    And, now, it courted Love; now, raving, called on Hate

With eyes upraised, as one inspired,
Pale Melancholy sat retired;
And from her wild sequestered seat,
In notes by distance made more sweet,
Poured through the mellow horn her pensive soul;
    And, dashing soft from rocks around,
    Bubbling runnels joined the sound.
Through glades and glooms the mingled measure stole,
    Or o'er some haunted stream, with fond delay,
      (Round a holy calm diffusing,
      Love of peace and lonely musing,)
    In hollow murmurs died away.

But, oh! how altered was its sprightlier tone,
When Cheerfulness, a nymph of healthiest hue,
    Her bow across her shoulder flung,
Her buskins gemmed with morning dew,
    Blew an inspiring air, that dale and thicket rung,
The hunter's call, to Faun and Dryad known!
      The oak-crowned Sisters, and their chaste-eyed Queen.
        Satyrs and sylvan boys were seen,
        Peeping from forth their alleys green;

Brown Exercise rejoiced to hear,
And Sport leaped up, and seized his beechen spear

Last, came Joy's ecstatic trial.
He, with viñy crown advancing,
    First to the lively pipe his hand addressed;
But soon he saw the brisk awakening viol,
    Whose sweet entrancing voice he loved the best.
They would have thought, who heard the strain,
    They saw, in Tempe's vale, her native maids,
    Amid the fatal-sounding shades,
To some unwearied minstrel dancing;
While, as his flying fingers kissed the strings,
    Love framed with Mirth a gay fantastic round:
    (Loose were her tresses seen, her zone unbound;)
    And he amidst his frolic play, —
    As if he would the charming air repay, —
Shook thousand odors from his dewy wings.

[1] XI. — THE USES OF KNOWLEDGE. — *Alison.*

The first end to which all wisdom or knowledge ought to be employed, is to illustrate the wisdom or goodness of the Father of Nature. Every science that is cultivated by men, leads naturally to religious thought, from the study of the plant that grows beneath our feet, to that of the Host of Heaven above us, who perform their stated revolutions in majestic silence, amid the expanse of infinity. When, in the youth of Moses, "the Lord appeared to him in Horeb," a voice was heard, saying, "draw nigh hither, and put off thy shoes from off thy feet; for the place where thou standest is holy ground." It is with such a reverential awe that every great or elevated mind will approach to the study of nature, and with such feelings of adoration and gratitude, that he will receive the illumination that gradually opens upon his soul.

It is not the lifeless mass of matter, he will then feel, that he is examining, — it is the mighty machine of Eternal Wisdom: the workmanship of Him, " in whom everything lives, and moves, and has its being." Under an aspect of this kind, it is impossible to pur-

---

[1] A few of the concluding pieces in the first edition, which were designed for the use of theological students, are now displaced by others of a more general character; as the author's new work, Pulpit Elocution, has since been prepared for the purpose of furnishing appropriate professional exercises.

sue knowledge without mingling with it the most elevated sentiments of devotion; — it is impossible to perceive the laws of nature without perceiving, at the same time, the presence and the Providence of the Lawgiver; — and thus it is, that, in every age, the evidences of religion have advanced with the progress of true philosophy; and that science in erecting a monument to herself, has, at the same time, erected an altar to the Deity.

The second great end to which all knowledge ought to be employed, is the welfare of humanity. Every science is the foundation of some art, beneficial to men; and while the study of it leads us to see the beneficence of the laws of nature, it calls upon us also to follow the great end of the Father of Nature in their employment and application. I need not say what a field is thus opened to the benevolence of knowledge: I need not tell you, that in every department of learning there is good to be done to mankind: I need not remind you, that the age in which we live has given us the noblest examples of this kind, and that science now finds its highest glory in improving the condition, or in allaying the miseries of humanity. But there is one thing of which it is proper ever to remind you, because the modesty of knowledge often leads us to forget it, — and that is, that the power of scientific benevolence is far greater than that of all others, to the welfare of society.

The benevolence of the great, or the opulent, however eminent it may be, perishes with themselves. The benevolence even of sovereigns is limited to the narrow boundary of human life; and, not unfrequently, is succeeded by different and discordant counsels. But the benevolence of knowledge is of a kind as extensive as the race of man, and as permanent as the existence of society. He, in whatever situation he may be, who, in the study of science, has discovered a new means of alleviating pain. or of remedying disease; who has described a wiser method of preventing poverty, or of shielding misfortune; who has suggested additional means of increasing or improving the beneficent productions of nature, has left a memorial of himself, which can never be forgotten; which will communicate happiness to ages yet unborn; and which, in the emphatic language of Scripture, renders him a " fellow-worker " with God himself, in he improvement of his Creation.

XII. — SCENE FROM THE LIGHTS AND SHADOWS OF SCOTTISH LIFE. — *Wilson.*

The rite of baptism had not been performed for several months in the kirk of Lanark It was now the hottest time of persecution, and the inhabitants of that parish found other places in which to worship God and celebrate the ordinances of religion. It was the Sabbath day,—and a small congregation, of about a hundred souls, had met for divine service in a place of worship more magnificent than any temple that human hands had ever built to Deity. Here, too, were three children about to be baptized. The congregation had not assembled to the toll of the bell,—but each heart knew the hour and observed it; for there are a hundred sun-dials among the hills, woods, moors, and fields, and the shepherds and the peasants see the hours passing by them in sunshine and shadow.

The church in which they were assembled, was hewn by God's hand, out of the eternal rocks. A river rolled its way through a mighty chasm of cliffs, several hundred feet high, of which the one side presented enormous masses, and the other corresponding recesses, as if the great stone girdle had been rent by a convulsion. The channel was overspread with prodigious fragments of rocks or large loose stones, some of them smooth and bare, others containing soil and verdure in their rents and fissures, and here and there crowned with shrubs and trees. The eye could at once command a long stretching vista, seemingly closed and shut up at both extremities, by the coalescing cliffs.

This majestic reach of river contained pools, streams, rushing shelves, and waterfalls innumerable; and when the water was low, which it now was in the common drought, it was easy to walk up this scene with the calm blue sky overhead, an utter and sublime solitude. On looking up, the soul was bowed down by the feeling of that prodigious height of unscalable and often overhanging cliff. Between the channel and the summit of the far-extended precipices, were perpetually flying rooks and wood-pigeons, and now and then a hawk, filling the profound abyss with their wild cawing, deep murmur, or shrilly shriek.

Sometimes a heron would stand erect and still on some little stone island, or rise up like a white cloud along the black walls of the chasm, and disappear. Winged creatures alone could inhabit this region. The fox and wild-cat chose more accessible haunts. Yet here came the persecuted Christians, and worshipped God, whose hand hung over their heads those magnificent pillars and arches, scooped out those galleries from the solid rock, and laid at their feet the calm water in its transparent beauty, in which they could see themselves sitting in reflected groups, with their Bibles in their hands.

The rite of baptism was over, and the religious service of the day closed by a Psalm. The mighty rocks hemmed in the holy sound and sent it, in a more compacted volume, clear, sweet, and strong, up to heaven. When the Psalm ceased, an echo, like a spirit's voice, was heard dying away high up among the magnificent architecture of the cliffs, and once more might be noticed in the silence the reviving voice of the waterfall.

Just then a large stone fell from the top of the cliff into the pool, a loud voice was heard, and a plaid hung over on the point of a shepherd's staff. Their watchful sentinel had descried danger, and this was his warning. Forthwith the congregation rose. There were paths dangerous to unpractised feet, along the ledges of the rocks, leading up to several caves and places of concealment. The more active and young assisted the elder — more especially the old pastor, and the women with the infants; and many minutes had not elapsed, till not a living creature was visible in the channel of the stream, but all of them hidden, or nearly so, in the clefts and caverns.

The shepherd who had given the alarm had lain down again in his plaid instantly on the green sward upon the summit of these precipices. A party of soldiers were immediately upon him, and demanded what signals he had been making, and to whom; when one of them, looking over the edge of the cliff, exclaimed, "See, see! Humphrey, we have caught the whole tabernacle of the Lord in a net at last. There they are, praising God among the stones of the river Mouss. These are the Cartland Craigs. By my soul's salvation, a noble cathedral!" "Fling the lying sentinel over the cliffs. Here is a canting covenanter for you, deceiving honest soldiers on the very Sabbath day. Over with him, over with him — out of the gallery into the pit."

But the shepherd had vanished like a shadow; and mixing with the tall green broom and bushes, was making his unseen way towards a wood. "Satan has saved his servant; but come, my lads — follow me; I know the way down into the bed of the stream — and the steps up to Wallace's Cave. They are called the 'Kittle Nine Stanes.' The hunt's up. We'll be all in at the death. Halloo — my boys — halloo!"

The soldiers dashed down a less precipitous part of the wooded banks, a little below the "craigs," and hurried up the channel. But when they reached the altar where the old gray-haired minister had been seen standing, and the rocks that had been covered with people, all was silent and solitary; not a creature to be seen

"Here is a Bible dropt by some of them," cried a soldier, and, with his foot, spun it away into the pool. "A bonnet, a bonnet," cried another,—now for the pretty sanctified face that rolled its demure eyes below it."

But, after a few jests and oaths, the soldiers stood still, eyeing with a kind of mysterious dread the black and silent walls of the rock that hemmed them in, and hearing only the small voice of the stream that sent a profounder stillness through the heart of that majestic so itude. "Curse these cowardly covenanters—what, if they tumble down upon our heads pieces of rock from their hiding-places? Ad vance? Or retreat?"

There was no reply. For a slight fear was upon every man; musket or bayonet could be of little use to men obliged to clamber up rocks, along slender paths, leading, they knew not where; and they were aware that armed men now-a-days, worshipped God,— men of iron hearts, who feared not the glitter of the soldier's arms —neither barrel nor bayonet—men of long stride, firm step, and broad breast, who, on the open field, would have overthrown the marshalled line, and gone first and foremost, if a city had to be taken by storm.

As the soldiers were standing together irresolute, a noise came upon their ears like distant thunder, but even more appalling; and a slight current of air, as if propelled by it, passed whispering along the sweet-briers, and the broom, and the tresses of the birch trees It came deepening, and rolling, and roaring on, and the very Cart land Craigs shook to their foundation as if in an earthquake. "The Lord have mercy upon us—what is this?" And down fell many of the miserable wretches on their knees, and some on their faces, upon the sharp-pointed rocks. Now, it was like the sound of many myriads of chariots rolling on their iron axles down the stony channel of the torrent.

The old gray-haired minister issued from the mouth of Wallace's Cave, and said, with a loud voice, "The Lord God terrible reigneth." A water-spout had burst up among the moorlands, and the river in its power, was at hand. There it came, tumbling along into that long reach of cliffs, and in a moment filled it with one mass of waves. Huge, agitated clouds of foam rode on the surface of a blood-red torrent An army must have been swept off by that flood. The soldiers perished in a moment; but high up in the cliffs, above the sweep of destruction, were the covenanters—men, women, and children, uttering prayers to God unheard by themselves in that raging thunder.

XVII. — SPECIMEN OF THE ELOQUENCE OF JOHN ADAMS. — *Webster*

The war must go on. We must fight it through. And if the war must go on, why put off longer the Declaration of Independence? That measure will strengthen us. It will give us character abroad.

Why then, sir, do we not, as soon as possible, change this from a civil to a national war? And since we must fight it through, why not put ourselves in a state to enjoy all the benefits of victory, if we gain the victory?

If we fail, it can be no worse for us. But we shall not fail. The cause will raise up armies; the cause will create navies. The people, the people, if we are true to them, will carry us, and will carry themselves, gloriously, through this struggle.

I care not how fickle other people have been found. I know the people of these colonies; and I know that resistance to British aggression is deep and settled in their hearts and cannot be eradicated. Every colony, indeed, has expressed its willingness to follow, if we but take the lead. Sir, the declaration will inspire the people with increased courage. Instead of a long and bloody war for restoration of privileges, for redress of grievances, for chartered immunities, held under a British king, set before them the glorious object of entire independence, and it will breathe into them anew the breath of life.

Read this declaration at the head of the army; every sword will be drawn from its scabbard, and the solemn vow uttered, to maintain it, or to perish on the bed of honor. Publish it from the pulpit; religion will approve it, and the love of religious liberty will cling round it, resolved to stand with it or fall with it. Send it to the public halls; proclaim it there; let them hear it, who heard the first roar of the enemy's cannon; let them see it, who saw their brothers and their sons fall on the field of Bunker Hill, and in the streets of Lexington and Concord, and the very walls will cry out in its support.

Sir, I know the uncertainty of human affairs, but I see, I see clearly through this day's business. You and I, indeed, may rue it. We may not live to the time, when this declaration shall be made good. We may die; die, colonists; die, slaves; die, it may be ignominiously and on the scaffold. Be it so. Be it so. If it be the pleasure of Heaven that my country shall require the poor offering of my life, the victim shall be ready, at the appointed hour of sacrifice, come when that hour may. But while I do live, let me have a country, or at least the hope of a country, and that a free country.

But whatever may be our fate, be assured, be assured, that this declaration will stand. It may cost treasure, and it may cost blood; out it will stand, and it will richly compensate for both. Through the thick gloom of the present, I see the brightness of the future, as the sun in heaven. We shall make this a glorious, an immortal day. When we are in our graves, our children will honor it. They will celebrate it with thanksgiving, with festivity, with bonfires, and iLuminations. On its annual return they will shed tears, copious, gushing tears, not of subjection and slavery, not of agony and distress, but of exultation, of gratitude, and of joy.

Sir, before God, I believe the hour is come. My judgment approves this measure, and my whole heart is in it. All that I have, and all that I am, and all that I hope, in this life, I am now ready here to stake upon it; and I leave off, as I began, that live or die, survive or perish, I am for the declaration. It is my living sentiment, and by the blessing of God it shall be my dying sentiment: independence, *now;* and INDEPENDENCE FOREVER.

XIV.— RESULTS OF THE HEROISM OF THE PILGRIMS.— *E. Everett.*

Methinks I see it now, that one solitary, adventurous vessel, the Mayflower of a forlorn hope, freighted with the prospects of a future state, and bound across the unknown sea. I behold it pursuing, with a thousand misgivings, the uncertain, the tedious voyage. Suns rise and set, and weeks and months pass, and winter surprises them on the deep, but brings them not the sight of the wished-for shore. I see them now, scantily supplied with provisions, crowded almost to suffocation in their ill-stored prison;— delayed by calms, pursuing a circuitous route,— and now driven in fury before the raging tempest, on the high and giddy waves. The awful voice of the storm howls through the rigging. The laboring masts seem straining from their base;— the dismal sound of the pumps is heard;— the ship leaps, as it were, madly, from billow to billow;— the ocean breaks, and settles with ingulphing floods over the floating deck, and beats with deadening, shivering weight, against the staggered vessel.— I see them, escaped from these perils, pursuing their all but desperate undertaking, and landed at last, after a five months' passage, on the ice-clad rocks of Plymouth,— weak and weary from the voyage,— poorly armed, scantily provisioned, depending on the charity of their ship-master for a draught of beer on board, drinking nothing but water on shore, — without shelter, — without means, — surrounded by hostile tribes.

Shut now the volume of history, and tell me, on any principle of human probability, what shall be the fate of this handful of adventurers. — Tell me, man of military science, in how many months were they all swept off by the thirty savage tribes, enumerated within the early limits of New England? Tell me, politician, how long did this shadow of a colony, on which your conventions and treaties had not smiled, languish on the distant coast? Student of history, compare for me the baffled projects, the deserted settlements, the abandoned adventures of other times, and find the parallel of this. Was it the winter's storm, beating upon the houseless heads of women and children; was it hard labor and spare meals; — was it disease, — was it the tomahawk, — was it the deep malady of a blighted hope, a ruined enterprise, and a broken heart, aching in its last moments at the recollection of the loved and left beyond the sea; was it some, or all of these united, that hurried this forsaken company to their melancholy fate? — And is it possible that neither of these causes, that not all combined, were able to blast this bud of hope? — Is it possible, that from a beginning so feeble, so frail, so worthy, not so much of admiration as of pity, there has gone forth a progress so steady, a growth so wonderful, an expansion so ample, a reality so important, a promise, yet to be fulfilled, so glorious!

END.

www.ingramcontent.com/pod-product-compliance
Lightning Source LLC
Chambersburg PA
CBHW032043230426
43672CB00009B/1451